The Evolving Presid

((The Evolving Presidency))

Addresses, Cases, Essays, Letters, Reports, Resolutions, Transcripts, and Other Landmark Documents,

1787–1998

Michael Nelson, Editor

Rhodes College

PRESS

A Division of Congressional Quarterly Inc.

Washington, D.C.

Printed in the United States of America

Text and cover design by Kachergis Book Design

Library of Congress Cataloging-in-Publication Data
Nelson, Michael, 1949–
    The evolving presidency : addresses, cases, essays, letters, reports,
resolutions, transcripts, and other landmark documents, 1787–1998 / Michael
Nelson.
        p.   cm.
    ISBN 1-56802-370-7. — —ISBN 1-56802-369-3 (pbk.)
    1. Presidents—United States—History—Sources.   I. Title.
JK511.N45   1998
352.23'0973—dc21   98-27073

To two admirable presidents:

❧ ❧

Alexander Heard *(Vanderbilt University)* and
James H. Daughdrill, Jr. *(Rhodes College)*

Contents

Preface: A User's Guide to *The Evolving Presidency*   xi

1. The Constitution: Provisions Concerning
   the Presidency (1787)   1
   *The presidency, the main innovation of the Constitutional
   Convention, is created and its structure and powers
   outlined*

2. Letters of Cato, Nos. 4 and 5 (1787)   10
   *An Anti-Federalist opponent of the proposed Constitution warns
   against the dangers of presidential power*

3. *The Federalist Papers*, Nos. 69 and 70 (1788)   16
   *A Federalist supporter of the proposed Constitution defends the
   republican character of the presidency*

4. George Washington's First Inaugural Address (1789)   30
   Washington establishes the model for inaugural addresses

5. James Madison's Defense of the President's
   Removal Power (1789)   34
   *Madison persuades Congress that the president should be chief
   executive of the bureaucracy*

6. The Pacificus-Helvidius Letters (1793)   39
   *Alexander Hamilton and James Madison debate the extent
   of the president's constitutional power in foreign affairs*

7. Thomas Jefferson's First Inaugural Address (1801)   44
   The first peaceful transfer of power from one party to another

8. Thomas Jefferson's Letter to the Vermont
   Legislature (1807)   50
   Jefferson establishes the two-term tradition for presidents

9. The Monroe Doctrine (1823)   52
   *An early assertion of presidential power in foreign policy-making
   at a time when the presidency was otherwise weak*

10. The Tennessee General Assembly's Protest against the
    Caucus System (1823)   56
    *The stage is set for the demise of the congressional caucus-centered
    presidential nominating process*

11. Andrew Jackson's First Message to Congress (1829)   61
    *The first outsider president grounds his authority in
    "the will of the majority"*

12. Andrew Jackson's Veto of the Bank Bill (1832)   66
    *Jackson activates the veto as a strong and effective power
    of the presidency*

13. Abraham Lincoln's Letter to Albert G. Hodges (1864)   70
    *Lincoln defends his use of prerogative power during the
    Civil War*

14. The Gettysburg Address (1863)   75
    *Lincoln, in an effort to give meaning to the war, invokes
    the Declaration of Independence's promise of equality and
    self-government*

15. *Ex Parte Milligan* (1866)   77
    *The Supreme Court proves more willing to curb presidential power
    after a war than during one*

16. Articles of Impeachment against Andrew Johnson (1868)   82
    *The only president to be impeached is charged with abusing the removal
    power and defaming Congress through intemperate rhetoric*

17. Theodore Roosevelt's and William Howard Taft's
    Theories of Presidential Power (1913, 1916)   93
    *The classic debate on the proper scope of presidential power
    and leadership*

18. Woodrow Wilson's First State of the Union Address (1913)   99
    Wilson ushers in the "rhetorical presidency"

19. The Teapot Dome Resolution (1924)   103
    *The nexus between congressional investigation and
    presidential scandal is forged*

20. Franklin D. Roosevelt's First Inaugural Address (1933)   106
    *FDR reassures a desperate nation and asks Congress for "broad executive
    power to wage war against the emergency" of economic depression*

21. *Humphrey's Executor v. United States* (1935)   112
The Supreme Court restricts the president's removal power

22. *United States v. Curtiss-Wright Export Corp.* (1936)   118
The Supreme Court declares that the president is the nation's "sole organ in the field of international relations"

23. Franklin D. Roosevelt's Court-packing Address (1937)   123
FDR overreaches by attacking the Supreme Court and, in the process, sparks the creation of the "conservative coalition" in Congress

24. Report of the Brownlow Committee (1937)   130
The origins of the modern White House staff

25. *Youngstown Sheet and Tube Co. v. Sawyer* (1952)   136
Justice Black's opinion of the Court and Justice Jackson's concurring opinion take different approaches to restraining presidential power

26. Dwight D. Eisenhower's Little Rock Executive Order (1957)   145
Eisenhower uses the president's "executive" and "take Care" powers to enforce the integration of an Arkansas high school

27. The First Kennedy-Nixon Debate (1960)   149
The first presidential debates take place during an important democratizing election

28. John F. Kennedy's Inaugural Address (1961)   159
The young president calls on the nation to "support any friend, oppose any foe" in the cold war

29. The Cuban Missile Crisis: John F. Kennedy's Letter to Soviet Premier Nikita Khrushchev (1962)   163
Crisis decision-making resolves the most dangerous international confrontation in history

30. Lyndon B. Johnson's "Great Society" Speech (1964)   166
Johnson rouses public support for his ambitious domestic agenda

31. Lyndon B. Johnson's Gulf of Tonkin Message (1964)   169
Congress writes a blank check to the president to wage war in Vietnam

32. Richard Nixon's China Trip Announcement (1971)   174
The ultimate anticommunist uses secret diplomacy to open a relationship with the People's Republic of China

33. The McGovern-Fraser Commission Report (1971)   177
     The modern presidential nominating process takes shape

34. The War Powers Resolution (1973)   184
     Congress tries to reclaim the war power from the president

35. Proposed Articles of Impeachment against
     Richard Nixon (1974)   190
     The Watergate crisis brings down the president and his closest advisers

36. *United States v. Nixon* (1974)   196
     The Supreme Court acknowledges but limits executive privilege

37. The "Smoking Gun" Watergate Tapes (1974)   201
     Incriminating White House tapes, released by order of the Supreme Court,
     spur Nixon's resignation

38. Gerald R. Ford's Pardon of Richard Nixon (1974)   207
     Ford jeopardizes his political standing by exercising the president's
     only unchecked constitutional power on behalf of his predecessor

39. Jimmy Carter's "Crisis of Confidence" Speech (1979)   211
     A president elected by praising the people blames them for the problems
     of his administration

40. Ronald Reagan's First Inaugural Address (1981)   218
     In a new-style inaugural address, Reagan ushers in an era
     by declaring that "government is not the solution to our problem;
     government is the problem"

41. *Immigration and Naturalization Service v. Chadha* (1983)   225
     The Supreme Court strikes down the legislative veto

42. George Bush's Persian Gulf War Address (1991)   235
     Bush's greatest triumph foreshadows his worst defeat

43. Bill Clinton's State of the Union Address (1998)   240
     A strong economy helps the president's political standing at a time of crisis

44. *Clinton v. City of New York* (1998)   247
     The Supreme Court declares the line item veto unconstitutional

45. Bill Clinton's "Apology" Address (1998)   252
     Clinton combines an admission of "wrong" personal behavior with an attack
     on the independent counsel

     Topical Guide to the Documents   255

Preface
A User's Guide to *The Evolving Presidency*

Sometimes new wine actually does fit into old wineskins. E-mail, for example, seems to have restored the lost art of letter writing, to the astonishment and delight of the parents and friends of college students. Similarly, the World Wide Web's vast store of information has revived interest in primary and documentary sources, which for so long have yielded to textbook summaries of, for example, what President James Monroe actually said in announcing his famous doctrine, or how the Supreme Court reasoned in its decision to order President Richard Nixon to turn over the Watergate tapes. Of course, as many mouse-wielding students have found from bitter experience, the Web's very abundance of information can be overwhelming, and it is sometimes unreliable.

This book is my effort to weave together for students of the American presidency the virtues of primary and documentary sources with those of careful, reliable editing and close treatment of political and historical context. The documentary record of the presidency is rich and varied, ranging from laws and Supreme Court decisions to speeches and tape recordings. Forty-five documents, spanning the 211 years from the Constitutional Convention of 1787 to the Supreme Court's June 1998 decision to overturn the Line Item Veto Act and the president's August 1998 apology to the nation, are included in this book. The emphasis is on the founding era, comprising one-fifth of the book, and the modern presidency, comprising two-thirds. Many documents are printed in full; others have been edited both to highlight those sections that have proven to be of enduring importance and to preserve the flavor of the original. All of the documents are preceded by short essays that place them in political and historical context. I have included a URL with each document, when available, for access to the complete, unedited text; however, because of the ever-changing nature of the Web, readers should not assume that documents will always be available at the listed sites.

Students and professors will find that *The Evolving Presidency* fits well in a course on the American presidency or American political institutions. The table of contents is chronological, but courses that are organized topically—the president and the Constitution, the president and Congress, presidential elections, the president and domestic policy, and so on—will benefit from the Topical Guide on pages 255–258.

The Topical Guide shows that a course unit on, say, the president and the bureaucracy can draw profitably on some or all of the following documents in this book: *The Federalist Papers* Nos. 69 and 70 (1788), the Pacificus-Helvidius Letters (1793), Andrew Jackson's First Message to Congress (1829), the Articles of Impeachment against Andrew Johnson (1868), *Humphrey's Executor v. United States* (1935), Report of the Brownlow Committee (1937), Proposed Articles of Impeachment against Richard Nixon (1974), *United States v. Nixon* (1974), the "Smoking Gun" Watergate Tapes (1974), and *Immigration and Naturalization Service v. Chadha* (1983). Some of these documents could be used in other units as well, providing ample flexibility for course use. The *Chadha* case, for example, could fit into units on the president and the Constitution, the president and Congress, the president and the Courts, or the president and domestic policy.

Librarians and researchers will find *The Evolving Presidency* a one-stop guide to the most important documents concerning the highest office in the land. Twenty-two presidents are represented in this book, many of them—including Abraham Lincoln (three documents), Franklin D. Roosevelt (six documents), John F. Kennedy (three documents), and Bill Clinton (three documents)—more than once. Seven landmark Supreme Court decisions are included. So are documents bearing on vital events in American history, such as the debate on the Constitution, the Civil War, the Great Depression, the Civil Rights Movement, and the Watergate scandal. Some library patrons will be satisfied with the edited versions of documents that highlight their most significant features; others will wish to follow the URLs to the complete text. All, I hope, will appreciate the essays that explain the significance of each document for its time and for the long-term history of the presidency.

Words generally serve me well, but they are inadequate to express my thanks to those involved in the publication of this book. I especially thank Brenda Carter, the director of CQ Press, who recognized the book's possibilities at an early stage and advised me well at every step on the way to completion, and Talia Greenberg, the book's copy editor and production editor, who among (many) other things saved me from several errors and infelicities great and small. I also wish to thank Jeffrey Cohen, Margaret Thompson, and four anonymous historians and political scientists for their helpful reviews of the prospectus for the book, along with historian Timothy S. Huebner of Rhodes College for reviewing the completed manuscript and Kachergis Book Design for creating the book's inviting and attractive design.

The Constitution*
Provisions Concerning the Presidency
(1787)

O N FEBRUARY 21, 1787, the Continental Congress passed a resolution calling for "a Convention of delegates who shall have been
appointed by the several states to be held in Philadelphia for the sole
and express purpose of revising the Articles of Confederation." The government that had been created by the Articles in 1781 was widely regarded as having a number of weaknesses, including insufficient powers
and the absence of an executive branch.

The convention (later dubbed the Constitutional Convention) met
from May 25 to September 17, 1787. It went far beyond its charter,
drafting an entirely new plan of government that, with the approval of
nine of the thirteen states, would replace the Articles. The proposed
Constitution was ratified by the ninth state (New Hampshire) on June
21, 1788, and took effect on March 4, 1789.

The presidency is arguably the most original feature of the Constitution. Yet although Virginia delegate James Madison often is referred to
as "the father of the Constitution," his paternity did not extend to the
executive branch. Madison's views about the national executive were
vague and variable. Like most of the delegates, he feared both executive
power and executive weakness, regarding the former as the seed of
tyranny and the latter as the wellspring of anarchy.

The convention considered a number of proposals for an executive.
These ranged from Connecticut delegate Roger Sherman's suggestion of
a committee-style executive that would be elected by Congress for the
sole purpose of "carrying the will of the Legislature into effect," to New
York delegate Alexander Hamilton's plan for a one-person "Governor"
chosen by electors and granted vast powers and lifetime tenure. Hamilton's plan was considered too extreme, but other delegates—notably
James Wilson and Gouverneur Morris, both of Pennsylvania—nonethe-

*Go to *http://www.law.ou.edu/hist/constitution*

less succeeded in persuading the convention to create a strong presidency. The near-certain knowledge that George Washington, who presided
over the convention, would be the first president was a source of reassurance to many at the convention.

Described mainly in Article II, the president was to be elected by an
electoral college to a four-year term and was empowered, among other
things, to recommend and veto congressional acts; to appoint, with the
Senate's advice and consent, judges and executive officials; to command
the army and navy; to negotiate treaties; and to issue pardons. Congress
could impeach and remove a president for committing acts of "Treason,
Bribery, or other high Crimes and Misdemeanors."

Other provisions of Article II included qualifications for president, a
presidential oath, and a restriction on the ability of Congress to change
the salary of an incumbent president. The Constitution also created the
vice presidency and charged the vice president (the second-place finisher
in the presidential election) to serve as president of the Senate and successor to the president should the office become vacant.

Several constitutional amendments have dealt with the presidency
and vice presidency. The Twelfth Amendment (1804) adapted the electoral college to the rise of political parties by requiring electors to cast
separate ballots for president and vice president. The Twentieth
Amendment (1933) advanced the start of the president's term from the
March 4 after the election to January 20. The Twenty-second Amendment (1951) imposed a two-term limit on the president. (The framers
had felt strongly that there should be no limit on presidential reeligibility.) The Twenty-fifth Amendment (1967) empowered the president,
with confirmation by Congress, to appoint a vice president when the
vice presidency becomes vacant. It also created procedures to govern situations of presidential disability. Other constitutional amendments
have affected the circumstances under which presidents are elected,
such as the Twenty-third Amendment (1961), which granted the District of Columbia the right to participate in presidential elections, and
the Twenty-fourth Amendment (1964), which barred the poll tax from
all federal elections.

                              ❧ ❧ ❧

Article I

SECTION 1. All legislative Powers herein granted shall be vested in a Congress of the United States, which shall consist of a Senate and House of Representatives. . . .

SECTION 2. . . . The House of Representatives shall chuse their Speaker and other Officers; and shall have the sole Power of Impeachment. . . .

SECTION 3. . . . The Vice President of the United States shall be President of the Senate, but shall have no Vote, unless they be equally divided.

The Senate shall chuse their other Officers, and also a President pro tempore, in the Absence of the Vice President, or when he shall exercise the Office of President of the United States.

The Senate shall have the sole Power to try all Impeachments. When sitting for that Purpose, they shall be on Oath or Affirmation. When the President of the United States is tried the Chief Justice shall preside: And no Person shall be convicted without the Concurrence of two thirds of the Members present.

Judgment in Cases of Impeachment shall not extend further than to removal from Office, and disqualification to hold and enjoy any Office of honor, Trust or Profit under the United States: but the Party convicted shall nevertheless be liable and subject to Indictment, Trial, Judgment and Punishment, according to Law. . . .

SECTION 6. . . . No Senator or Representative shall, during the Time for which he was elected, be appointed to any civil Office under the Authority of the United States, which shall have been created, or the Emoluments whereof shall have been increased during such time; and no Person holding any Office under the United States, shall be a Member of either House during his Continuance in Office. . . .

SECTION 7. . . . Every Bill which shall have passed the House of Representatives and the Senate, shall, before it become a Law, be presented to the President of the United States; If he approve he shall sign it, but if not he shall return it, with his Objections to that House in which it shall have originated, who shall enter the Objections at large on their Journal, and proceed to reconsider it. If after such Reconsideration two thirds of that House shall agree to pass the Bill, it shall be sent, together with the Objections, to the other House, by which it shall likewise be reconsidered, and if approved by two thirds of that House, it shall become a Law. But in all such Cases the Votes of both Houses shall be determined by yeas and Nays, and the Names of the Persons voting for and against the Bill shall be entered on the Journal of each House respectively. If any Bill shall not be returned by the President within ten Days (Sundays excepted) after it shall have been presented to him, the Same shall be a Law, in like Manner as if he had signed it, unless the Congress by their Adjournment prevent its Return, in which Case it shall not be a Law.

Every Order, Resolution, or Vote to which the Concurrence of the Senate and House of Representatives may be necessary (except on a question of Adjournment) shall be presented to the President of the United States; and before the Same shall take Effect, shall be approved by him, or being disapproved by him, shall be repassed by two thirds of the Senate and House of Representatives, according to the Rules and Limitations prescribed in the Case of a Bill. . . .

Article II

SECTION 1. The executive Power shall be vested in a President of the United States of America. He shall hold his Office during the Term of four Years, and, together with the Vice President, chosen for the same Term, be elected, as follows.

Each State shall appoint, in such Manner as the Legislature thereof may direct, a Number of Electors, equal to the whole Number of Senators and Representatives to which the State may be entitled in the Congress: but no Senator or Representative, or Person holding an Office of Trust or Profit under the United States, shall be appointed an Elector.

[The Electors shall meet in their respective States, and vote by Ballot for two Persons, of whom one at least shall not be an Inhabitant of the same State with themselves. And they shall make a List of all the Persons voted for, and of the Number of Votes for each; which List they shall sign and certify, and transmit sealed to the Seat of the Government of the United States, directed to the President of the Senate. The President of the Senate shall, in the Presence of the Senate and House of Representatives, open all the Certificates, and the Votes shall then be counted. The Person having the greatest Number of Votes shall be the President, if such Number be a Majority of the whole Number of Electors appointed; and if there be more than one who have such Majority, and have an equal Number of Votes, then the House of Representatives shall immediately chuse by Ballot one of them for President; and if no Person have a Majority, then from the five highest on the list the said House shall in like Manner chuse the President. But in chusing the President, the Votes shall be taken by States, the Representation from each State having one Vote; a quorum for this Purpose shall consist of a Member or Members from two thirds of the States, and a Majority of all the States shall be necessary to a Choice. In every

Case, after the Choice of the President, the Person having the greatest Number of Votes of the Electors shall be the Vice President. But if there should remain two or more who have equal Votes, the Senate shall chuse from them by Ballot the Vice President.]*

The Congress may determine the Time of chusing the Electors, and the Day on which they shall give their Votes; which Day shall be the same throughout the United States.

No Person except a natural born Citizen, or a Citizen of the United States, at the time of the Adoption of this Constitution, shall be eligible to the Office of President; neither shall any Person be eligible to that Office who shall not have attained to the Age of thirty five Years, and been fourteen Years a Resident within the United States.

In Case of the Removal of the President from Office, or of his Death, Resignation, or Inability to discharge the Powers and Duties of the said Office, the Same shall devolve on the Vice President, and the Congress may by Law provide for the Case of Removal, Death, Resignation or Inability, both of the President and Vice President, declaring what Officer shall then act as President, and such Officer shall act accordingly, until the Disability be removed, or a President shall be elected.

The President shall, at stated Times, receive for his Services, a Compensation, which shall neither be encreased nor diminished during the Period for which he shall have been elected, and he shall not receive within that Period any other Emolument from the United States, or any of them.

Before he enter on the Execution of his Office, he shall take the following Oath or Affirmation: —"I do solemnly swear (or affirm) that I will faithfully execute the Office of President of the United States, and will to the best of my Ability, preserve, protect and defend the Constitution of the United States."

SECTION 2. The President shall be Commander in Chief of the Army and Navy of the United States, and of the Militia of the several States, when called into the actual Service of the United States; he may require the Opinion, in writing, of the principal Officer in each of the executive Departments, upon any Subject relating to the Duties of their respective Offices, and he shall have Power to grant Reprieves and Pardons for Offenses against the United States, except in Cases of Impeachment.

He shall have Power, by and with the Advice and Consent of the Senate, to make Treaties, provided two thirds of the Senators present concur; and he shall nominate, and by and with the Advice and Consent of the Senate, shall appoint

*Superseded by Amendment XII, section 2.

Ambassadors, other public Ministers and Consuls, Judges of the supreme Court, and all other Officers of the United States, whose Appointments are not herein otherwise provided for, and which shall be established by Law: but the Congress may by Law vest the Appointment of such inferior Officers, as they think proper, in the President alone, in the Courts of Law, or in the Heads of Departments.

The President shall have Power to fill up all Vacancies that may happen during the Recess of the Senate, by granting Commissions which shall expire at the End of their next Session.

SECTION 3. He shall from time to time give to the Congress Information of the State of the Union, and recommend to their Consideration such Measures as he shall judge necessary and expedient; he may, on extraordinary Occasions, convene both Houses, or either of them, and in Case of Disagreement between them, with Respect to the Time of Adjournment, he may adjourn them to such Time as he shall think proper; he shall receive Ambassadors and other public Ministers; he shall take Care that the Laws be faithfully executed, and shall Commission all the Officers of the United States.

SECTION 4. The President, Vice President and all Civil Officers of the United States, shall be removed from office on Impeachment for, and Conviction of, Treason, Bribery, or other high Crimes and Misdemeanors. . . .

Article III

SECTION 1. The judicial Power of the United States, shall be vested in one supreme Court, and in such inferior Courts as the Congress may from time to time ordain and establish. . . .

Amendment XII
(Ratified June 15, 1804)

The Electors shall meet in their respective states and vote by ballot for President and Vice-President, one of whom, at least, shall not be an inhabitant of the same state with themselves; they shall name in their ballots the person voted for as President, and in distinct ballots the person voted for as Vice-President, and they shall make distinct lists of all persons voted for as President, and of all persons voted for as Vice-President, and of the number of votes for each, which lists they shall sign and certify, and transmit sealed to the seat of the government of the United States, directed to the President of the Senate; —The President of the Senate shall, in the presence of the Senate and House of Representatives, open all the certificates and the votes shall then be counted; —The person having the greatest number of votes for President, shall be the President, if such number be a majority of the whole number of Electors appointed; and if no person have such majority, then from the persons having the highest numbers not exceeding three on the list of those voted for as President, the House of Representatives shall choose immediately, by ballot, the President. But in choosing the President, the votes shall be taken by states, the representation from each state having one vote; a quorum for this purpose shall consist of a member or members from two-thirds of the states, and a majority of all the states shall be necessary to a choice. [And if the House of Representatives shall not choose a President whenever the right of choice shall devolve upon them, before the fourth day of March next following, then the Vice-President shall act as President, as in the case of the death or other constitutional disability of the President—]* The person having the greatest number of votes as Vice-President, shall be the Vice-President, if such number be a majority of the whole number of Electors appointed, and if no person have a majority, then from the two highest numbers on the list, the Senate shall choose the Vice-President; a quorum for the purpose shall consist of two-thirds of the whole number of Senators, and a majority of the whole number shall be necessary to a choice. But no person constitutionally ineligible to the office of President shall be eligible to that of Vice-President of the United States. . . .

Amendment XX
(Ratified January 23, 1933)

SECTION 1. The terms of the President and Vice President shall end at noon on the 20th day of January, and the terms of Senators and Representatives at noon on the 3d day of January, of the years in which such terms would have ended if this article had not been ratified; and the terms of their successors shall then begin. . . .

SECTION 3. If, at the time fixed for the beginning of the term of the President, the President elect shall have died, the Vice President elect shall become President. If a President shall not have been chosen before the time fixed for the beginning of his term, or if the President elect shall have failed to qualify, then the Vice President elect shall act as President until a President shall have qualified; and the Congress may by law provide for the case wherein neither a President elect nor a Vice President elect shall have qualified, declaring who shall then act as President, or the manner in which one who is to act shall be

---

*Superseded by Amendment XX, section 3.

selected, and such person shall act accordingly until a President or Vice President shall have qualified.

SECTION 4. The Congress may by law provide for the case of the death of any of the persons from whom the House of Representatives may choose a President whenever the right of choice shall have devolved upon them, and for the case of the death of any of the persons from whom the Senate may choose a Vice President whenever the right of choice shall have devolved upon them.

SECTION 5. Sections 1 and 2 shall take effect on the 15th day of October following the ratification of this article.

SECTION 6. This article shall be inoperative unless it shall have been ratified as an amendment to the Constitution by the legislatures of three-fourths of the several States within seven years from the date of its submission. . . .

Amendment XXII
(Ratified February 27, 1951)

SECTION 1. No person shall be elected to the office of the President more than twice, and no person who has held the office of President, or acted as President, for more than two years of a term to which some other person was elected President shall be elected to the office of the President more than once. But this Article shall not apply to any person holding the office of President when this Article was proposed by the Congress, and shall not prevent any person who may be holding the office of President, or acting as President, during the term within which this Article becomes operative from holding the office of President or acting as President during the remainder of such term.

SECTION 2. This Article shall be inoperative unless it shall have been ratified as an amendment to the Constitution by the legislatures of three-fourths of the several States within seven years from the date of its submission to the States by the Congress.

Amendment XXIII
(Ratified March 29, 1961)

SECTION 1. The District constituting the seat of Government of the United States shall appoint in such manner as the Congress may direct:

A number of electors of President and Vice President equal to the whole number of Senators and Representatives in Congress to which the District would be entitled if it were a State, but in no event more than the least populous State; they shall be in addition to those appointed by the States, but they shall be considered, for the purposes of the election of President and Vice President, to be electors appointed by a State; and they shall meet in the District and perform such duties as provided by the twelfth article of amendment.

SECTION 2. The Congress shall have power to enforce this article by appropriate legislation.

Amendment XXIV
(Ratified January 23, 1964)

SECTION 1. The right of citizens of the United States to vote in any primary or other election for President or Vice President, for electors for President or Vice President, or for Senator or Representative in Congress, shall not be denied or abridged by the United States or any State by reason of failure to pay any poll tax or other tax.

SECTION 2. The Congress shall have power to enforce this article by appropriate legislation.

Amendment XXV
(Ratified February 10, 1967)

SECTION 1. In case of the removal of the President from office or of his death or resignation, the Vice President shall become President.

SECTION 2. Whenever there is a vacancy in the office of the Vice President, the President shall nominate a Vice President who shall take office upon confirmation by a majority vote of both Houses of Congress.

SECTION 3. Whenever the President transmits to the President pro tempore of the Senate and the Speaker of the House of Representatives his written declaration that he is unable to discharge the powers and duties of his office, and until he transmits to them a written declaration to the contrary, such powers and duties shall be discharged by the Vice President as Acting President.

SECTION 4. Whenever the Vice President and a majority of either the principal officers of the executive departments or of such other body as Congress may by law provide, transmit to the President pro tempore of the Senate and the Speaker of the House of Representatives their written declaration that the President is unable to discharge the powers and duties of his office, the Vice President shall immediately assume the powers and duties of the office as Acting President.

Thereafter, when the President transmits to the President pro tempore of the Senate and the Speaker of the House of Representatives his written declaration that no inability exists, he shall resume the powers and duties of his office unless the Vice President and a majority of either the principal officers of the executive department or of such other body as Congress may by law provide, transmit within four days to the President pro tempore of the Senate and the

Speaker of the House of Representatives their written declaration that the President is unable to discharge the powers and duties of his office. Thereupon Congress shall decide the issue, assembling within forty-eight hours for that purpose if not in session. If the Congress, within twenty-one days after receipt of the latter written declaration, or, if Congress is not in session, within twenty-one days after Congress is required to assemble, determines by two-thirds vote of both houses that the President is unable to discharge the powers and duties of his office, the Vice President shall continue to discharge the same as Acting President; otherwise, the President shall resume the powers and duties of his office.

⋙ 2 ⋘

Letters of Cato, Nos. 4 and 5
(1787)

ARTICLE II POSED a political problem for those who were trying to persuade the states to ratify the Constitution. Not only was the presidency the most obvious innovation in the proposed plan of government, but its unitary nature and strong powers roused fears of the most horrifying political specter that most Americans could imagine: an all-powerful monarchy like the one they had overthrown in the Revolutionary War. Opponents of the Constitution—the so-called Anti-Federalists—effectively exploited these fears.

One of the first Anti-Federalist writers to publish his objections to the Constitution was "Cato," whose first letter (he wrote seven altogether) was published in the *New York Journal* on September 27, 1787, only ten days after the Constitutional Convention concluded its business. The author is believed to have been either Gov. George Clinton of New York or Abraham Yates Jr., a New York delegate to the convention who had left it in silent protest. Pseudonymous political writings, often under a name from Roman antiquity, were customary at the time. "Brutus," "Marcus," "Agrippa," and, of course, "Publius," the author of *The Federalist Papers,* were among the writers who contributed to the ratification debate, along with "The Federal Farmer" and "The Republican."

In his fourth (November 8) and fifth (November 22) letters, Cato attacked the president as a monarch in disguise, surrounded by a royal court, "oppressing his fellow-citizens and raising himself to permanent grandeur on the ruins of his country." Some of Cato's warnings now seem farfetched (he charged that the Constitution required that only one election ever be held), but others were prescient, especially his concern that the national capital in general, and the president in particular, could become isolated from the rest of the country.

Cato's identification of the presidency with monarchy was echoed by many other Anti-Federalists. At the Virginia ratifying convention, for example, Gov. Patrick Henry charged: "This Constitution is said to have beautiful features, but when I come to examine these features, Sir, they appear to me to be horridly frightful: Among other deformities, it has an awful squinting; it squints toward monarchy: And does this not raise indignation in the breast of every American?"

Cato No. 4

To the Citizens of the State of New York.

. . . I shall begin with observations on the executive branch of this new system; and though it is not the first in order, as arranged therein, yet being the *chief,* is perhaps entitled by the rules of rank to the first consideration. The executive power as described in the 2d article, consists of a president and vice-president, who are to hold their offices during the term of four years; the same article has marked the manner and time of their election, and established the qualifications of the president; it also provides against the removal, death, or inability of the president and vice-president—regulates the salary, of the president, delineates his duties and powers; and, lastly, declares the causes for which the president and vice-president shall be removed from office.

Notwithstanding, the great learning and abilities of the gentlemen who composed the convention, it may be here remarked with deference, that the construction of the first paragraph of the first section of the second article is vague and inexplicit, and leaves the mind in doubt as to the election of a president and vice-president, after the expiration of the election for the first term of four years; in every other case, the election of these great officers is expressly provided for; but there is no explicit provision for their election in case of expiration of their offices, subsequent to the election which is to set this political machine in motion, no certain and express terms as in your state constitution, that *statedly* once in every four years, and as often as these offices shall become vacant, by expiration or otherwise, as is therein expressed, an election shall be held as follows, &c., this inexplicitness perhaps may lead to an establishment for life.

It is remarked by Mon[t]esquieu, in treating of republics, that *in all magistracies, the greatness of the power must, be compensated by the brevity of the duration, and that a longer time than a year would be dangerous.* It is, therefore, obvious to the least intelligent mind to account why great power in the hands of a magistrate, and that power connected with considerable duration, may be dangerous to the liberties of a republic, the deposit of vast trusts in the hands of a single magistrate, enables him in their exercise to create a numerous train of dependents; this tempts his *ambition,* which in a republican magistrate is also remarked, to be *pernicious,* and the duration of his office for any considerable time favors his views, gives him the means and time to perfect and execute his designs, *he therefore fancies that he may be great and glorious by oppressing his fellow-citizens, and raising himself to permanent grandeur on the ruins of his country.* And here it may be necessary to compare the vast and important powers of the president, together with his continuance in office, with the foregoing doctrine—his eminent magisterial situation will attach many adherents to him, and he will be surrounded by expectants and courtiers, his power of nomination and influence on all appointments, the strong posts in each state comprised within his superintendence, and garrisoned by troops under his direction, his control over the army, militia, and navy, the unrestrained power of granting pardons for treason, which may be used to screen from punishment those whom he had secretly instigated to commit the crime, and thereby prevent a discovery of his own guilt, his duration in office for four years: these, and various other principles evidently prove the truth of the position, that if the president is possessed of ambition, he has power and time sufficient to ruin his country.

Though the president, during the sitting of the legislature, is assisted by the senate, yet he is without a constitutional council in their recess; he will therefore be unsupported by proper information and advice, and will generally be directed by minions and favorites, or a council of state will grow out of the principal officers of the great departments, the most dangerous council in a free country.

The ten miles square, which is to become the seat of government, will of course be the place of residence for the president and the great officers of state;

the same observations of a great man will apply to the court of a president possessing the powers of a monarch, that is observed of that of a *monarch — ambition with idleness — baseness with pride — the thirst of riches without labor — aversion to truth — flattery — treason — perfidy — violation of engagements — contempt of civil duties — hope from the magistrate's weakness: but above all the perpetual ridicule of* virtue — these, he remarks, are the characteristics by which the courts in all ages have been distinguished.

The language and the manners of this court will be what distinguishes them from the rest of the community, not what assimilates them to it; and in being remarked for a behavior that shows they are not *meanly-born,* and in adulation to people of fortune and power.

The establishment of a vice-president is as unnecessary as it is dangerous. This officer, for want of other employment, is made president of the senate, thereby blending the executive and legislative powers, besides always giving to some one state, from which he is to come, an unjust pre-eminence.

It is a maxim in republics that the representative of the people should be of their immediate choice; but by the manner in which the president is chosen, he arrives to this office at the fourth or fifth hand, nor does the highest vote, in the way he is elected, determine the choice, for it is only necessary that he should be taken from the highest of five, who may have a plurality of votes.

Compare your past opinions and sentiments with the present proposed establishment, and you will find, that if you adopt it, that it will lead you into a system which you heretofore reprobated as odious. Every American Whig, not long since, bore his emphatic testimony against a monarchical government, though limited, because of the dangerous inequality that it created among citizens as relative to their rights and property; and wherein does this president, invested with his powers and prerogatives, essentially differ from the king of Great Britain (save as to name, the creation of nobility, and some immaterial incidents, the offspring of absurdity and locality). The direct prerogatives of the president, as springing from his political character, are among the following: It is necessary, in order to distinguish him from the rest of the community, and enable him to keep, and maintain his court, that the compensation for his services, or in other words, his revenue, should be such as to enable him to appear with the splendor of a prince; he has the power of receiving ambassadors from, and a great influence on their appointments to foreign courts; as also to make treaties, leagues, and alliances with foreign states, assisted by the Senate, which when made become the supreme law of the land: he is a constituent part of the legislative power, for every bill which shall pass the House of Representatives and Senate is to be presented to him for approbation: if he approves of it he is to sign it, if he disapproves he is to return it with objections, which in many cases will amount to a complete negative; and in this view he will have a great share in the power of making peace, coining money, etc., and all the various objects of legislation, expressed or implied in this Constitution: for though it may be asserted that the king of Great Britain has the express power of making peace or war, yet he never thinks it prudent to do so without the advice of his Parliament, from whom he is to derive his support, and therefore these powers, in both president and king, are substantially the same: he is the generalissimo of the nation, and of course has the command and control of the army, navy and militia; he is the general conservator of the peace of the union—he may pardon all offences, except in cases of impeachment, and the principal fountain of all offices and employments. Will not the exercise of these powers therefore tend either to the establishment of a vile and arbitrary aristocracy or monarchy? The safety of the people in a republic depends on the share or proportion they have in the government; but experience ought to teach you, that when a man is at the head of an elective government invested with great powers, and interested in his re-election, in what circle appointments will be made; by which means an *imperfect aristocracy* bordering on monarchy may be established.

You must, however, my countrymen, beware that the advocates of this new system do not deceive you by a fallacious resemblance between it and your own state government which you so much prize; and, if you examine, you will perceive that the chief magistrate of this state is your immediate choice, controlled and checked by a just and full representation of the people, divested of the prerogative of influencing war and peace, making treaties, receiving and sending embassies, and commanding standing armies and navies, which belong to the power of the confederation, and will be convinced that this government is no more like a true picture of your own than an Angel of Darkness resembles an Angel of Light.

Cato No. 5

To the Citizens of the State of New York.

In my last number I endeavored to prove that the language of the article relative to the establishment of the executive of this new government was vague and inexplicit; that the great powers of the president, connected with his duration in office, would lead to oppression and ruin; that he would be governed by favorites and flatterers, or that a dangerous council would be collected from the great officers of state; that the ten miles square, if the remarks of one of the wisest men, drawn from the experience of mankind, may be credited, would be the asylum of the base, idle, avaricious and ambitious, and that the court would possess a language and manners different from yours; that a vice-president is as unnecessary as he is dangerous in his influence; that the president cannot represent you because he is not of your own immediate choice; that if you adopt this government you will incline to an arbitrary and odious aristocracy or monarchy; that the president, possessed of the power given him by this frame of government, differs but very immaterially from the establishment of monarchy in Great Britain; and I warned you to beware of the fallacious resemblance that is held out to you by the advocates of this new system between it and your own state governments.

And here I cannot help remarking that inexplicitness seems to pervade this whole political fabric; certainly in political compacts, which Mr. Coke calls *the mother and nurse of repose and quietness* the want of which induced men to engage in political society, has ever been held by a wise and free people as essential to their security; as on the one hand it fixes barriers which the ambitious and tyrannically disposed magistrate dare not overleap, and on the other, becomes a wall of safety to the community—otherwise stipulations between the governors and governed are nugatory; and you might as well deposit the important powers of legislation and execution in one or a few and permit them to govern according to their disposition and will; but the world is too full of examples, which prove that *to live by one man's will became the cause of all men's misery.* Before the existence of expressed compacts it was reasonably implied that the magistrate should govern with wisdom and justice; but mere implication was too feeble to restrain the unbridled ambition of a bad man, or afford security against negligence, cruelty or any other defect of mind. It is alleged that the opinions and manners of the people of America are capable to resist and prevent an extension of prerogative or oppression, but you must recollect that opinion and manners are mutable, and may not always be a permanent obstruction against the encroachments of government; that the progress of a commercial society begets luxury, the parent of inequality, the foe to virtue, and the enemy to restraint; and that ambition and voluptuousness, aided by flattery, will teach magistrates where limits are not explicitly fixed to have separate and distinct interests from the people; besides, it will not be denied that government assimilates the manners and opinions of the community to it. Therefore, a general presumption that rulers will govern well is not a sufficient security. You are then under a sacred obligation to provide for the safety of your posterity, and would you now basely desert their interests, when by a small share of prudence you may transmit to them a beautiful political patrimony, which will prevent the necessity of their travelling through seas of blood to obtain that which your wisdom might have secured? It is a duty you owe likewise to your own reputation, for you have a great name to lose; you are characterized as cautious, prudent and jealous in politics; whence is it therefore that you are about to precipitate yourselves into a sea of uncertainty, and adopt a system so vague, and which has discarded so many of your valuable rights? Is it because you do not believe that an American can be a tyrant? If this be the case, you rest on a weak basis: Americans are like other men in similar situations, when the manners and opinions of the community are changed by the causes I mentioned before; and your political compact inexplicit, your posterity will find that great power connected with ambition, luxury and flattery, will as readily produce a Caesar, Caligula, Nero and Domitian in America, as the same causes did in the Roman Empire. . . .

<hr>

✵ 3 ✵

The Federalist Papers, Nos. 69 and 70*

(1788)

PROPONENTS OF THE Constitution at the state ratifying conventions—the Federalists—answered "Cato" and other Anti-Federalist opponents by stressing both the virtues of the presidency and the restraints that the Constitution placed on the office. In doing so they leaned heavily on the explanations and defenses of the Constitution that Alexander Hamilton and John Jay (both New Yorkers) and James Madison (a Virginian) were putting forth in a series of eighty-five newspaper articles that Hamilton had commissioned. These articles, gathered together in late 1788 in a book called *The Federalist Papers,* appeared pseudonymously under the name "Publius" in several New York newspapers between October 27, 1787, and May 28, 1788. They were widely reprinted around the country.

Hamilton wrote more than fifty of the articles that dealt with the presidency, including Nos. 69–77. No. 69, which appeared in the *New York Packet* on March 14, 1788, squarely addressed the Anti-Federalist

*Go to *http://www.law.ou.edu/hist/federalist*

charge that the presidency was a disguised monarchy. Hamilton argued that, in contrast to the British king, who secures his office by inheritance and serves for life, the president is freely elected for a limited term. The king rules for life; the president can be impeached and removed from office. The king has an absolute veto over laws passed by the legislature; the president's vetoes can be overridden. The king can both declare war and raise an army and navy; the president can do neither. The king can create offices and appoint people to fill them; the president cannot create offices and can fill those that Congress creates only after securing the approval of the Senate.

Federalist No. 70 was published on March 15 in another New York newspaper, the *Independent Journal.* Less defensive in tone than No. 69, it described the virtues of the presidency. Hamilton's theme was "energy," a quality that he regarded as essential to the defense of the nation and the steady administration of the laws. In the government created by the Constitution, energy was to be provided by the presidency, mostly because of its unitary character. Unity, Hamilton argued, imbues the office with a host of virtues—"decision, activity, secrecy, and dispatch . . . vigor and expedition."

In the days that followed, Hamilton continued his defense of the presidency. In *Federalist* Nos. 71–77 he praised the office for having additional qualities indispensable to energy: "duration" from both the four-year term (No. 71) and eligibility for reelection (No. 72); "adequate provision for its support" in the form of salary (No. 73); and "competent powers" (Nos. 73–77). The great irony of these essays is that Hamilton, who would have preferred that the Constitutional Convention create a much stronger presidency than it did, became the office's most effective defender.

Federalist No. 69

To the People of the State of New-York.

I proceed now to trace the real characters of the proposed executive, as they are marked out in the plan of the convention. This will serve to place in a strong light the unfairness of the representations which have been made in regard to it.

The first thing which strikes our attention is that the executive authority, with few exceptions, is to be vested in a single magistrate. This will scarcely, however, be considered as a point upon which any comparison can be grounded; for if, in this particular, there be a resemblance to the king of Great Britain, there is not less a resemblance to the Grand Seignior, to the khan of Tartary, to the Man of the Seven Mountains, or to the governor of New York.

That magistrate is to be elected for *four* years; and is to be re-eligible as often as the people of the United States shall think him worthy of their confidence. In these circumstances there is a total dissimilitude between *him* and a king of Great Britain, who is an *hereditary* monarch, possessing the crown as a patrimony descendible to his heirs forever; but there is a close analogy between *him* and a governor of New York, who is elected for *three* years, and is re-eligible without limitation or intermission. If we consider how much less time would be requisite for establishing a dangerous influence in a single State than for establishing a like influence throughout the United States, we must conclude that a duration of *four* years for the Chief Magistrate of the Union is a degree of permanency far less to be dreaded in that office, than a duration of *three* years for a corresponding office in a single State.

The President of the United States would be liable to be impeached, tried, and, upon conviction of treason, bribery, or other high crimes or misdemeanors, removed from office; and would afterwards be liable to prosecution and punishment in the ordinary course of law. The person of the King of Great Britain is sacred and inviolable; there is no constitutional tribunal to which he is amenable; no punishment to which he can be subjected without involving the crisis of a national revolution. In this delicate and important circumstance of personal responsibility, the President of Confederated America would stand upon no better ground than a governor of New York, and upon worse ground than the governors of Virginia and Delaware.

The President of the United States is to have power to return a bill, which shall have passed the two branches of the legislature, for reconsideration; but the bill so returned is not to become a law unless, upon that reconsideration, it be approved by two thirds of both houses. The king of Great Britain, on his part, has an absolute negative upon the acts of the two houses of Parliament. The disuse of that power for a considerable time past does not affect the reality of its existence and is to be ascribed wholly to the crown's having found the means of substituting influence to authority, or the art of gaining a majority in one or the other of the two houses, to the necessity of exerting a prerogative which could seldom be exerted without hazarding some degree of national agitation. The qualified negative of the President differs widely from this absolute negative of the British sovereign and tallies exactly with the revisionary authority of the council of revision of this State, of which the governor is a constituent part. In this respect the power of the President would exceed that of the governor of New York, because the former would possess, singly, what the latter shares with the chancellor and judges; but it would be precisely the same with that of the governor of Massachusetts, whose constitution, as to this article, seems to have been the original from which the convention have copied.

The President is to be the "commander-in-chief of the army and navy of the United States, and of the militia of the several States, when called into the actual service of the United States. He is to have power to grant reprieves and pardons for offenses against the United States, *except in cases of impeachment;* to recommend to the consideration of Congress such measures as he shall judge necessary and expedient; to convene, on extraordinary occasions, both houses of the legislature, or either of them, and, in case of disagreement between them *with respect to the time of adjournment,* to adjourn them to such time as he shall think proper; to take care that the laws be faithfully executed; and to commission all officers of the United States." In most of these particulars, the power of the President will resemble equally that of the king of Great Britain and of the governor of New York. The most material points of difference are these:— *First.* The President will have only the occasional command of such part of the militia of the nation as by legislative provision may be called into the actual service of the Union. The king of Great Britain and the governor of New York have at all times the entire command of all the militia within their several jurisdictions. In this article, therefore, the power of the President would be inferior to that of either the monarch or the governor. *Second.* The President is to be commander-in-chief of the army and navy of the United States. In this respect his authority would be nominally the same with that of the king of Great Britain, but in substance much inferior to it. It would amount to nothing more than the supreme command and direction of the military and naval forces, as first general and admiral of the Confederacy; while that of the British king extends to the *declaring* of war and to the *raising* and *regulating* of fleets and armies—all which, by the Constitution under consideration, would appertain to the legislature.[1] The governor of New York, on the other hand, is by the constitution of the State vested only with the command of its militia and navy. But the constitutions of several of the States expressly declare their governors to be commanders-in-chief, as well of the army as navy; and it may well be a question whether those of New Hampshire and Massachusetts, in particular, do not, in this instance, confer larger powers upon their respective governors than could be claimed by a President of the United States. *Third.* The power of the President, in respect to pardons, would extend to all cases, *except those of impeachment.* The governor of New York may pardon in all cases, even in those of impeachment, except for treason and murder. Is not the power of the governor, in this article, on a calculation of political consequences, greater than that of the President? All conspiracies and plots against the government which have not been matured into actual treason may be screened from punishment of every kind by the interposition of the prerogative of pardoning. If a governor of New York, therefore, should be at the head of any such conspiracy, until the design had been ripened into actual hostility he could insure his accomplices and adherents an entire impunity. A President of the Union, on the other hand, though he may even pardon treason, when prosecuted in the ordinary course of law, could shelter no offender, in any degree, from the effects of impeachment and conviction. Would not the prospect of a total indemnity for all the preliminary steps be a greater temptation to undertake and persevere in an enterprise against the public liberty, than the mere prospect of an exemption from death and confiscation, if the final execution of the design, upon an actual appeal to arms, should miscarry? Would this last expectation have any influence at all, when the probability was computed that the person who was to afford that exemption might himself be involved in the consequences of the measure, and might be incapacitated by his agency in it from affording the desired impunity? The better to judge of this matter, it will be necessary to recollect that, by the proposed Constitution, the offense of treason is limited "to levying war upon the United States, and adhering to their enemies, giving them aid and comfort"; and that by the laws of New York it is confined within similar bounds. *Fourth.* The President can only adjourn the national legislature in the single case of disagreement about the time of adjournment. The British monarch may prorogue or even dissolve the Parliament. The governor of New York may also prorogue the legislature of this State for a limited time; a power which, in certain situations, may be employed to very important purposes.

The President is to have power, with the advice and consent of the Senate, to make treaties, provided two thirds of the senators present concur. The king of Great Britain is the sole and absolute representative of the nation in all foreign transactions. He can of his own accord make treaties of peace, commerce, alliance, and of every other description. It has been insinuated that his authority in this respect is not conclusive, and that his conventions with foreign powers are subject to the revision, and stand in need of the ratification, of Parliament. But I believe this doctrine was never heard of until it was broached upon the present occasion. Every jurist[2] of that kingdom, and every other man acquainted with its Constitution knows, as an established fact, that the prerogative of making treaties exists in the crown in its utmost plenitude; and that the compacts entered into by the royal authority have the most complete legal validity and perfection, independent of any other sanctions. The Parliament, it is true, is sometimes seen employing itself in altering the existing laws to conform them to the stipulations in a new treaty; and this may have possibly given birth to the imagination that its co-operation was necessary to the obligatory efficacy of the treaty. But this parliamentary interposition proceeds from a different cause: from the necessity of adjusting a most artificial and intricate system of revenue and commercial laws, to the changes made in them by the operation of the treaty; and of adapting new provisions and precautions to the new state of things, to keep the machine from running into disorder. In this respect, therefore, there is no comparison between the intended power of the President and the actual power of the British sovereign. The one can perform alone what the other can only do with the concurrence of a branch of the legislature. It must be admitted that in this instance the power of the federal executive would exceed that of any State executive. But this arises naturally from the exclusive possession by the Union of that part of the sovereign power which relates to treaties. If the Confederacy were to be dissolved, it would become a question whether the executives of the several States were not solely invested with that delicate and important prerogative.

The President is also to be authorized to receive ambassadors and other public ministers. This, though it has been a rich theme of declamation, is more a matter of dignity than of authority. It is a circumstance which will be without consequence in the administration of the government; and it was far more convenient that it should be arranged in this manner than that there should be a necessity of convening the legislature, or one of its branches, upon every arrival of a foreign minister, though it were merely to take the place of a departed predecessor.

The President is to nominate, and, *with the advice and consent of the Senate,* to appoint ambassadors and other public ministers, judges of the Supreme Court, and in general all officers of the United States established by law, and whose appointments are not otherwise provided for by the Constitution. The king of Great Britain is emphatically and truly styled the fountain of honor. He not only appoints to all offices, but can create offices. He can confer titles of nobility at pleasure, and has the disposal of an immense number of church preferments. There is evidently a great inferiority in the power of the President, in this particular, to that of the British king; nor is it equal to that of the governor of New York, if we are to interpret the meaning of the constitution of the State by the practice which has obtained under it. The power of appointment is with us lodged in a council, composed of the governor and four members of the Senate, chosen by the Assembly. The governor *claims,* and has frequently *exercised,* the right of nomination, and is *entitled* to a casting vote in the appointment. If he really has the right of nominating, his authority is in this respect equal to that of the President, and exceeds it in the article of the casting vote. In the national government, if the Senate should be divided, no appointment could be made; in the government of New York, if the council should be divided, the governor can turn the scale and confirm his own nomination.[3] If we compare the publicity which must necessarily attend the mode of appointment by the President and an entire branch of the national legislature, with the privacy in the mode of appointment by the governor of New York, closeted in a secret apartment with at most four, and frequently with only two persons; and if we at the same time consider how much more easy it must be to influence the small number of which council of appointment consists than the considerable number of which the national Senate would consist, we cannot hesitate to pronounce that the power of the chief magistrate of this State, in the disposition of offices, must, in practice, be greatly superior to that of the Chief Magistrate of the Union.

Hence it appears that, except as to the concurrent authority of the President in the article of treaties, it would be difficult to determine whether that magistrate would, in the aggregate, possess more or less power than the governor of New York. And it appears yet more unequivocally that there is no pretense for the parallel which has been attempted between him and the king of Great Britain. But to render the contrast in this respect still more striking, it may be of use to throw the principal circumstances of dissimilitude into a closer group.

The President of the United States would be an officer elected by the people for *four* years; the king of Great Britain is a perpetual and *hereditary* prince. The one would be amenable to personal punishment and disgrace; the person of the other is sacred and inviolable. The one would have a qualified negative upon the acts of the legislative body; the other has an *absolute* negative. The one would have a right to command the military and naval forces of the nation; the other, in addition to this right, possesses that of *declaring* war, and of *raising* and *regulating* fleets and armies by his own authority. The one would have a concurrent power with a branch of the legislature in the formation of treaties; the other is the *sole possessor* of the power of making treaties. The one would have a like concurrent authority in appointing to offices; the other is the sole author of all appointments. The one can confer no privileges whatever; the other can make denizens of aliens, noblemen of commoners; can erect corporations with all the rights incident to corporate bodies. The one can prescribe no rules concerning the commerce or currency of the nation; the other is in several respects the arbiter of commerce, and in this capacity can establish markets and fairs, can regulate weights and measures, can lay embargoes for a limited time, can coin money, can authorize or prohibit the circulation of foreign coin. The one has no particle of spiritual jurisdiction; the other is the supreme head and governor of the national church! What answer shall we give to those who would persuade us that things so unlike resemble each other? The same that ought to be given to those who tell us that a government, the whole power of which would be in the hands of the elective and periodical servants of the people, is an aristocracy, a monarchy, and a despotism.

NOTES

1. A writer in a Pennsylvania paper, under the signature of Tamony, has asserted that the king of Great Britain owes his prerogative as commander-in-chief to an annual mutiny bill. The truth is, on the contrary, that his prerogative in this respect is immemorial, and was only disputed "contrary to all reason and precedent," as Blackstone, vol. i, page 262, expresses it, by the Long Parliament of Charles I; but by the statute the 13th of Charles II, chap. 6, it was declared to be in the king alone, for that the sole supreme government and command of the militia within his Majesty's realms and dominions, and of all forces by sea and land, and of all forts and places of strength, *ever was and is* the undoubted right of his Majesty and his royal predecessors, kings and queens of England, and that both or either house of Parliament cannot nor ought to pretend to the same.

2. *Vide Blackstone's Commentaries,* Vol. I, p. 257.

3. Candor, however, demands an acknowledgment that I do not think the claim of the governor to a right of nomination well founded. Yet it is always justifiable to reason from the practice of a government till its propriety has been constitutionally questioned. And independent of this claim, when we take into view the other considerations and pursue them through all their consequences, we shall be inclined to draw much the same conclusion.

Federalist No. 70

To the People of the State of New-York.

There is an idea, which is not without its advocates, that a vigorous executive is inconsistent with the genius of republican government. The enlightened well-wishers to this species of government must at least hope that the supposition is destitute of foundation; since they can never admit its truth, without at the same time admitting the condemnation of their own principles. Energy in the executive is a leading character in the definition of good government. It is essential to the protection of the community against foreign attacks; it is not less essential to the steady administration of the laws; to the protection of property against those irregular and high-handed combinations which sometimes interrupt the ordinary course of justice; to the security of liberty against the enterprises and assaults of ambition, of faction, and of anarchy. Every man the least conversant in Roman history knows how often that republic was obliged to take refuge in the absolute power of a single man, under the formidable title of dictator, as well against the intrigues of ambitious individuals who aspired to the tyranny, and the seditions of whole classes of the community whose conduct threatened the existence of all government, as against the invasions of external enemies who menaced the conquest and destruction of Rome.

There can be no need, however, to multiply arguments or examples on this head. A feeble executive implies a feeble execution of the government. A feeble execution is but another phrase for a bad execution; and a government ill executed, whatever it may be in theory, must be, in practice, a bad government.

Taking it for granted, therefore, that all men of sense will agree in the necessity of an energetic executive, it will only remain to inquire, what are the ingredients which constitute this energy? How far can they be combined with those other ingredients which constitute safety in the republican sense? And how far does this combination characterize the plan which has been reported by the convention?

The ingredients which constitute energy in the executive are unity; duration; an adequate provision for its support; and competent powers.

The ingredients which constitute safety in the republican sense are a due dependence on the people, and a due responsibility.

Those politicians and statesmen who have been the most celebrated for the soundness of their principles and for the justness of their views have declared in favor of a single executive and a numerous legislature. They have, with great propriety, considered energy as the most necessary qualification of the former, and have regarded this as most applicable to power in a single hand; while they have, with equal propriety, considered the latter as best adapted to deliberation and wisdom, and best calculated to conciliate the confidence of the people and to secure their privileges and interests.

That unity is conducive to energy will not be disputed. Decision, activity, secrecy, and dispatch will generally characterize the proceedings of one man in a much more eminent degree than the proceedings of any greater number; and in proportion as the number is increased, these qualities will be diminished.

This unity may be destroyed in two ways: either by vesting the power in two or more magistrates of equal dignity and authority, or by vesting it ostensibly in one man, subject in whole or in part to the control and cooperation of others, in the capacity of counselors to him. Of the first, the two consuls of Rome may serve as an example; of the last, we shall find examples in the constitutions of several of the States. New York and New Jersey, if I recollect right, are the only States which have intrusted the executive authority wholly to single men.[1] Both these methods of destroying the unity of the executive have their partisans; but the votaries of an executive council are the most numerous. They are both liable, if not equal, to similar objections, and may in most lights be examined in conjunction.

The experience of other nations will afford little instruction on this head. As far, however, as it teaches anything, it teaches us not to be enamored of plurality in the executive. We have seen that the Achaeans, on an experiment of two Praetors, were induced to abolish one. The Roman history records many instances of mischiefs to the republic from the dissensions between the consuls, and between the military tribunes, who were at times substituted for the consuls. But it gives us no specimens of any peculiar advantages derived to the state from the circumstance of the plurality of those magistrates. That the dissensions between them were not more frequent or more fatal is matter of astonishment, until we advert to the singular position in which the republic was almost continually placed, and to the prudent policy pointed out by the circumstances of the state, and pursued by the consuls, of making a division of the government between them. The patricians engaged in a perpetual struggle with the plebeians for the preservation of their ancient authorities and dignities; the consuls, who were generally chosen out of the former body, were commonly united by the personal interest they had in the defense of privileges of their order. In addition to this motive of union, after the arms of the republic had considerably expanded the bounds of its empire, it became an established custom with the consuls to divide the administration between themselves by lot—one of them remaining at Rome to govern the city and its environs, the other taking command in the more distant provinces. This expedient must no doubt have had great influence in preventing those collisions and rivalships which might otherwise have embroiled the peace of the republic.

But quitting the dim light of historical research, and attaching ourselves purely to the dictates of reason and good sense, we shall discover much greater cause to reject than to approve the idea of plurality in the executive, under any modification whatever.

Whenever two or more persons are engaged in any common enterprise or pursuit, there is always danger of difference of opinion. If it be a public trust or office in which they are clothed with equal dignity and authority, there is peculiar danger of personal emulation and even animosity. From either, and especially from all these causes, the most bitter dissensions are apt to spring. Whenever these happen, they lessen the respectability, weaken the authority, and distract the plans and operations of those whom they divide. If they should unfortunately assail the supreme executive magistracy of a country, consisting of a plurality of persons, they might impede or frustrate the most important measures of the government in the most critical emergencies of the state. And what is still worse, they might split the community into the most violent and irreconcilable factions, adhering differently to the different individuals who composed the magistracy.

Men often oppose a thing merely because they have had no agency in planning it, or because it may have been planned by those whom they dislike. But if they have been consulted, and have happened to disapprove, opposition then becomes, in their estimation, an indispensable duty of self-love. They seem to think themselves bound in honor, and by all the motives of personal infallibility, to defeat the success of what has been resolved upon contrary to their sentiments. Men of upright, benevolent tempers have too many opportunities of remarking, with horror, to what desperate lengths this disposition is sometimes carried, and how often the great interests of society are sacrificed to the vanity, to the conceit, and to the obstinacy of individuals, who have credit enough to make their passions and their caprices interesting to mankind. Perhaps the question now before the public may, in its consequences, afford melancholy proofs of the effects of this despicable frailty, or rather detestable vice, in the human character.

Upon the principles of a free government, inconveniences from the source just mentioned must necessarily be submitted to in the formation of the legislature; but it is unnecessary, and therefore unwise, to introduce them into the constitution of the executive. It is here too that they may be most pernicious. In the legislature, promptitude of decision is oftener an evil than a benefit. The differences of opinion, and the jarring of parties in that department of the government, though they may sometimes obstruct salutary plans, yet often promote deliberation and circumspection, and serve to check excesses in the majority. When a resolution too is once taken, the opposition must be at an end. That resolution is a law, and resistance to it punishable. But no favorable circumstances palliate or atone for the disadvantages of dissension in the executive department. Here they are pure and unmixed. There is no point at which they cease to operate. They serve to embarrass and weaken the execution of the plan or measure to which they relate, from the first step to the final conclusion of it. They constantly counteract those qualities in the executive which are the most necessary ingredients in its composition, vigor and expedition, and this without any counterbalancing good. In the conduct of war, in which the energy of the executive is the bulwark of the national security, everything would be to be apprehended from its plurality.

It must be confessed that these observations apply with principal weight to the first case supposed—that is, to a plurality of magistrates of equal dignity and authority, a scheme, the advocates for which are not likely to form a numerous sect; but they apply, though not with equal yet with considerable weight to the project of a council, whose concurrence is made constitutionally necessary to the operations of the ostensible executive. An artful cabal in that council would be able to distract and to enervate the whole system of administration. If no such cabal should exist, the mere diversity of views and opinions would alone be sufficient to tincture the exercise of the executive authority with a spirit of habitual feebleness and dilatoriness.

But one of the weightiest objections to a plurality in the executive, and which lies as much against the last as the first plan, is that it tends to conceal faults and destroy responsibility. Responsibility is of two kinds—to censure and to punishment. The first is the more important of the two, especially in an elective office. Men in public trust will much oftener act in such a manner as to render them unworthy of being any longer trusted, than in such a manner as to make them obnoxious to legal punishment. But the multiplication of the executive adds to the difficulty of detection in either case. It often becomes impossible, amidst mutual accusations, to determine on whom the blame or the punishment of a pernicious measure, or series of pernicious measures, ought really to fall. It is shifted from one to another with so much dexterity, and under such plausible appearances, that the public opinion is left in suspense about the real author. The circumstances which may have led to any national miscarriage or misfortune are sometimes so complicated that where there are a number of actors who may have had different degrees and kinds of agency, though we may clearly see upon the whole that there has been mismanagement, yet it may be impracticable to pronounce to whose account the evil which may have been incurred is truly chargeable.

"I was overruled by my council. The council were so divided in their opinions that it was impossible to obtain any better resolution on the point." These and similar pretexts are constantly at hand, whether true or false. And who is there that will either take the trouble or incur the odium of a strict scrutiny into the secret springs of the transaction? Should there be found a citizen zealous enough to undertake the unpromising task, if there happened to be a collusion between the parties concerned, how easy it is to clothe the circumstances with so much ambiguity as to render it uncertain what was the precise conduct of any of those parties.

In the single instance in which the governor of this State is coupled with a council—that is, in the appointment to offices, we have seen the mischiefs of it in the view now under consideration. Scandalous appointments to important offices have been made. Some cases, indeed, have been so flagrant that *all parties* have agreed in the impropriety of the thing. When inquiry has been made, the blame has been laid by the governor on the members of the council, who, on their part, have charged it upon his nomination; while the people remain altogether at a loss to determine by whose influence their interests have been committed to hands so unqualified and so manifestly improper. In tenderness to individuals, I forbear to descend to particulars.

It is evident from these considerations that the plurality of the executive tends to deprive the people of the two greatest securities they can have for the faithful exercise of any delegated power; *first,* the restraints of public opinion, which lose their efficacy as well, on account of the division of the censure attendant on bad measures among a number, as on account of the uncertainty on whom it ought to fall; and, *second,* the opportunity of discovering with facility and clearness the misconduct of the persons they trust, in order either to their removal from office or to their actual punishment in cases which admit of it.

In England, the king is a perpetual magistrate; and it is a maxim which has obtained for the sake of the public peace that he is unaccountable for his administration, and his person sacred. Nothing, therefore, can be wiser in that kingdom than to annex to the king a constitutional council, who may be responsible to the nation for the advice they give. Without this, there would be no responsibility whatever in the executive department—an idea inadmissible in a free government. But even there the king is not bound by the resolutions of his council, though they are answerable for the advice they give. He is the absolute master of his own conduct in the exercise of his office and may observe or disregard the counsel given to him at his sole discretion.

But in a republic where every magistrate ought to be personally responsible for his behavior in office, the reason which in the British Constitution dictates the propriety of a council not only ceases to apply, but turns against the institution. In the monarchy of Great Britain, it furnishes a substitute for the prohibited responsibility of the Chief Magistrate, which serves in some degree as a hostage to the national justice for his good behavior. In the American republic, it would serve to destroy, or would greatly diminish, the intended and necessary responsibility of the Chief Magistrate himself.

The idea of a council to the executive, which has so generally obtained in the State constitutions, has been derived from that maxim of republican jealousy which considers power as safer in the hands of a number of men than of a single man. If the maxim should be admitted to be applicable to the case, I should contend that the advantage on that side would not counterbalance the numerous disadvantages on the opposite side. But I do not think the rule at all applicable to the executive power. I clearly concur in opinion, in this particular, with a writer whom the celebrated Junius pronounces to be "deep, solid, and ingenious," that "the executive power is more easily confined when it is one";[2] that it is far more safe there should be a single object for the jealousy and watchfulness of the people; and, in a word, that all multiplication of the executive is rather dangerous than friendly to liberty.

A little consideration will satisfy us that the species of security sought for in the multiplication of the executive is unattainable. Numbers must be so great as to render combination difficult, or they are rather a source of danger than of security. The united credit and influence of several individuals must be more formidable to liberty than the credit and influence of either of them separately. When power, therefore, is placed in the hands of so small a number of men as to admit of their interests and views being easily combined in a common enterprise, by an artful leader, it becomes more liable to abuse, and more dangerous when abused, than if it be lodged in the hands of one man, who, from the very circumstance of his being alone, will be more narrowly watched and more readily suspected, and who cannot unite so great a mass of influence as when he is associated with others. The decemvirs of Rome, whose name denotes their number,[3] were more to be dreaded in their usurpation than any *one* of them would have been. No person would think of proposing an executive much more numerous than that body; from six to a dozen have been suggested for the number of the council. The extreme of these numbers is not too great for an easy combination; and from such a combination America would have more to fear than from the ambition of any single individual. A council to a magistrate, who is himself responsible for what he does, are generally nothing better than a clog upon his good intentions, are often the instruments and accomplices of his bad, and are almost always a cloak to his faults.

I forbear to dwell upon the subject of expense; though it be evident that if the council should be numerous enough to answer the principal end aimed at by the institution, the salaries of the members, who must be drawn from their homes to reside at the seat of government, would form an item in the catalogue of public expenditures too serious to be incurred for an object of equivocal utility.

I will only add that, prior to the appearance of the Constitution, I rarely met with an intelligent man from any of the States who did not admit, as the result of experience, that the UNITY of the executive of this State was one of the best of the distinguishing features of our Constitution.

NOTES

1. New York has no council except for the single purpose of appointing to offices; New Jersey has a council whom the governor may consult. But I think, from the terms of the Constitution, their resolutions do not bind him.

2. De Lolme.

3. Ten.

George Washington's First
Inaugural Address*

(1789)

THE CONSTITUTION makes no provision for presidential inaugu-
rations. It requires only that the new president take the oath stated
in Article II: "I do solemnly swear (or affirm) that I will faithfully execute the Office of President of the United States, and will to the best of
my Ability preserve, protect and defend the Constitution of the United
States." Tradition is the wellspring of every other aspect of inaugural
ceremonies. The 1789 inauguration of George Washington of Virginia
as the first president began many of these traditions, such as swearing
the oath with left hand on an opened Bible and right hand raised to
heaven, adding the words "so help me God," delivering an inaugural
address, and holding a public celebration afterward.

Washington had been elected president on February 4, 1789. The
election was organized by the outgoing Continental Congress, which
existed under the Articles of Confederation. After declaring on July 2,
1788, that the Constitution was ratified, Congress had passed a resolution on September 13 that each state should appoint presidential electors on the first Wednesday in January 1789 (January 7). When these
electors convened in their state capitals on the first Wednesday in February (February 4), they voted unanimously for Washington. They also
elected John Adams of Massachusetts as vice president.

Although the Continental Congress had set the first Wednesday in
March (March 4) as the day the government created by the Constitution
was to begin, not enough members of the newly elected Congress arrived
in New York City (still the U.S. capital) to constitute a quorum. Thus,
the electoral votes for president were not opened by Congress, and Washington was not declared elected, until April 6. The president-elect wait-

*Go to *http://www.law.ou.edu/hist/wash1.html*

ed at Mount Vernon, his Virginia home, until he was officially informed by messenger of his election on April 14. Washington proceeded slowly northward to New York by coach. He was greeted by ecstatic crowds, pealing church bells, and cannon salutes at every stop along the way. On April 30 Washington arrived in New York to be sworn in as president.

Washington took the constitutional oath of office on the outdoor balcony of New York's Federal Hall before an exuberant crowd. Observing the oath-taking custom of the time, he placed his left hand on the Bible and his right hand heavenward and appended the words "so help me God" to the official language of the Constitution. The first president then went inside to the Senate chamber to deliver an inaugural address.

Washington's address sounded two themes that have been echoed in the inaugural addresses of most of his successors. First, he paid "homage to the Great Author of every public and private good," noting the benign workings of "providential agency" in the birth of the United States and urging Congress and the American people to earn "the propitious smiles of Heaven" by acting with justice and magnanimity. Second, Washington spoke of national unity and dedication to the Constitution. What he did not do was equally precedent setting, namely, use the inaugural address as an occasion to exercise his constitutional power to make "recommendation of particular measures" to Congress.

The final event of the first presidential inauguration was a public fireworks display. After it was over, the president walked to his new home.

❧ ❧ ❧

Fellow-Citizens of the Senate and of the House of Representatives:

Among the vicissitudes incident to life no event could have filled me with greater anxieties than that of which the notification was transmitted by your order, and received on the 14th day of the present month. On the one hand, I was summoned by my country, whose voice I can never hear but with veneration and love, from a retreat which I had chosen with the fondest predilection, and, in my flattering hopes, with an immutable decision, as the asylum of my declining years—a retreat which was rendered every day more necessary as well as more dear to me by the addition of habit to inclination, and of frequent interruptions in my health to the gradual waste committed on it by time. On the other hand, the magnitude and difficulty of the trust to which the voice of my country called me, being sufficient to awaken in the wisest and most experienced of her citizens a distrustful scrutiny into his qualifications, could not but overwhelm with despondence one who (inheriting inferior endowments from nature and unpracticed in the duties of civil administration) ought to be peculiarly conscious of his own deficiencies. In this conflict of emotions all I dare aver is that it has been my faithful study to collect my duty from a just appreciation of every circumstance by which it might be affected. All I dare hope is that if, in executing this task, I have been too much swayed by a grateful remembrance of former instances, or by an affectionate sensibility to this transcendent proof of the confidence of my fellow-citizens, and have thence too little consulted my incapacity as well as disinclination for the weighty and untried cares before me, my error will be palliated by the motives which mislead me, and its consequences be judged by my country with some share of the partiality in which they originated.

Such being the impressions under which I have, in obedience to the public summons, repaired to the present station, it would be peculiarly improper to omit in this first official act my fervent supplications to that Almighty Being who rules over the universe who presides in the councils of nations, and whose providential aids can supply every human defect, that His benediction may consecrate to the liberties and happiness of the people of the United States a Government instituted by themselves for these essential purposes, and may enable every instrument employed in its administration to execute with success the functions allotted to his charge. In tendering this homage to the Great Author of every public and private good, I assure myself that it expresses your sentiments not less than my own, nor those of my fellow-citizens at large less than either. No people can be bound to acknowledge and adore the Invisible Hand which conducts the affairs of men more than those of the United States. Every step by which they have advanced to the character of an independent nation seems to have been distinguished by some token of providential agency; and in the important revolution just accomplished in the system of their united government the tranquil deliberations and voluntary consent of so many distinct communities from which the event has resulted can not be compared with the means by which most governments have been established without some return of pious gratitude, along with an humble anticipation of the future blessings which the past seem to presage. These reflections, arising out of the present crisis, have forced themselves too strongly on my mind to be suppressed. You will join with me, I trust, in thinking that there are none under the influence of which the proceedings of a new and free government can more auspiciously commence.

By the article establishing the executive department it is made the duty of the President "to recommend to your consideration such measures as he shall judge necessary and expedient." The circumstances under which I now meet you will acquit me from entering into that subject further than to refer to the great constitutional charter under which you are assembled, and which, in defining your powers, designates the objects to which your attention is to be given. It will be more consistent with those circumstances, and far more congenial with the feelings which actuate me, to substitute, in place of a recommendation of particular measures, the tribute that is due to the talents, the rectitude, and the patriotism which adorn the characters selected to devise and adopt them. In these honorable qualifications I behold the surest pledges that as on one side no local prejudices or attachments, no separate views nor party animosities, will misdirect the comprehensive and equal eye which ought to watch over this great assemblage of communities and interests, so, on another, that the foundation of our national policy will be laid in the pure and immutable principles of private morality, and the preeminence of free government be exemplified by all the attributes which can win the affections of its citizens and command the respect of the world. I dwell on this prospect with every satisfaction which an ardent love for my country can inspire, since there is no truth more thoroughly established than that there exists in the economy and course of nature an indissoluble union between virtue and happiness; between duty and advantage; between the genuine maxims of an honest and magnanimous policy and the solid rewards of public prosperity and felicity; since we ought to be no less persuaded that the propitious smiles of Heaven can never be expected on a nation that disregards the eternal rules of order and right which Heaven itself has ordained; and since the preservation of the sacred fire of liberty and the destiny of the republican model of government are justly considered, perhaps, as deeply, as finally, staked on the experiment intrusted to the hands of the American people.

Besides the ordinary objects submitted to your care, it will remain with your judgement to decide how far an exercise of the occasional power delegated by the fifth article of the Constitution is rendered expedient at the present juncture by the nature of objections which have been urged against the system, or by the degree of inquietude which has given birth to them. Instead of undertaking particular recommendations on this subject, in which I could be guided by no lights derived from official opportunities, I shall again give way to my entire confidence in your discernment and pursuit of the public good; for I assure myself that whilst you carefully avoid every alteration which might endanger the benefits of an united and effective government, or which ought to await the future lessons of experience, a reverence for the characteristic rights of freemen and a regard for the public harmony will sufficiently influence your deliberations on the question how far the former can be impregnably fortified or the latter be safely and advantageously promoted.

To the foregoing observations I have one to add, which will be most properly addressed to the House of Representatives. It concerns myself, and will therefore be as brief as possible. When I was first honored with a call into the service of my country, then on the eve of an arduous struggle for its liberties, the light in which I contemplated my duty required that I should renounce every pecuniary compensation. From this resolution I have in no instance departed; and being still under the impressions which produced it, I must decline as inapplicable to myself any share in the personal emoluments which may be indispensably included in a permanent provision for the executive department, and must accordingly pray that the pecuniary estimates for the station in which I am placed may during my continuance in it be limited to such actual expenditures as the public good may be thought to require.

Having thus imparted to you my sentiments as they have been awakened by the occasion which brings us together, I shall take my present leave; but not without resorting once more to the benign Parent of the Human Race in humble supplication that, since He has been pleased to favor the American people with opportunities for deliberating in perfect tranquility, and dispositions for deciding with unparalleled unanimity on a form of government for the security of their union and the advancement of their happiness, so His divine blessing may be equally conspicuous in the enlarged views, the temperate consultations, and the wise measures on which the success of this Government must depend.

❧ 5 ☙

James Madison's Defense of the President's Removal Power

(1789)

GEORGE WASHINGTON was not the only one trying to sort out the ambiguities in the Constitution once the new government was under way; the First Congress was involved in this process as well. One prominent example: although the Constitution said that major presidential appointments to the executive branch required the "Advice and

Consent of the Senate," it was silent concerning the removal power. In enacting the laws that created the first three executive departments— state (or foreign affairs), Treasury, and war—Congress had to address this constitutional silence. In doing so, legislators would implicitly be addressing a larger issue: Who is supposed to control the bureaucracy?

Rep. James Madison of Virginia believed strongly that the president was the chief executive. On May 19, 1789, he introduced a resolution that "there should be established for the aid of the chief magistrate in executing the duties of his office the following departments, to wit: a department for foreign affairs . . . Treasury . . . [and] war." The House of Representatives signaled its initial reluctance to recognize the executive nature of the departments by voting to strike the phrase "for the aid of the chief magistrate in executing the duties of his office" from Madison's resolution. A month later, when the state department bill came before the House, this reluctance was made manifest in the debate over a provision that the secretary of state "shall be removed from office by the President of the United States," acting alone.

Several positions emerged in the debate. Rep. Roger Sherman of Connecticut, who, like Madison, had been a prominent participant in the Constitutional Convention, argued that Congress had the power to assign the removal power in any way it wanted. Rep. William Smith of South Carolina interpreted the Constitution to mean that the only appropriate process for removing an executive official was impeachment. Others argued that because the Constitution required the Senate's consent for appointments, it must also require the Senate's consent for removals. Much to Madison's dismay, they were able to cite an offhand remark by Alexander Hamilton in *Federalist* No. 77 in defense of their argument.

On June 17, Madison attacked all of these positions and defended the president's exclusive power of removal. He agreed that the Constitution's appointment provision, taken by itself, was ambiguous. "But there is another part of the constitution . . . ," Madison argued; "it is that part which declares that the executive power shall be vested in a president of the United States." How could presidents be held accountable for their execution of the laws if they lacked the authority to remove officials who were impeding their efforts?

One week later, the House voted 29–22 to enact the state department bill, including the presidential removal clause. On July 14, the Senate split 10–10 on a motion to strike the clause from the bill. Vice President John Adams broke the tie in favor of presidential removal, which the Washington administration favored. The Senate approved the entire bill on July 18 by a 10–9 vote, and Washington signed it into law nine days later.

The state department bill established a precedent: every department's principal officers are removable by the president alone. Beginning in the late nineteenth century, however, the creation of independent regulatory agencies reopened the removal question. (See Document 21, p. 112.)

🎋 🎋 🎋

. . . Several constructions have been put upon the constitution relative to the point in question. The gentleman from Connecticut (Mr. SHERMAN) has advanced a doctrine which was not touched upon before. He seems to think (if I understood him rightly) that the power of displacing from office is subject to legislative discretion; because it is having a right to create, it may limit or modify as it thinks proper. I shall not say but at first view this doctrine may seem to have some plausibility. But when I consider, that the constitution clearly intended to maintain a marked distinction between the legislative, executive, and judicial powers of Government; and when I consider, that if the Legislature has a power, such as contended for, they may subject and transfer at discretion powers from one department of our Government to another; they may, on that principle, exclude the President altogether from exercising any authority in the removal of officers; they may give it to the Senate alone, or the President and Senate combined; they may vest it in the whole Congress; or they may reserve it to be exercised by this House. When I consider the consequences of this doctrine, and compare them with the true principles of the constitution, I own that I cannot subscribe to it.

Another doctrine, which has found very respectable friends, has been particularly advocated by the gentleman from South Carolina, (Mr. SMITH). It is this: when an officer is appointed by the President and Senate, he can only be displaced for malfeasance in his office by impeachment. I think this would give a stability to the executive department, so far as it may be described by the heads of departments, which is more incompatible with the genius of republican Governments in general, and this constitution in particular, than any doctrine which has yet been proposed. The danger to liberty, the danger of mal-administration, has not been found to lie so much in the facility of introducing improper persons into office, as in the difficulty of displacing those who are unworthy of the public trust. If it is said, that an officer once appointed shall not be displaced without the formality required by impeachment, I shall be glad to know what security we have for the faithful administration of the Government? Every individual, in the long chain which extends from the highest to the lowest link of the Executive Magistracy, would find a security in his situation which would relax his fidelity and promptitude in the discharge of his duty.

The doctrine, however, which seems to stand most in opposition to the principles I contend for, is, that the power to annul an appointment is, in the nature of things, incidental to the power which makes the appointment. I agree that if nothing more was said in the constitution than that the President, by and with the advice and consent of the Senate, should appoint to office, there would be great force in saying that the power of removal resulted by a natural implication from the power of appointing. But there is another part of the constitution, no less explicit than the one on which the gentleman's doctrine is founded; it is that part which declares that the executive power shall be vested in a President of the United States. The association of the Senate with the President in exercising that particular function, is an exception to this general rule; and exception to general rules, I conceive, are ever to be taken strictly. But there is another part of the constitution which inclines, in my judgment, to favor the construction I put upon it; the President is required to take care that the laws be faithfully executed. If the duty to see the laws faithfully executed be required at the hands of the Executive Magistrate, it would seem that it was generally intended he should have that species of power which is necessary to accomplish that end. Now, if the officer when once appointed is not to depend upon the President for his official existence, but upon a distinct body (for where there are two negatives required, either can prevent the removal), I confess I do not see how the President can take care that the laws be faithfully executed. It is true, by circuitous operation, he may obtain an impeachment, and even without this it is possible he may obtain the concurrence of the Senate for the purpose of displacing an officer; but would this give that species of control to the Executive Magistrate which seems to be required by the constitution? I own, if my opinion was not contrary to that entertained by what I suppose to be the minority on this question, I should be doubtful of being mistaken, when I discovered how inconsistent that construction would make the constitution with itself. I can hardly bring myself to imagine the wisdom of the convention who framed the constitution contemplated such incongruity.

There is another maxim which ought to direct us in expounding the constitution, and is of great importance. It is laid down, in most of the constitutions or bills of rights in the republics of America; it is to be found in the political writings of the most celebrated civilians, and is every where held as essential to the preservation or liberty, that the three great departments of Government be kept separate and distinct; and if in any case they are blended, it is in order to admit a partial qualification, in order more effectually to guard against an entire consolidation. I think, therefore, when we review the several parts of this constitution, when it says that the legislative powers shall be vested in a Congress of the United States under certain exceptions, and the executive power vested in the President with certain exceptions, we must suppose they were intended to be kept separate in all cases in which they are not blended, and ought, consequently, to expound the constitution so as to blend them as little as possible.

Every thing relative to the merits of the question as distinguished from a constitutional question, seems to turn on the danger of such a power vested in the President alone. But when I consider the checks under which he lies in the exercise of this power, I own to you I feel no apprehensions but what arise from the dangers incidental to the power itself; for dangers will be incidental to it, vest it where you please. I will not reiterate what was said before with respect to the mode of election, and the extreme improbability that any citizen will be selected from the mass of citizens who is not highly distinguished by his abilities and worth; in this alone we have no small security for the faithful exercise of this power. But, throwing that out of the question, let us consider the restraints he will feel after he is placed in that elevated station. It is to be remarked, that the power in this case will not consist so much in continuing a bad man in office, as in the danger of displacing a good one. Perhaps the great danger, as has been observed, of abuse in the executive power, lies in the improper continuance of bad men in office. But the power we contend for will not enable him to do this; for if an unworthy man be continued in office by an unworthy President, the House of Representatives can at any time impeach him, and the Senate can remove him, whether the President chooses or not. The danger then consists merely in this: the President can displace from office a man whose merits require that he should be continued in it. What will be the motives which the President can feel for such abuse of his power, and the restraints that operate to prevent it? In the first place, he will be impeachable by this House, before the Senate, for such an act of mal-administration; for I contend that the wanton removal of meritorious officers would subject him to impeachment and removal from his own high trust. But what can be his motives for displacing a worthy man? It must be that he may fill the place with an unworthy creature of his own. Can he accomplish this end? No; he can place no man in the vacancy whom the Senate shall not approve. . . .

But let us not consider the question on one side only; there are dangers to be contemplated on the other. Vest this power in the Senate jointly with the President, and you abolish at once that great principle of unity and responsibility in the executive department, which was intended for the security of liberty and the public good. If the President should possess alone the power of removal from office, those who are employed in the execution of the law will be in their proper situation, and the chain of dependence be preserved; the lowest officers, the middle grade, and the highest, will depend, as they ought, on the President, and the President on the community. The chain of dependence therefore terminates in the supreme body, namely, in the people, who will possess, besides, in aid of their original power, the decisive engine of impeachment. . . .

❧ 6 ❧

The Pacificus-Helvidius Letters

(1793)

ALTHOUGH GEORGE WASHINGTON had hoped to preserve unity within the new government, a rift developed between Secretary of the Treasury Alexander Hamilton and Secretary of State Thomas Jefferson, along with their political allies in Congress. This division emerged during Washington's first term when Jefferson opposed several of Hamilton's proposals to involve the federal government actively in the nation's economy. It was aggravated during the first year of Washington's second term when the president issued the Neutrality Proclamation of 1793, declaring that the United States would not take sides in the war between England and France. Jefferson had urged Washington to support France, which had helped the Americans win the Revolutionary War against England.

Hamilton, a partisan of England, defended the proclamation in a series of newspaper articles written pseudonymously as "Pacificus." Jefferson, who as a member of the administration was unwilling to attack the president's proclamation in public, recruited Rep. James Madison of Virginia to answer Hamilton as "Helvidius." "For God's sake, my dear Sir," Jefferson urged Madison, "take up your pen, select the most striking heresies, and cut him to pieces in the face of the public."

The opening letters in the exchange between Hamilton (Pacificus) and Madison (Helvidius), the erstwhile coauthors (as Publius) of *The Federalist Papers*, were published in the *Gazette of the United States*, a Philadelphia newspaper, during the summer of 1793. The debate focused less on the merits of Washington's policy than on whether the president has the constitutional power to issue a proclamation of neutrality without securing Congress's support.

Hamilton, arguing for a broad construction of presidential power, emphasized the difference between the vesting clauses of Article I and Article II of the Constitution. Article I begins: "All legislative Powers herein granted shall be vested in a Congress of the United States." The opening sentence of Article II omits the words "herein granted" and states: "The executive Power shall be vested in a President of the United States of America." From this difference, Hamilton concluded that although the powers of Congress are strictly limited to those enumerated in the remainder of Article I, the "executive Power" enjoyed by the president extends beyond the list of specific powers granted in Article II to include any other powers that may be construed as executive in nature—including the power to declare American neutrality.

Madison refused to accept Hamilton's characterization of neutrality as a "naturally" executive power. Because it is an aspect of the treaty-making and war-making powers, Madison argued, neutrality is, if anything, essentially a legislative power. Madison even echoed the rhetoric of his erstwhile Anti-Federalist opponents during the fight to ratify the Constitution, finding "royal prerogatives" lurking in Hamilton's argument.

Pacificus No. I

. . . The objections which have been raised against the Proclamation of Neutrality lately issued by the President have been urged in a spirit of acrimony and invective, which demonstrates, that more was in view than merely a free discussion of an important public measure; that the discussion covers a design of weakening the confidence of the People in the author of the measure; in order to remove or lessen a powerful obstacle to the success of an opposition to the Government, which however it may change its form, according to circumstances, seems still to be adhered to and pursued with persevering Industry.

This Reflection adds to the motives connected with the measure itself to recommend endeavours by proper explanations to place it in a just light. . . .

The inquiry then is—what department of the Government of the U[nited] States is the prop[er] one to make a declaration of Neutrality in the cases in which the engagements [of] the Nation permit and its interests require such a declaration.

A correct and well informed mind will discern at once that it can belong neit[her] to the Legislative nor Judicial Department and of course must belong to the Executive.

The Legislative Department is not the *organ* of intercourse between the U[nited] States and foreign Nations. It is charged neither with *making* nor *interpreting* Treaties. It is therefore not naturally that Organ of the Government which is to pronounce the existing condition of the Nation, with regard to foreign Powers, or to admonish the Citizens of their obligations and duties as rounded upon that condition of things. Still less is it charged with enforcing the execution and observance of these obligations and those duties.

It is equally obvious that the act in question is foreign to the Judiciary Department of the Government. The province of that Department is to decide litigations in particular cases. . . .

It must then of necessity belong to the Executive Department to exercise the function in Question—when a proper case for the exercise of it occurs.

It appears to be connected with that department in various capacities, as the *organ* of intercourse between the Nation and foreign Nations—as the interpreter of the National Treaties in those cases in which the Judiciary is not competent, that is in the cases between Government and Government—as that Power, which is charged with the Execution of the Laws, of which Treaties form a part—as that Power which is charged with the command and application of the Public Force.

This view of the subject is so natural and obvious—so analogous to general theory and practice—that no doubt can be entertained of its justness, unless such doubt can be deduced from particular provisions of the Constitution of the U[nited] States.

Let us see then if cause for such doubt is to be found in that constitution.

The second Article of the Constitution of the U[nited] States, section 1st, establishes this general Proposition, that "The EXECUTIVE POWER shall be vested in a President of the United States of America.". . .

The general doctrine then of our constitution is, that the EXECUTIVE POWER of the Nation is vested in the President; subject only to the *exceptions* and *qu{a}lifications* which are expressed in the instrument.

Two of these [are] the participation of the Senate in the appointment of Officers and the making of Treaties. A third remains to be mentioned[:] the right of the Legislature "to declare war and grant letters of marque and reprisal."

With these exceptions the EXECUTIVE POWER of the Union is completely lodged in the President. This mode of construing the Constitution has indeed been recognized by Congress in formal acts, upon full consideration and debate. The power of removal from office is an important instance.

And since upon general principles for reasons already given, the issuing of a proclamation of neutrality is merely an Executive Act; since also the general Executive Power of the Union is vested in the President, the conclusion is, that the step, which has been taken by him, is liable to no just exception on the score of authority. It may be observed that this Inference w[ould] be Just if the power of declaring war had [not] been vested in the Legislature, but that [this] power naturally includes the right of judg[ing] whether the Nation is under obligations to m[ake] war or not.

The answer to this is, that however true it may be, that th[e] right of the Legislature to declare wa[r] includes the right of judging whether the N[ation] be under obligations to make War or not—it will not follow that the Executive is in any case excluded from a similar right of Judgment, in the execution of its own functions.

If the Legislature have a right to make war on the one hand—it is on the other the duty of the Executive to preserve Peace till war is declared; and in fulfilling that duty, it must necessarily possess a right of judging what is the nature of the obligations which the treaties of the Country impose on the Government; and when in pursuance of this right it has concluded that there is nothing in them inconsistent with a *state* of neutrality, it becomes both its province and its duty to enforce the laws incident to that state of the Nation. The Executive is charged with the execution of all laws, the laws of Nations as well as the Municipal law, which recognises and adopts those laws. It is consequently bound, by faithfully executing the laws of neutrality, when that is the state of the Nation, to avoid giving a cause of war to foreign Powers. . . .

In this distribution of powers the wisdom of our constitution is manifested. It is the province and duty of the Executive to preserve to the Nation the blessings of peace. The Legislature alone can interrupt those blessings, by placing the Nation in a state of War. . . .

The President is the constitutional Executor of the laws. Our Treaties and the laws of Nations form a part of the law of the land. He who is to execute the laws must first judge for himself of their meaning. In order to the observance of that conduct, which the laws of nations combined with our treaties prescribed to this country, in reference to the present War in Europe, it was necessary for the President to judge for himself whether there was any thing in our treaties incompatible with an adherence to neutrality. Having judged that there was not, he had a right, and if in his opinion the interests of the Nation required it, it was his duty, as Executor of the laws, to proclaim the neutrality of the Nation, to exhort all persons to observe it, and to warn them of the penalties which would attend its non observance. . . .

Helvidius No. I

. . . [U]nder colour of vindicating an important public act, of a chief magistrate, who enjoys the confidence and love of his country, principles are advanced [by Pacificus] which strike at the vitals of its constitution, as well as at its honor and true interest. . . .

If we consult for a moment, the nature and operation of the two powers to declare war and make treaties, it will be impossible not to see that they can never fall within a proper definition of executive powers. The natural province of the executive magistrate is to execute laws, as that of the legislature is to make laws. All his acts therefore, properly executive, must pre-suppose the existence of the laws to be executed. A treaty is not an execution of laws: it does not pre-suppose the existence of laws. It is, on the contrary, to have itself the force of a *law,* and to be carried into *execution,* like all *other laws,* by the *executive magistrate.* To say then that the power of making treaties which are confessedly laws, belongs naturally to the department which is to executive laws, is to say, that the executive department naturally includes a legislative power. In theory, this is an absurdity—in practice a tyranny.

The power to declare war is subject to similar reasoning. A declaration that there shall be war, is not an execution of laws: it does not suppose pre-existing laws to be executed: it is not in any respect, an act merely executive. It is, on the contrary, one of the most deliberative acts that can be performed; and when performed, has the effect of *repealing* all the *laws* operating in a state of peace, so far as they are inconsistent with a state of war: and of *enacting* as a *rule for the executive,* a *new code* adapted to the relation between the society and its foreign enemy. In like manner a conclusion of peace *annuls* all the *laws* peculiar to a state of war, and *revives* the general *laws* incident to a state of peace.

These remarks will be strengthened by adding that treaties, particularly treaties of peace, have sometimes the effect of changing not only the external laws of the society, but operate also on the internal code, which is purely municipal, and to which the legislative authority of the country is of itself competent and compleat. . . .

In the general distribution of powers, we find that of declaring war expressly vested in the Congress, where every other legislative power is declared to be vested, and without any other qualification than what is common to every other legislative act. The constitutional idea of this power would seem then clearly to be, that it is of a legislative and not an executive nature. . . .

The power of treaties is vested jointly in the President and in the Senate, which is a branch of the legislature. From this arrangement merely, there can be no interference that would necessarily exclude the power from the executive class: since the senate is joined with the President in another power, that of appointing to offices, which as far as relate to executive offices at least, is considered as of an executive nature. Yet on the other hand, there are sufficient indications that the power of treaties is regarded by the constitution as materially different from mere executive power, and as having more affinity to the legislative than to the executive character.

One circumstance indicating this, is the constitutional regulation under which the senate give their consent in the case of treaties. In all other cases the consent of the body is expressed by a majority of voices. In this particular case, a concurrence of two thirds at least is made necessary, as a substitute or compensation for the other branch of the legislature, which on certain occasions, could not be conveniently a party to the transaction.

But the conclusive circumstance is, that treaties when formed according to the constitutional mode, are confessedly to have the force and operation of *laws,* and are to be a rule for the courts in controversies between man and man, as much as any *other laws.* They are even emphatically declared by the constitution to be "the supreme law of the land.". . .

Thus it appears that by whatever standard we try this doctrine, it must be condemned as no less vicious in theory than it would be dangerous in practice. It is countenanced neither by the writers on law; nor by the nature of the powers themselves; nor by any general arrangements or particular expressions, or plausible analogies, to be found in the constitution.

Whence then can the writer have borrowed it?

There is but one answer to this question.

The power of making treaties and the power of declaring war, are *royal prerogatives* in the *British government.* . . .

❧ 7 ❧

Thomas Jefferson's First Inaugural Address*

(1801)

A S THE DEBATE between Pacificus and Helvidius illustrated (see Document 6, p. 39), strong factional disagreements existed even

*Go to *http://www.law.ou.edu/hist/jeff1.html*

within George Washington's avowedly nonpartisan administration. Washington's 1796 announcement that he would retire from the presidency the following year loosed these spirits of partisanship into the larger political system. The Federalist Party, which won the election of 1796, passed laws (notably the Alien and Sedition Acts of 1798) to stifle public criticism of the government and thus to undermine the opposition Democratic-Republican Party. In response, the Democratic-Republicans quickly passed resolutions in Kentucky and Virginia that denied the federal government's right to impose its laws on resisting states.

In 1800, in a rematch of the 1796 presidential election, Thomas Jefferson of Virginia, the Democratic-Republican candidate, defeated President John Adams of Massachusetts, the Federalist nominee. But the very act of tallying the votes aggravated partisan tensions. Under the Constitution, electors did not vote separately for president and vice president; instead, they each cast two votes for president, with the candidate who received the largest majority of electoral votes elected as president and the runner-up as vice president. The anomalous consequence of this system in 1800 was that when all seventy-three Democratic-Republican electors cast their two votes for both Jefferson and Aaron Burr of New York, the party's vice-presidential nominee, the result was recorded as a tie vote for president between Jefferson and Burr.

Constitutionally, the House of Representatives is charged to choose the president in the event that the electoral college fails to elect someone, with each state delegation casting one vote and the support of a majority of states needed for victory. Federalist mischief-makers, who still dominated the House, delayed Jefferson's election through six days and thirty-six ballots. (Burr tacitly encouraged them.) Finally, on February 17, 1801, partly at the behest of Federalist leader Alexander Hamilton, who feared for both the reputation of his party and the stability of the still-fragile constitutional government he had worked so hard to create, the House chose Jefferson.

Under the circumstances, Jefferson's inaugural address on March 4, 1801, was uniquely significant—it marked the first peaceful transfer of power from one elected political party to another in the new nation, and one of the first in the world. It also was the first inauguration to take place in the new capital city of Washington, still basically a construction site.

In addition to the occasion itself, the address was significant because of what Jefferson said. Resisting the temptation to proclaim a partisan triumph, the new president insisted that "every difference of opinion is not a difference of principle. We have called by different names brethren of the same principle. We are all republicans, we are all federalists." Jefferson did not eschew all differences with his partisan opponents, however. Later in the address he stated his minimalist and distinctly un-Federalist philosophy of government: "a wise and frugal Government, which shall restrain men from injuring one another, shall leave them otherwise free to regulate their own pursuits of industry and improvement, and shall not take from the mouth of labor the bread it has earned. This is the sum of good government. . . ."

As president, Jefferson worked to undo some Federalist policies—he persuaded Congress to repeal the Alien and Sedition Acts, for example—but he preserved many others. His administration is best remembered for the Louisiana Purchase of 1803, a remarkable assertion of presidential power that nearly doubled the size of the United States by acquiring French territory west of the Appalachian Mountains.

In 1804 Congress passed and the states ratified the Twelfth Amendment, which separated the voting for president and vice president. (See Document 1, p. 1.) The amendment preserved the electoral college but ensured that the confusion of the 1800 election could not recur.

Friends and Fellow-Citizens:

Called upon to undertake the duties of the first executive office of our country, I avail myself of the presence of that portion of my fellow-citizens which is here assembled to express my grateful thanks for the favor with which they have been pleased to look toward me, to declare a sincere consciousness that the task is above my talents, and that I approach it with those anxious and awful presentiments which the greatness of the charge and the weakness of my powers so justly inspire. A rising nation, spread over a wide and fruitful land, traversing all the seas with the rich productions of their industry, engaged in commerce with nations who feel power and forget right, advancing rapidly to destinies beyond the reach of mortal eye—when I contemplate these transcendent objects, and see the honor, the happiness, and the hopes of this beloved country committed to the issue and the auspices of this day, I shrink from the contemplation, and humble myself before the magnitude of the undertaking.

Utterly, indeed, should I despair did not the presence of many whom I here see remind me that in the other high authorities provided by our Constitution I shall find resources of wisdom, of virtue, and of zeal on which to rely under all difficulties. To you, then, gentlemen, who are charged with the sovereign functions of legislation, and to those associated with you, I look with encouragement for that guidance and support which may enable us to steer with safety the vessel in which we are all embarked amidst the conflicting elements of a troubled world.

During the contest of opinion through which we have passed the animation of discussions and of exertions has sometimes worn an aspect which might impose on strangers unused to think freely and to speak and to write what they think; but this being now decided by the voice of the nation, announced according to the rules of the Constitution, all will, of course, arrange themselves under the will of the law, and unite in common efforts for the common good. All, too, will bear in mind this sacred principle, that though the will of the majority is in all cases to prevail, that will to be rightful must be reasonable; that the minority possess their equal rights, which equal law must protect, and to violate would be oppression. Let us, then, fellow-citizens, unite with one heart and one mind. Let us restore to social intercourse that harmony and affection without which liberty and even life itself are but dreary things. And let us reflect that, having banished from our land that religious intolerance under which mankind so long bled and suffered, we have yet gained little if we countenance a political intolerance as despotic, as wicked, and capable of as bitter and bloody persecutions. During the throes and convulsions of the ancient world, during the agonizing spasms of infuriated man, seeking through blood and slaughter his long-lost liberty, it was not wonderful that the agitation of the billows should reach even this distant and peaceful shore; that this should be more felt and feared by some and less by others, and should divide opinions as to measures of safety. But every difference of opinion is not a difference of principle. We have called by different names brethren of the same principle. We are all republicans, we are all federalists. If there be any among us who would wish to dissolve this Union or to change its republican form, let them stand undisturbed as monuments of the safety with which error of opinion may be tolerated where reason is left free to combat it. I know, indeed, that some honest men fear that a republican government can not be strong, that this Government is not strong enough; but would the honest patriot, in the full tide of successful experiment, abandon a government which has so far kept us free and firm on the theoretic and visionary fear that this Government, the world's best hope, may by possibility want energy to preserve itself? I trust not. I believe this, on the contrary, the strongest Government on earth. I believe it the only one where every man, at the call of the law, would fly to the standard of the law, and would meet invasions of the public order as his own personal concern. Sometimes it is said that man can not be trusted with the government of himself. Can he, then, be trusted with the government of others? Or have we found angels in the forms of kings to govern him? Let history answer this question.

Let us, then, with courage and confidence pursue our own federal and republican principles, our attachment to union and representative government. Kindly separated by nature and a wide ocean from the exterminating havoc of one quarter of the globe; too high-minded to endure the degradations of the others; possessing a chosen country, with room enough for our descendants to the thousandth and thousandth generation; entertaining a due sense of our equal right to the use of our faculties, to the acquisitions of our own industry, to honor and confidence from our fellow-citizens, resulting not from birth, but from our actions and their sense of them; enlightened by a benign religion, professed, indeed, and practiced in various forms, yet all of them inculcating honesty, truth, temperance, gratitude, and the love of man; acknowledging and adoring an overruling Providence, which by all its dispensations proves that it delights in the happiness of man here and his greater happiness hereafter—with all these blessings, what more is necessary to make us a happy and a prosperous people? Still one thing more, fellow-citizens—a wise and frugal Government, which shall restrain men from injuring one another, shall leave them otherwise free to regulate their own pursuits of industry and improvement, and shall not take from the mouth of labor the bread it has earned. This is the sum of good government, and this is necessary to close the circle of our felicities.

About to enter, fellow-citizens, on the exercise of duties which comprehend everything dear and valuable to you, it is proper you should understand what I deem the essential principles of our Government, and consequently those which ought to shape its Administration. I will compress them within the narrowest compass they will bear, stating the general principle, but not all its limitations. Equal and exact justice to all men, of whatever state or persuasion, religious or political; peace, commerce, and honest friendship with all nations, entangling alliances with none; the support of the State governments in all their rights, as the most competent administrations for our domestic concerns and the surest bulwarks against antirepublican tendencies; the preservation of the General Government in its whole constitutional vigor, as the sheet anchor of our peace at home and safety abroad; a jealous care of the right of election by the people—a mild and safe corrective of abuses which are lopped by the sword of revolution where peaceable remedies are unprovided; absolute acquiescence in the decisions of the majority, the vital principle of republics, from which is not appeal but to force, the vital principle and immediate parent of despotism; a well-disciplined militia, our best reliance in peace and for the first moments of war, till regulars may relieve them; the supremacy of the civil over the military authority; economy in the public expense, that labor may be lightly burthened; the honest payment of our debts and sacred preservation of the public faith; encouragement of agriculture, and of commerce as its handmaid; the diffusion of information and arraignment of all abuses at the bar of the public reason; freedom of religion; freedom of the press, and freedom of person under the protection of the habeas corpus, and trial by juries impartially selected. These principles form the bright constellation which has gone before us and guided our steps through an age of revolution and reformation. The wisdom of our sages and blood of our heroes have been devoted to their attainment. They should be the creed of our political faith, the text of civic instruction, the touchstone by which to try the services of those we trust; and should we wander from them in moments of error or of alarm, let us hasten to retrace our steps and to regain the road which alone leads to peace, liberty, and safety.

I repair, then, fellow-citizens, to the post you have assigned me. With experience enough in subordinate offices to have seen the difficulties of this the greatest of all, I have learnt to expect that it will rarely fall to the lot of imperfect man to retire from this station with the reputation and the favor which bring him into it. Without pretensions to that high confidence you reposed in our first and greatest revolutionary character, whose preëminent services had entitled him to the first place in his country's love and destined for him the fairest page in the volume of faithful history, I ask so much confidence only as may give firmness and effect to the legal administration of your affairs. I shall often go wrong through defect of judgment. When right, I shall often be thought wrong by those whose positions will not command a view of the whole ground. I ask your indulgence for my own errors, which will never be intentional, and your support against the errors of others, who may condemn what they would not if seen in all its parts. The approbation implied by your suffrage is a great consolation to me for the past, and my future solicitude will be to retain the good opinion of those who have bestowed it in advance, to conciliate that of others by doing them all the good in my power, and to be instrumental to the happiness and freedom of all.

Relying, then, on the patronage of your good will, I advance with obedience to the work, ready to retire from it whenever you become sensible how much better choice it is in your power to make. And may that Infinite Power which rules the destinies of the universe lead our councils to what is best, and give them a favorable issue for your peace and prosperity.

8

Thomas Jefferson's Letter to the Vermont Legislature

(1807)

THOMAS JEFFERSON did not attend the Constitutional Convention of 1787. Like John Adams, who was the American minister to Great Britain, Jefferson was representing his country abroad at the time, as the minister to France.

Although Jefferson generally admired both the delegates to the convention (an "assembly of demigods," he observed from Paris, only half ironically) and the plan of government that they produced, he objected strongly to the absence of a term limit on the president. "Their President seems like a bad edition of a Polish king," Jefferson lamented in a letter to Adams on November 13, 1787. "He may be reelected from 4. years to 4. years for life. . . . Once in office, and possessing the military force of the union, without either the aid or check of a council, he would not be easily dethroned, even if the people could be induced to withdraw their votes from him. I wish that at the end of the 4. years they had made him for ever ineligible a second time."

As president, Jefferson managed to temper his objections to presidential reeligibility long enough to run for a second term in 1804. He was reelected easily, by a margin of 162 electoral votes to 14 electoral votes for the Federalist candidate, Charles Cotesworth Pinckney of South Carolina.

Still, the bounds of Jefferson's expediency on the term-limit issue extended only so far. In 1806 and 1807, six state legislatures petitioned him to run for a third term. Undoubtedly, Jefferson would have been reelected if he had allowed his name to go forward: the Federalist Party was growing steadily weaker, the president's hold on the Democratic-Republican Party was strong, and his popularity, although not as great as in 1804, was more than adequate to win a third term.

But two terms was Jefferson's limit. On December 10, 1807, in a letter to the legislature of Vermont, he stated his belief that no president should serve in office any longer than eight years. Echoing his two-decade-old letter to Adams, Jefferson wrote, "If some termination to the services of the Chief Magistrate be not fixed by the Constitution, or supplied by practice, his office, nominally four years, will in fact become for life, and history shows how easily that degenerates into an inheritance." To strengthen his argument for a two-term tradition, Jefferson even invoked "the sound precedent set by an illustrious predecessor," George Washington. In truth, Washington had retired more for personal reasons than for reasons of state. As he confessed in his farewell address, Washington longed for "the shade of retirement."

Jefferson's long-standing desire to impose a limit on presidential reeligibility stood in sharp contrast to the intention of the Constitution's framers, who believed that the president should always have a political incentive to do the best possible job and the voters should always be free to reelect (or reject) the president. Yet he won his argument in the court of history. No president was even nominated for a third term until 1940, when Franklin D. Roosevelt ran. Far from shattering the two-term tradition, Roosevelt's successful reelection campaigns in 1940 and 1944 triggered such a strong conservative backlash that the Twenty-second Amendment was enacted in 1951 to forbid third terms.

⁂ ⁂ ⁂

To the Legislature of Vermont.
Washington, December 10, 1807

I received in due season the *address* of the legislature of Vermont, bearing date the 5th of November, 1806, in which, with their approbation of the general course of my administration, they were so good as to express their desire that I would consent to be proposed again, to the public voice, on the expiration of my present term of office. Entertaining, as I do, for the legislature of Vermont those sentiments of high respect which would have prompted an immediate answer, I was certain, nevertheless, they would approve a delay which had for its object to avoid a premature agitation of the public mind, on a subject so interesting as the election of a chief magistrate.

That I should lay down my charge at a proper period, is as much a duty as to have borne it faithfully. If some termination to the services of the chief magistrate be not fixed by the Constitution, or supplied by practice, his office, nominally for years, will, in fact, become for life; and history shows how easily that degenerates into an inheritance. Believing that a representative government, responsible at short periods of election, is that which produces the greatest sum of happiness to mankind, I feel it a duty to do no act which shall essentially impair that principle; and I should unwillingly be the person who, disregarding the sound precedent set by an illustrious predecessor, should furnish the first example of prolongation beyond the second term of office.

Truth, also, requires me to add, that I am sensible of that decline which advancing years bring on; and feeling their physical, I ought not to doubt their mental effect. Happy if I am the first to perceive and to obey this admonition of nature, and to solicit a retreat from cares too great for the wearied faculties of age.

For the approbation which the legislature of Vermont has been pleased to express of the principles and measures pursued in the management of their affairs, I am sincerely thankful; and should I be so fortunate as to carry into retirement the equal approbation and good will of my fellow citizens generally, it will be the comfort of my future days, and will close a service of forty years with the only reward it ever wished.

❧ 9 ☙

The Monroe Doctrine*
(1823)

JAMES MONROE, a Democratic-Republican from Virginia who was elected president in 1816 and reelected without opposition in 1820, is best known for the doctrine that bears his name. Like most nineteenth-century presidents, Monroe faced an assertive Congress that dominated his administration in matters of domestic policy. In foreign affairs, however, Monroe reinforced the constitutional right of the president to take the initiative in establishing American policy. (See Document 6, p. 39.)

The Monroe Doctrine was proclaimed, with the support of the British, in response to two foreign policy disputes in which the United

*Go to *http://www.law.ou.edu/hist/monrodoc.html*

States was involved during the early 1820s. The first was a Russian claim to exclusive trading rights in an area along the Pacific coast, from the Bering Strait south to some unspecified location on the shore of the Oregon territory. The other was a variety of rumored European plans, most involving France, to recolonize the newly independent nations of previously Spanish South America.

After frequent consultations with the cabinet and with former presidents James Madison and Thomas Jefferson during the fall of 1823, Monroe and Secretary of State John Quincy Adams resolved to declare the "new world" of the Americas off-limits to any attempts at colonization by the "old world" of Europe.

The Monroe Doctrine was included in Monroe's annual written message to Congress on December 2, 1823. Presidents from Jefferson to, a century later, William Howard Taft fulfilled their constitutional obligation to "give to the Congress Information of the State of the Union" in writing rather than in a speech before Congress, which was the practice followed by George Washington and John Adams, as well as by every president since Woodrow Wilson in 1913. (See Document 18, p. 99.)

No consultation with Congress preceded the declaration of the Monroe Doctrine, and some legislators believed that the president had exceeded the powers of his office by unilaterally enunciating a major foreign policy on behalf of the entire government. Yet the doctrine stood as an accomplished fact: Congress took no action either to affirm or to repudiate it. Public reaction around the country was generally positive.

The Monroe Doctrine had little immediate effect. As it turned out, European nations were not planning to recolonize South America; as for the Russians, they defied Monroe by continuing for a time their efforts in the Pacific Northwest. Nonetheless, the doctrine was widely understood, both at home and abroad, to be a bold assertion of American power and of presidential control of foreign policy.

Around the turn of the century, the Monroe Doctrine was officially endorsed by Congress (1899) and expanded by President Theodore Roosevelt. In 1904 Roosevelt declared in his annual message to Congress that the United States had the right to intervene if "chronic wrongdoing or impotence" in a country of the Western Hemisphere seemed to require such intervention. Protest from Latin America led to the withdrawal of the so-called Roosevelt Corollary in 1928.

In recent years, the Monroe Doctrine has seldom been explicitly invoked. Even when Soviet nuclear missiles were installed in Cuba in 1962, President John F. Kennedy demanded their withdrawal on other diplomatic grounds. (See Document 29, p. 163.) Nonetheless, the United States has continued to regard Latin America as a sphere of influence, interfering both in its domestic politics and in its relations with other parts of the world when deemed necessary to protect American interests.

※ ※ ※

Fellow Citizens of the Senate and House of Representatives:

. . . At the proposal of the Russian Imperial Government, made through the minister of the Emperor residing here, a full power and instructions have been transmitted to the minister of the United States at St. Petersburg [Russia] to arrange by amicable negotiation the respective rights and interests of the two nations on the northwest coast of this continent. A similar proposal had been made by His Imperial Majesty to the Government of Great Britain, which has likewise been acceded to. The Government of the United States has been desirous by this friendly proceeding of manifesting the great value which they have invariably attached to the friendship of the [Russian] Emperor and their solicitude to cultivate the best understanding with his Government. In the discussions to which this interest has given rise and in the arrangements by which they may terminate the occasion has been judged proper for asserting, as a principle in which the rights and interests of the United States are involved, that the American continents, by the free and independent condition which they have assumed and maintain, are henceforth not to be considered as subjects for future colonization by any European powers. . . .

In the wars of the European powers in matters relating to themselves we have never taken any part, nor does it comport with our policy to do so. It is only when our rights are invaded or seriously menaced that we resent injuries or make preparation for our defense. With the movements in this hemisphere we are of necessity more immediately connected, and by causes which must be obvious to all enlightened and impartial observers. The political system of the allied powers [of Europe] is essentially different in this respect from that of America. This difference proceeds from that which exists in their respective Governments; and to the defense of our own, which has been achieved by the loss of so much blood and treasure, and matured by the wisdom of their most enlightened citizens, and under which we have enjoyed unexampled felicity, this whole nation is devoted. We owe it, therefore, to candor and to the amicable relations existing between the United States and those powers to declare that we should consider any attempt on their part to extend their system to any portion of this hemisphere as dangerous to our peace and safety. With the existing colonies or dependencies of any European power we have not interfered and shall not interfere. But with the [South American] Governments who have declared their independence and maintained it, and whose independence we have, on great consideration and on just principles, acknowledged, we could not view any interposition for the purpose of oppressing them, or controlling in any other manner their destiny, by any European power in any other light than as the manifestation of an unfriendly disposition toward the United States. In the war between those new Governments and Spain we declared our neutrality at the time of their recognition, and to this we have adhered, and shall continue to adhere, provided no change shall occur which, in the judgment of the competent authorities of this Government, shall make a corresponding change on the part of the United States indispensable to their security. . . .

Our policy in regard to Europe, which was adopted at an early stage of the wars which have so long agitated that quarter of the globe, nevertheless remains the same, which is, not to interfere in the internal concerns of any of its powers; to consider the government de facto as the legitimate government for us; to cultivate friendly relations with it, and to preserve those relations by a frank, firm, and manly policy, meeting in all instances the just claims of every power, submitting to injuries from none. But in regard to those continents circumstances are eminently and conspicuously different. It is impossible that the allied powers should extend their political system to any portion of either continent without endangering our peace and happiness; nor can anyone believe that our southern brethren, if left to themselves, would adopt it of their own accord. It is equally impossible, therefore, that we should behold such interposition in any form with indifference. If we look to the comparative strength and resources of Spain and those new Governments, and their distance from each other, it must be obvious that she can never subdue them. It is still the true policy of the United States to leave the parties to themselves, in the hope that other powers will pursue the same course.

If we compare the present condition of our Union with its actual state at the close of our Revolution, the history of the world furnishes no example of a progress in improvement in all the important circumstances which constitute the happiness of a nation which bears any resemblance to it. At the first epoch our population did not exceed 3,000,000. By the last census it amounted to about 10,000,000, and, what is more extraordinary, it is almost altogether native, for the immigration from other countries has been inconsiderable. At the first epoch half the territory within our acknowledged limits was uninhabited and a wilderness. Since then new territory has been acquired of vast extent, comprising within it many rivers, particularly the Mississippi, the navigation of which to the ocean was of the highest importance to the original States. Over this territory our population has expanded in every direction, and new States have been established almost equal in number to those which formed the first bond of our Union. This expansion of our population and accession of new States to our Union have had the happiest effect on all its highest interests. That it has eminently augmented our resources and added to our strength and respectability as a power is admitted by all. But it is not in these important circumstances only that this happy effect is felt. It is manifest that by enlarging the basis of our system and increasing the number of States the system itself has been greatly strengthened in both its branches. Consolidation and disunion have thereby been rendered equally impracticable. Each Government, confiding in its own strength, has less to apprehend from the other, and in consequence each, enjoying a greater freedom of action, is rendered more efficient for all the purposes for which it was instituted. It is unnecessary to treat here of the vast improvement made in the system itself by the adoption of this Constitution and of its happy effect in elevating the character and in protecting the rights of the nation as well as of individuals. To what, then, do we owe these blessings? It is known to all that we derive them from the excellence of our institutions. Ought we not, then, to adopt every measure which may be necessary to perpetuate them?

❧ 10 ❧

The Tennessee General Assembly's Protest against the Caucus System

(1823)

THE PRESIDENTIAL SELECTION PROCESS underwent some wrenching changes during the four decades after the Constitution took effect. The delegates to the Constitutional Convention had explicitly rejected the simple expedient of having Congress elect the president, creating instead an electoral college in which the candidate who received the most electoral votes became president and the runner-up became vice president. The early rise of political parties that nominated both presidential and vice-presidential candidates upset this arrangement, causing a tie vote for president between Thomas Jefferson and his running mate, Aaron Burr, in 1800 (see Document 7, p. 44) and prompting passage of the Twelfth Amendment to separate the balloting for president and vice president in 1804.

The rise of political parties also meant that a mechanism had to be developed to nominate the candidates who would represent each party in the election. Beginning in 1796, the Federalist and Democratic-Republican delegations in Congress met (or "caucused") separately every four years to choose their respective nominees. The Democratic-Republican caucus nominated Jefferson in 1796, 1800, and 1804; James Madison in 1808 and 1812; and James Monroe in 1816 and 1820. (It also chose their vice-presidential running mates.) The Federalist caucus nominated John Adams in 1796 and 1800, then fell into disuse as the party's fortunes in Congress drastically declined.

Almost from the beginning, "King Caucus," as its critics began to call it, was attacked by some as elitist and unrepresentative of the party rank and file. Indeed, any state or district that did not elect a party's candidate to Congress was, by definition, left out of its nominating process entirely. When the Federalist Party's demise before the 1820 election left voters only the Democratic-Republican ticket to choose, these criticisms intensified. With just one party in the field, nomination by caucus was tantamount to election.

In late 1823, Tennessee felt particularly aggrieved by the caucus system because its candidate for president, Gen. Andrew Jackson, seemed unlikely to be nominated. On November 1, the state's General Assembly published a resolution that condemned the caucus for, among other things, violating "the spirit of the Constitution," whose framers had rejected congressional election of the president. Other states registered protests of their own.

The Democratic-Republican caucus that took place in mid-February 1824 was a disaster. Only 66 of 261 members of Congress attended. Their nominee, Secretary of the Treasury William Crawford of Georgia, ran a distant third in the presidential election, trailing both Jackson and

Secretary of State John Quincy Adams of Massachusetts. Because neither Jackson, who finished first, nor Adams received a majority of electoral votes, the House of Representatives was called on to choose the
winner. In a very controversial decision, the House elected Adams.

The 1824 election marked the demise of King Caucus. By the 1830s,
political parties were nominating their candidates for president and vice
president at national conventions. These conventions, consisting of delegates chosen by local party organizations all around the country, have
taken place in presidential election years ever since.

༚ ༚ ༚

The General Assembly of the state of Tennessee has taken into consideration the practice which, on former occasions, has prevailed at the city of Washington, of members of the Congress of the United States meeting in caucus,
and nominating persons to be voted for as President and Vice-President of the
United States; and, upon the best view of the subject which this General Assembly has been able to take, it is believed that the practice of congressional
nominations is a violation of the spirit of the Constitution of the United
States.

That instrument provides that there shall be three separate and distinct departments of the government, and great care and caution seems to have been
exercised by its framers to prevent any one department from exercising the
smallest degree of influence over another; and such solicitude was felt on this
subject, that, in the 2nd Section of the 2nd Article, it is expressly declared,
"That no senator or representative, or person holding an office of trust or profit
under the United States, shall be appointed an elector." From this provision, it
is apparent that the Convention intended that the members of Congress should
not be the principal and primary agents or actors in electing the President and
Vice-President of the United States; so far from it, they are expressly disqualified from being placed in a situation to vote for these high officers.

Is there not more danger of undue influence to be apprehended when the
members of Congress meet in caucus and mutually and solemnly pledge themselves to support the individuals who may have the highest number of votes in
such meeting than there would be in permitting them to be eligible to the appointment of electors? In the latter case, a few characters rendered ineligible by
the Constitution might succeed; but, in the former, a powerful combination of
influential men is formed, who may fix upon the American people their highest officers against the consent of a clear majority of the people themselves; and

this may be done by the very men whom the Constitution intended to prohibit from acting on the subject.

Upon an examination of the Constitution of the United States, there is but one case in which the members of Congress are permitted to act, which is in the event of a failure to make an election by the electoral college; and then the members of the House of Representatives vote by states. With what propriety the same men, who, in the year 1825, may be called on to discharge a constitutional duty, can, in the year 1824, go into a caucus and pledge themselves to support the men then nominated, cannot be discerned, especially when it might so happen that the persons thus nominated could not, under any circumstances, obtain a single vote from the state whose members stand pledged to support them. . . .

It has been said that the members of Congress in caucus only recommend to the people for whom to vote, and that such recommendation is not obligatory. This is true and clearly proves that it is a matter which does not belong to them—that, in recommending candidates, they go beyond the authority committed to them as members of Congress and thus transcend the trust delegated to them by their constituents. If their acts had any obligatory force, then the authority must be derived from some part of the Constitution of the United States and might be rightfully exercised; but when they say they only *recommend,* it is an admission, on their part, that they are acting without authority and are attempting, by a usurped influence, to effect an object not confided to them and not within their powers, even by implication.

It cannot be admitted that there is any weight in the argument drawn from the fact that both the [Federalist and Democratic-Republican] parties, heretofore contending for the superiority in the United States, have, in former times, resorted to this practice. The actions of public or private men, heated by party zeal and struggling for ascendency and power, ought not to be urged as precedents when circumstances have entirely changed. All political precedents are of doubtful authority and should never be permitted to pass unquestioned, unless made in good times and for laudable purposes. In palliation of the practice of resorting to caucus nominations in former times, it was said that each party must of necessity consult together in the best practicable way and select the most suitable persons from their respective parties so that the united efforts of all those composing it might be brought to bear upon their opponents. It is to be recollected that there is no danger of a departure from or violation of the Constitution, except when strong temptations are presented, and this will seldom occur, except when parties are arrayed against each other and their feelings violently excited.

The state of things, however, in the United States is entirely changed; it is no longer a selection made by members of Congress of different parties, but it is an election by the two houses of Congress, in which all the members must be permitted to attend and vote. It is not difficult to perceive that this practice may promote and place men in office who could not be elected were the constitutional mode pursued. It is placing the election of the President and Vice-President of the United States—an election in which all the states have an equal interest and equal rights—more in the power of a few of the most populous states than was contemplated by the Constitution. This practice is considered objectionable on other accounts: so long as Congress is considered as composed of the individuals on whom the election depends, the executive will is subjected to the control of that body, and it ceases, in some degree, to be a separate and independent branch of the government; and the expectation of executive patronage may have an unhappy influence on the deliberations of Congress.

Upon a review of the whole question, the following reasons which admit of much amplification and enlargement, more than has been urged in the foregoing, might be conclusively relied on to prove the impolicy and unconstitutionality of the congressional nominations of candidates for the presidency and vice-presidency of the United States: 1. A caucus nomination is against the spirit of the Constitution. 2. It is both inexpedient and impolitic. 3. Members of Congress may become the final electors and therefore ought not to prejudge the case by pledging themselves previously to support particular candidates. 4. It violates the equality intended to be secured by the Constitution to the weaker states. 5. Caucus nominations may, in time (by the interference of the states), acquire the force of precedents and become authoritative and, thereby, endanger the liberties of the American people.

This General Assembly, believing that the true spirit of the Constitution will be best preserved by leaving the election of President and Vice-President to the *people themselves,* through the medium of electors chosen by them, uninfluenced by any previous nomination made by members of Congress, have adopted the following resolutions:

1. *Resolved,* that the senators in Congress from this state be instructed, and our representatives be requested, to use their exertions to prevent a nomination being made during the next session of Congress, by the members thereof in caucus, of persons to fill the offices of President and Vice-President of the United States.

2. *Resolved,* that the General Assembly will, at its present session, divide the state into as many districts, in convenient form, as this state is entitled to elec-

toral votes, for the purpose of choosing an elector in each to vote for the President and Vice-President of the United States.

3. *Resolved,* that the governor of this state transmit a copy of the foregoing preamble and resolutions to the executive of each of the United States, with a request that the same be laid before each of their respective legislatures.

4. *Resolved,* that the governor transmit a copy to each of the senators and representatives in Congress from this state.

⊷ II ⊷

Andrew Jackson's First Message to Congress
(1829)

ANDREW JACKSON MAY FAIRLY be described as the first "outsider" president. For one thing, he was the first president to lack extensive experience in national affairs. (His four immediate predecessors had been secretary of state before becoming president.) Only briefly a member of Congress, Jackson had made his reputation as the general who defeated the British in the Battle of New Orleans, the greatest American victory in the War of 1812. Jackson also was a political outsider: he viewed the national government with suspicion, as a bastion of privilege for a ruling eastern commercial elite. Finally, Jackson, a Tennessean, was the first president from west of the Appalachian Mountains. Each of the first six presidents had been from Virginia or Massachusetts.

In all of these ways, Jackson represented rising tendencies in the country that were broadening the base of the American political system. The system was becoming broader geographically: settlement in the West (roughly the area between the Appalachians and the Mississippi River) had almost doubled the number of states from thirteen in 1776 to twenty-four in 1828. The system was also broader socially. Virtually every state had abandoned the traditional requirement that to vote one must own property. And the system had become broader politically. In the 1828 election, almost all presidential electors were selected by vote of the people, not the state legislatures. (The Constitution allowed states to choose their electors either way.)

The 1828 election was a rematch between Jackson and John Quincy Adams. In 1824, when Jackson won a plurality but not the constitutionally required majority of electoral votes, the House of Representatives had chosen Adams to be president. Sullied by the circumstances of his election, Adams had been unpopular and politically ineffective in office. Jackson easily defeated him in 1828 by an electoral vote majority of 178–83, thus becoming the first president nominated by the recently formed Democratic Party. Jackson's majority consisted mainly of those whom he called "the humble members of society," especially the farmers, mechanics, and laborers of the South and West.

An outsider president who was elected by a coalition of outsider voters, Jackson used his first annual message to Congress, sent on December 8, 1829, to state officially his view that "the first principle of our system" is that "the majority is to govern." Among the proposals that he offered in the message were direct election of the president, a single six-year presidential term, and restoration of power to the states. He also announced his intention to give government jobs to the common people who had supported him in the election. Dubbed the "spoils system" by critics, Jackson defended the policy on the grounds that it would foster "efficiency, . . . industry and integrity" in government.

※ ※ ※

Fellow Citizens of the Senate and of the House of Representatives:

It affords me pleasure to tender my friendly greetings to you on the occasion of your assembling at the Seat of Government, to enter upon the important duties to which you have been called by the voice of our countrymen. The task devolves on me, under a provision of the Constitution, to present to you, as the Federal Legislature of twenty-four sovereign States, and twelve millions of happy people, a view of our affairs; and to propose such measures as, in the discharge of my official functions, have suggested themselves as necessary to promote the objects of our Union.

In communicating with you for the first time, it is, to me, a source of unfeigned satisfaction, calling for mutual gratulation and devout thanks to a benign Providence, that we are at peace with all mankind; and that our country exhibits the most cheering evidence of general welfare and progressive improvement. Turning our eyes to other nations, our great desire is to see our brethren of the human race secured in the blessings enjoyed by ourselves, and advancing in knowledge, in freedom, and in social happiness. . . .

I consider it one of the most urgent of my duties to bring to your attention the propriety of amending that part of our Constitution which relates to the election of President and Vice President. Our system of government was, by its framers, deemed an experiment; and they, therefore, consistently provided a mode of remedying its defects.

To the People belongs the right of electing their Chief Magistrate: it was never designed that their choice should, in any case, be defeated, either by the intervention of electoral colleges, or by the agency confided, under certain contingencies, to the House of Representatives. Experience proves, that, in proportion as agents to execute the will of the People are multiplied, there is danger of their wishes being frustrated. Some may be unfaithful: all are liable to err. So far, therefore, as the People can, with convenience, speak, it is safer for them to express their own will. . . .

There are perhaps few men who can for any great length of time enjoy [appointed government] office and power, without being more or less under the influence of feelings unfavorable to the faithful discharge of their public duties. Their integrity may be proof against improper considerations immediately addressed to themselves; but they are apt to acquire a habit of looking with indifference upon the public interests, and of tolerating conduct from which an unpractised man would revolt. Office is considered as a species of property; and Government, rather as a means of promoting individual interests, than as an instrument created solely for the service of the People. Corruption in some, and, in others, a perversion of correct feelings and principles, divert Government from its legitimate ends, and make it an engine for the support of the few at the expense of the many. The duties of all public officers are, or, at least, admit of being made, so plain and simple, that men of intelligence may readily qualify themselves for their performance; and I cannot but believe that more is lost by the long continuance of men in office, than is generally to be gained by their experience. I submit therefore to your consideration, whether the efficiency of the Government would not be promoted, and official industry and integrity better secured, by a general extension of the law which limits appointments to four years.

In a country where offices are created solely for the benefit of the People, no one man has any more intrinsic right to official station than another. Offices were not established to give support to particular men, at the public expense.

No individual wrong is therefore done by removal, since neither appointment to, nor continuance in, office, is a matter of right. The incumbent became an officer with a view to public benefits; and when these require his removal, they are not to be sacrificed to private interests. It is the People, and they alone, who have a right to complain, when a bad officer is substituted for a good one. He who is removed has the same means of obtaining a living, that are enjoyed by the millions who never held office. The proposed limitation would destroy the idea of property, now so generally connected with official station; and although individual distress may be sometimes produced, it would, by promoting that rotation which constitutes a leading principle in the republican creed, give healthful action to the system. . . .

[The] state of the finances exhibits the resources of the nation in an aspect highly flattering to its industry; and auspicious of the ability of Government, in a very short time, to extinguish the public debt. When this shall be done, our population will be relieved from a considerable portion of its present burthens; and will find, not only new motives to patriotic affection, but additional means for the display of individual enterprise. The fiscal power of the States will also be increased; and may be more extensively exerted in favor of education and other public objects; while ample means will remain in the Federal Government to promote the general weal, in all the modes permitted to its authority.

After the extinction of the public debt, it is not probable that any adjustment of the tariff, upon principles satisfactory to the People of the Union, will, until a remote period, if ever, leave the Government without a considerable surplus in the Treasury, beyond what may be required for its current service. . . . It appears to me that the most safe, just, and federal disposition which could be made of the surplus revenue, would be its apportionment among the several States according to their ratio of representation; and should this measure not be found warranted by the Constitution, that it would be expedient to propose to the States an amendment authorizing it. I regard an appeal to the source of power, in cases of real doubt, and where its exercise is deemed indispensable to the general welfare, as among the most sacred of all our obligations. Upon this country, more than any other, has, in the providence of God, been cast the special guardianship of the great principle of adherence to written constitutions. If it fail here, all hope in regard to it will be extinguished. That this was intended to be a Government of limited and specific, and not general powers, must be admitted by all; and it is our duty to preserve for it the character intended by its framers. If experience points out the necessity for an enlargement of these powers, let us apply for it to those for whose benefit it is to be exercised; and not undermine the whole system by a resort to overstrained constructions. The scheme has worked well. It has exceeded the hopes of those who devised it, and become an object of admiration to the world. We are responsible to our country, and to the glorious cause of self-government, for the preservation of so great a good. The great mass of legislation relating to our internal affairs, was intended to be left where the Federal Convention found it—in the State Governments. Nothing is clearer, in my view, than that we are chiefly indebted for the success of the Constitution under which we are now acting, to the watchful and auxiliary operation of the State authorities. This is not the reflection of a day, but belongs to the most deeply rooted convictions of my mind. I cannot, therefore, too strongly or too earnestly, for my own sense of its importance, warn you against all encroachments upon the legitimate sphere of State sovereignty. Sustained by its healthful and invigorating influence, the Federal system can never fall. . . .

I would suggest, also, an inquiry, whether the provisions of the act of Congress, authorizing the discharge of the persons of debtors to the Government, from imprisonment, may not, consistently with the public interest, be extended to the release of the debt, where the conduct of the debtor is wholly exempt from the imputation of fraud. Some more liberal policy than that which now prevails, in reference to this unfortunate class of citizens, is certainly due to them, and would prove beneficial to the country. The continuance of the liability, after the means to discharge it have been exhausted, can only serve to dispirit the debtor; or, where his resources are but partial, the want of power in the government to compromise and release the demand, instigates to fraud, as the only resource for securing a support to his family. He thus sinks into a state of apathy, and becomes a useless drone in society, or a vicious member of it, if not a feeling witness of the rigor and inhumanity of his country. All experience proves, that oppressive debt is the bane of enterprise; and it should be the care of a Republic not to exert a grinding power over misfortune and poverty. . . .

I now commend you, fellow-citizens, to the guidance of Almighty God, with a full reliance on his merciful providence for the maintenance of our free institutions; and with an earnest supplication, that, whatever errors it may be my lot to commit, in discharging the arduous duties which have devolved on me, will find a remedy in the harmony and wisdom of your counsels.

Andrew Jackson's Veto of the Bank Bill

(1832)

ANDREW JACKSON'S VETO of the bill passed by Congress in 1832 to renew the Second Bank of the United States was politically important at the time and has been enduringly important as a precedent-setting assertion of presidential power.

Politically, Jackson regarded the bank as the leading institutional bastion of everything he opposed: favoritism for the eastern commercial and financial elite, excessive power for the federal government, and political bias in favor of the opposition National Republican, or Whig, Party. Indeed, bank president Nicholas Biddle, encouraged by Sen. Henry Clay of Kentucky, Jackson's opponent in the 1832 presidential election, asked Congress to renew the bank's charter four years before the old charter was scheduled to expire because Clay thought that a veto by Jackson would be a good issue for the Whigs in the election. Despite Jackson's opposition, Congress acceded to Biddle's request.

All of Jackson's predecessors as president had used the veto sparingly: in forty years, they had vetoed nine bills, only three of them important. The belief of Federalist and Democratic-Republican presidents alike had been that the veto should be reserved for legislation that was of doubtful constitutionality.

Jackson interpreted the veto power differently, grounding his view in a new and expansive conception of the presidency. The president, Jackson believed, was a truer representative of the people than Congress. He was their "tribune," the only person in the government who had been elected by the entire country and who thus could claim to articulate the national interest. As a consequence, Jackson regarded the president's judgment that an act of Congress was unwise as sufficient grounds for a veto.

On July 10, 1832, seven days after Congress voted to renew the charter of the national bank, Jackson sent his veto message to Capitol Hill. He took pains to explain his constitutional objections to the bank, re-

fusing to defer to the Supreme Court on matters of constitutional interpretation. (In 1819, the Court had upheld the constitutionality of a national bank in *McCulloch v. Maryland.*) "The Congress, the executive,
and the court must each for itself be guided by its own opinion of the
Constitution," Jackson wrote. But he also made clear that he regarded
his opinion that the bank was bad for the country as reason enough to
cast a veto.

Congress failed to muster the two-thirds majority needed to override
Jackson's veto of the bank bill. In the 1832 election, the president was
resoundingly reelected over Clay by a margin of 219–49 in the electoral
college and 54 percent to 37 percent in the popular vote.

Both the veto and the theory of the presidency that underlay it established precedents that were of lasting significance. In the short term,
President John Tyler and Jackson's other successors institutionalized his
practice of vetoing bills on political as well as constitutional grounds. In
the long term, the attitude that the president is the people's main representative in government took root widely and deeply in the American
political system.

🏇 🏇 🏇

The bill "to modify and continue" the act entitled "An act to incorporate
the subscribers to the Bank of the United States" was presented to me on the
4th July instant. Having considered it with that solemn regard to the principles of the Constitution which the day was calculated to inspire, and come to
the conclusion that it ought not to become a law, I herewith return it to the
Senate, in which it originated, with my objections.

A bank of the United States is in many respects convenient for the government and useful to the people. Entertaining this opinion, and deeply im-
pressed with the belief that some of the powers and privileges possessed by the
existing bank are unauthorized by the Constitution, subversive of the rights of
the states, and dangerous to the liberties of the people, I felt it my duty at an
early period of my administration to call the attention of Congress to the prac-
ticability of organizing an institution combining all its advantages and obviat-
ing these objections. I sincerely regret that in the act before me I can perceive
none of those modifications of the bank charter which are necessary, in my
opinion, to make it compatible with justice, with sound policy, or with the
Constitution of our country.

The present corporate body, denominated the president, directors, and company of the Bank of the United States, will have existed at the time this act is intended to take effect twenty years. It enjoys an exclusive privilege of banking under the authority of the general government, a monopoly of its favor and support, and, as a necessary consequence, almost a monopoly of the foreign and domestic exchange. The powers, privileges, and favors bestowed upon it in the original charter, by increasing the value of the stock far above its par value, operated as a gratuity of many millions to the stockholders.

An apology may be found for the failure to guard against this result in the consideration that the effect of the original act of incorporation could not be certainly foreseen at the time of its passage. The act before me proposes another gratuity to the holders of the same stock, and in many cases to the same men, of at least $7 million more. This donation finds no apology in any uncertainty as to the effect of the act. On all hands it is conceded that its passage will increase at least 20 or 30 percent more the market price of the stock, subject to the payment of the annuity of $200,000 per year secured by the act, thus adding in a moment one-fourth to its par value. It is not our own citizens only who are to receive the bounty of our government. More than $8 million of the stock of this bank are held by foreigners. By this act the American republic proposes virtually to make them a present of some millions of dollars. For these gratuities to foreigners and to some of our own opulent citizens the act secures no equivalent whatever. They are the certain gains of the present stockholders under the operation of this act, after making full allowance for the payment of the bonus.

Every monopoly and all exclusive privileges are granted at the expense of the public, which ought to receive a fair equivalent. The many millions which this act proposes to bestow on the stockholders of the existing bank must come directly or indirectly out of the earnings of the American people. It is due to them, therefore, if their government sell monopolies and exclusive privileges, that they should at least exact for them as much as they are worth in open market. The value of the monopoly in this case may be correctly ascertained. The $28 million of stock would probably be at an advance of 50 percent and command in market at least $42 million, subject to the payment of the present bonus. The present value of the monopoly, therefore, is $17 million, and this the act proposes to sell for $3 million, payable in fifteen annual installments of $200,000 each. . . .

It is maintained by the advocates of the bank that its constitutionality in all its features ought to be considered as settled by precedent and by the decision of the Supreme Court. To this conclusion I cannot assent. Mere precedent is a dangerous source of authority and should not be regarded as deciding questions of constitutional power except where the acquiescence of the people and the states can be considered as well settled. So far from this being the case on this subject, an argument against the bank might be based on precedent. One Congress in 1791 decided in favor of a bank; another in 1811 decided against it. One Congress in 1815 decided against a bank; another in 1816 decided in its favor. Prior to the present Congress, therefore, the precedents drawn from that source were equal. If we resort to the states, the expressions of legislative, judicial, and executive opinions against the bank have been probably to those in its favor as four to one. There is nothing in precedent, therefore, which, if its authority were admitted, ought to weigh in favor of the act before me.

If the opinion of the Supreme Court covered the whole ground of this act, it ought not to control the coordinate authorities of this government. The Congress, the executive, and the court must each for itself be guided by its own opinion of the Constitution. Each public officer who takes an oath to support the Constitution swears that he will support it as he understands it and not as it is understood by others. It is as much the duty of the House of Representatives, of the Senate, and of the President to decide upon the constitutionality of any bill or resolution which may be presented to them for passage or approval as it is of the supreme judges when it may be brought before them for judicial decision. The opinion of the judges has no more authority over Congress than the opinion of Congress has over the judges, and on that point the President is independent of both. The authority of the Supreme Court must not, therefore, be permitted to control the Congress or the executive when acting in their legislative capacities, but to have only such influence as the force of their reasoning may deserve. . . .

It is to be regretted that the rich and powerful too often bend the acts of government to their selfish purposes. Distinctions in society will always exist under every just government. Equality of talents, of education, or of wealth cannot be produced by human institutions. In the full enjoyment of the gifts of Heaven and the fruits of superior industry, economy, and virtue, every man is equally entitled to protection by law; but when the laws undertake to add to these natural and just advantages artificial distinctions, to grant titles, gratuities, and exclusive privileges, to make the rich richer and the potent more powerful, the humble members of society—the farmers, mechanics, and laborers—who have neither the time nor the means of securing like favors to themselves, have a right to complain of the injustice of their government. There are no necessary evils in government. Its evils exist only in its abuses. If it would confine itself to equal protection, and, as Heaven does its rains, shower its favors alike on the high and the low, the rich and the poor, it would be an unqualified blessing. In the act before me there seems to be a wide and unnecessary departure from these just principles.

Nor is our government to be maintained or our Union preserved by invasions of the rights and powers of the several states. In thus attempting to make our general government strong, we make it weak. Its true strength consists in leaving individuals and states as much as possible to themselves—in making itself felt, not in its power, but in its beneficence; not in its control, but in its protection; not in binding the states more closely to the center, but leaving each to move unobstructed in its proper orbit.

Experience should teach us wisdom. Most of the difficulties our government now encounters and most of the dangers which impend over our Union have sprung from an abandonment of the legitimate objects of government by our national legislation and the adoption of such principles as are embodied in this act. Many of our rich men have not been content with equal protection and equal benefits but have besought us to make them richer by act of Congress. By attempting to gratify their desires, we have in the results of our legislation arrayed section against section, interest against interest, and man against man, in a fearful commotion which threatens to shake the foundations of our Union.

It is time to pause in our career to review our principles and, if possible, revive that devoted patriotism and spirit of compromise which distinguished the sages of the Revolution and the fathers of our Union. If we cannot at once, in justice to interests vested under improvident legislation, make our government what it ought to be, we can at least take a stand against all new grants of monopolies and exclusive privileges, against any prostitution of our government to the advancement of a few at the expense of the many, and in favor of compromise and gradual reform in our code of laws and system of political economy.

❧ 13 ❧

Abraham Lincoln's Letter to Albert G. Hodges

(1864)

DURING THE QUARTER-CENTURY that followed the presidency of Andrew Jackson, the rapidly expanding nation was torn by disagreement over the extension of slavery into new territories and states. In 1860, two years after his unsuccessful but widely admired campaign for U.S. senator from Illinois against Democrat Stephen A. Douglas, Abraham Lincoln was nominated for president by the recently formed Republican Party. Despite winning only 40 percent of the popular vote, Lincoln carried every free state (but no slave states) and triumphed over three opponents: Douglas, the nominee of the northern Democrats; Vice President John C. Breckinridge of Kentucky, who was nominated by southern Democrats; and Tennessean John Bell, the nominee of the newly formed Constitutional Union Party.

Although Lincoln had pledged not to attack the rights of slaveowners in the southern and border states, his opposition to extending slavery beyond its existing bounds prompted seven Deep South states to secede from the United States and, on February 7, 1861 (nearly a month before Lincoln's inauguration), to form the Confederate States of America. Before leaving office, President James Buchanan had told Congress that although the southern states had no constitutional right to secede, he had no constitutional power to stop them. Lincoln strongly disagreed. He used his March 4 inaugural address to warn secessionists that they would not be allowed to leave the Union peacefully: "You have no oath registered in Heaven to destroy the government, while I shall have the most solemn one 'to preserve, protect, and defend' it. You can forbear the assault; I can *not* shrink from the *defense* of it."

Notwithstanding Lincoln's warning, rebel forces massed near Fort Sumter in Charleston, South Carolina, the next day. On April 12 they fired on the fort, which soon fell. On May 3 Lincoln issued a proclamation that called out the state militia and asked for seventy-five thousand volunteers to assist in executing the national laws. Four other southern states seceded and joined the Confederacy in short order. Border states, notably Kentucky and Maryland, considered secession seriously.

Although calling out the militia was clearly within the president's constitutional powers, other actions taken by Lincoln during the spring of 1861 were not. With Congress not yet convened in Washington (and the president reluctant to summon it into special session before getting the war effort under way), Lincoln substantially increased the size of the army and navy, ordered a blockade of southern ports, suspended the writ of *habeas corpus* (the constitutional guarantee against detention without legal cause by government authorities) in certain militarily vital parts of the country, instructed the Treasury to pay $2 million to two secret agents to purchase military supplies, imposed new passport regulations on foreign visitors, and barred "treasonable correspondence" from being delivered by the post office.

On New Year's Day 1863, Lincoln, again acting on his own authority, issued the Emancipation Proclamation, which freed "all persons held as slaves within any State or designated part of a State, the people whereof shall then be in rebellion against the United States." Some time later, Kentuckian Albert G. Hodges, the editor of the *Frankfort Commonwealth,* asked the president why he had felt compelled to abandon his long-standing pledge not to interfere with slavery where it already existed. Lincoln replied in a letter to Hodges on April 4, 1864.

In his letter, Lincoln argued that it made no sense to observe constitutional niceties while the ultimate purpose of the Constitution—to preserve the Union—was under siege. "Was it possible to lose the nation and yet preserve the Constitution?" he asked, rhetorically. "By general law, life and limb must be protected, yet often a limb must be amputated to save a life; but a life is never wisely given to save a limb." Defending the actions of his first few months in office and afterward, Lincoln added: "I felt that measures otherwise unconstitutional might become lawful by becoming indispensable to the preservation of the Constitution through the preservation of the nation."

Although Lincoln did not mention John Locke, his letter to Hodges was reminiscent of the seventeenth-century English philosopher's discussion of prerogative in his *Second Treatise on Government.* In the absence and sometimes in defiance of law, Locke had argued, an executive must obey "this fundamental law of nature and government, viz., that, as much as may be, all the members of society are to be preserved." Such is prerogative: "the people's permitting their rulers to do several things of their own free choice, where the law was silent, and sometimes, too, against the direct letter of the law, for the public good, and their acquiescing in it when so done." The check on executive power in such an instance is the elected legislature's subsequent decision to accept or reject the propriety of the executive's actions.

Certainly Lincoln could claim that, for the most part, his own exercises of prerogative had been vindicated. To be sure, the president was denounced by some as a dictator. But in August 1861, after several weeks of debate, Congress declared most of the president's early actions as "hereby approved and in all respects legalized and made valid, to the same effect as if they had been issued and done under the previous express authority and direction of the Congress of the United States." In 1862 and 1863, Congress retroactively validated most of Lincoln's other actions.

Not just Congress but the voters endorsed the president's unusual wartime leadership. Lincoln won 55 percent of the popular vote and carried all but three Union states in his bid for reelection in November 1864.

⁂ ⁂ ⁂

My dear Sir:

You ask me to put in writing the substance of what I verbally said the other day in your presence, to Governor [Thomas E.] Bramlette and [former] Senator [Archibald] Dixon, [both of Kentucky]. It was about as follows:

"I am naturally antislavery. If slavery is not wrong, nothing is wrong. I cannot remember when I did not so think and feel, and yet I have never understood that the presidency conferred upon me an unrestricted right to act officially upon this judgment and feeling. It was in the oath I took that I would, to the best of my ability, preserve, protect, and defend the Constitution of the United States. I could not take the office without taking the oath. Nor was it my view that I might take an oath to get power, and break the oath in using the power. I understood, too, that in ordinary civil administration this oath even forbade me to practically indulge my primary abstract judgment on the moral question of slavery. I had publicly declared this many times, and in many ways. And I aver that, to this day, I have done no official act in mere deference to my abstract judgment and feeling on slavery. I did understand, however, that my oath to preserve the Constitution to the best of my ability imposed upon me the duty of preserving, by every indispensable means, that government—that nation, of which that Constitution was the organizing law. Was it possible to lose the nation and yet preserve the Constitution? By general law, life and limb must be protected, yet often a limb must be amputated to save a life; but a life is never wisely given to save a limb. I felt that measures otherwise unconstitutional might become lawful by becoming indispensable to the preservation of the Constitution through the preservation of the nation. Right or wrong, I assume this ground, and now avow it. I could not feel that, to the best of my ability, I had even tried to preserve the Constitution if, to save slavery or any minor matter, I should permit the wreck of government, country, and Constitution all together. When, early in the war, General [John C.] Frémont attempted military emancipation, I forbade it, because I did not then think it an indispensable necessity. When, a little later, General [Simon] Cameron, then Secretary of War, suggested the arming of the blacks, I objected because I did not yet think it an indispensable necessity. When, still later, General [David] Hunter attempted military emancipation, I again forbade it, because I did not yet think the indispensable necessity had come. When in March and May and July, 1862, I made earnest and successive appeals to the border States to favor compensated emancipation, I believed the indispensable necessity to military emancipation and arming the blacks would come unless averted by that measure. They declined the proposition, and I was, in my best judgment, driven to the alternative of either surrendering the Union, and with it the Constitution, or of laying strong hand upon the colored element. I chose the latter. In choosing it, I hoped for greater gain than loss; but of this, I was not entirely confident. More than a year of trial now shows no loss by it in our foreign relations, none in our home popular sentiment, none in our white military force—no loss by it anyhow or anywhere. On the contrary it shows a gain of quite a hundred and thirty thousand soldiers, seamen, and laborers. These are palpable facts, about which, as facts, there can be no caviling. We have the men; and we could not have had them without the measure.

"And now let any Union man who complains of the measure test himself by writing down in one line that he is for subduing the rebellion by force of arms; and in the next, that he is for taking these hundred and thirty thousand men from the Union side and placing them where they would be but for the measure he condemns. If he cannot face his case so stated, it is only because he cannot face the truth."

I add a word which was not in the verbal conversation. In telling this tale I attempt no compliment to my own sagacity. I claim not to have controlled events, but confess plainly that events have controlled me. Now, at the end of three years' struggle, the nation's condition is not what either party, or any man, devised or expected. God alone can claim it. Whither it is tending seems plain. If God now wills the removal of a great wrong, and wills also that we of the North, as well as you of the South, shall pay fairly for our complicity in that wrong, impartial history will find therein new cause to attest and revere the justice and goodness of God. *Yours truly,*

A. Lincoln

❧ 14 ❧
The Gettysburg Address*
(1863)

O N JULY 4, 1863, the northern armies won two victories that almost ensured that the Union would prevail in the Civil War. In
the West, the Confederate fortification at Vicksburg, Mississippi, fell to
the forces of Gen. Ulysses S. Grant, bringing the strategically vital Mississippi River under complete northern control. In Gettysburg, Pennsylvania, Union forces beat back a Confederate incursion into the North
led by Gen. Robert E. Lee.

Four months after these victories, President Abraham Lincoln rode a
train from Washington to Gettysburg to attend the November 19 dedication of the cemetery in which six thousand casualties of the Battle of
Gettysburg were to be buried. Lincoln was not the main speaker at the
dedication—that honor fell to former senator and renowned orator Edward Everett, who delivered a lengthy and moving address to the assembled crowd of around fifteen thousand people. Instead, Lincoln
spoke briefly after Everett was finished, his high, clear voice audible to
all. On his hat he wore a mourning band for his recently deceased young
son, Willie.

Lincoln's theme was the "nation"—the word appears three times in
the first two sentences of the address and is reinvoked in the peroration.
Brief as the Gettysburg Address is, it thematically traces the American
experience from past to present to future. The treatment of the past is
especially interesting. Lincoln dates the founding of the nation not to
the Constitution in 1787, but rather "four score and seven years ago" to
1776, the year that the Declaration of Independence proclaimed that
"all men are created equal." To Lincoln, equality is the "proposition" to
which the new nation was thereby "dedicated."

The brilliance of the Gettysburg Address is that, in the space of only
three minutes and 272 words, it solemnly and honestly acknowledges

*Go to *http://www.law.ou.edu/hist/getty.html*

75

the awful pain suffered by "these honored dead" while defining the war in which they fought as part of the enduring struggle to attain "government of the people, by the people, for the people." Following in the great tradition of Pericles's funeral oration for the Athenian soldiers slain in the Peloponnesian War, and employing the grand cadences of the King James Version of the Bible, Lincoln vowed that because "this nation, under God, shall have a new birth of freedom," the fallen soldiers will not have "died in vain." So profound was the address, one modern scholar has written, that those who heard it "walked off, from those curving graves on the hillside, under a changed sky, into a different America."

❧ ❧ ❧

Four score and seven years ago our fathers brought forth on this continent, a new nation, conceived in Liberty, and dedicated to the proposition that all men are created equal.

Now we are engaged in a great civil war, testing whether that nation or any nation so conceived and so dedicated, can long endure. We are met on a great battle-field of that war. We have come to dedicate a portion of that field, as a final resting place for those who here gave their lives that that nation might live. It is altogether fitting and proper that we should do this.

But, in a larger sense, we can not dedicate—we can not consecrate—we can not hallow—this ground. The brave men, living and dead, who struggled here, have consecrated it, far above our poor power to add or detract. The world will little note, nor long remember what we say here, but it can never forget what they did here. It is for us the living, rather, to be dedicated here to the unfinished work which they who fought here have thus far so nobly advanced. It is rather for us to be here dedicated to the great task remaining before us— that from these honored dead we take increased devotion to that cause for which they gave the last full measure of devotion—that we here highly resolve that these dead shall not have died in vain—that this nation, under God, shall have a new birth of freedom—and that government of the people, by the people, for the people, shall not perish from the earth.

15

Ex Parte Milligan

(1866)

C AN THE PRESIDENT legitimately claim emergency powers in wartime beyond those that are enumerated in the Constitution? The typical answer of the Supreme Court to this question has been variable: *yes* in the heat of war but *no* on later reflection. (For an exception, see Document 25, p. 136.) This pattern of oscillation on matters of presidential war-making was established by the Court during the Civil War and its aftermath.

Midway through the war, the Court was asked to rule on the legality of the naval blockade that President Abraham Lincoln had unilaterally imposed on southern ports after the Confederates seized Fort Sumter in April 1861. The foreign owners of four vessels captured by the Union navy sued for redress (their ships and cargo—the "prizes" of capture—had been sold at public auction) on the grounds that Congress had not yet declared war on the Confederacy.

The Court rejected this appeal in an 1863 decision known as the *Prize Cases.* Writing for the majority, Justice Robert C. Grier explained that when American territory is taken by hostile forces, the absence of a congressional declaration of war does not mean that no war exists. In such circumstances, the decision continued, "the President was bound to meet [the insurrection] in the shape it presented itself, without waiting for Congress to baptise it with a name; and no name given to it by him or them could change that fact." Justice Grier went on to say that in crises such as the one Lincoln faced, the Court must defer to the president's judgment.

In 1866, a year after the Civil War ended and Lincoln was assassinated, the Court took a more critical view of another of the president's wartime actions. Two years earlier, on October 5, 1864, an outspoken southern sympathizer named Lambdin P. Milligan had been arrested in Indiana by order of Gen. Alvin P. Hovey, the Union commander at Indianapolis, on charges of conspiracy to help Confederate prisoners escape and rejoin their army. Even though Indiana was far from the fighting and the state's regular civil courts were open and operating, Milligan was tried by a military commission. (Lincoln had imposed martial law on portions of some northern states whose loyalty to the Union he doubted.) The military commission found Milligan guilty and sentenced him to be hanged.

In the case of *Ex Parte Milligan,* the Supreme Court ruled in favor of Milligan's claim that the commission had no constitutional authority to try him. Ordering Milligan released from prison, the Court condemned the government's assertion that it had the power, even in time of war, to impose military trials on civilians while the regular courts were functioning.

Justice David Davis, a close friend and longtime political ally of the late president, wrote the majority opinion in the case. He began by taking note of the changed circumstances brought about by the cessation of hostilities: "*Now* that the public safety is assured, this question, as well as others, can be discussed and decided without passion or the admixture of any element not required to form a legal judgment." From the vantage point of restored domestic tranquillity, Davis ruled that "No doctrine involving more pernicious consequences was ever invented by the wit of man than that any of the [Constitution's] provisions can be suspended during any of the great exigencies of war."

🦋 🦋 🦋

MR. JUSTICE DAVIS delivered the opinion of the court. . . .

The importance of the main question . . . cannot be overstated; for it involves the very framework of the government and the fundamental principles of American liberty.

During the late wicked Rebellion, the temper of the times did not allow that calmness in deliberation and discussion so necessary to a correct conclusion of a purely judicial question. *Then,* considerations of safety were mingled with the exercise of power; and feelings and interests prevailed which are happily terminated. *Now* that the public safety is assured, this question, as well as all others, can be discussed and decided without passion or the admixture of any element not required to form a legal judgment. We approach the investigation of this case, fully sensible of the magnitude of the inquiry and the necessity of full and cautious deliberation. . . .

The controlling question in the case is this: Upon the *facts* stated in Milligan's petition, and the exhibits filed, had the military commission mentioned in it *jurisdiction,* legally, to try and sentence him? Milligan, not a resident of one of the rebellious states, or a prisoner of war, but a citizen of Indiana for twenty years past, and never in the military or naval service, is, while at his home, arrested by the military power of the United States, imprisoned, and, on certain criminal charges preferred against him, tried, convicted, and sentenced to be hanged by a military commission, organized under the direction of the military commander of the military district of Indiana. Had this tribunal the *legal* power and authority to try and punish this man?

No graver question was ever considered by this court, nor one which more nearly concerns the rights of the whole people; for it is the birthright of every American citizen when charged with crime, to be tried and punished according to law. The power of punishment is, alone through the means which the laws have provided for that purpose, and if they are ineffectual, there is an immunity from punishment, no matter how great an offender the individual may be, or how much his crimes may have shocked the sense of justice of the country, or endangered its safety. By the protection of the law human rights are secured; withdraw that protection, and they are at the mercy of wicked rulers, or the clamor of an excited people. . . .

The Constitution of the United States is a law for rulers and people, equally in war and in peace, and covers with the shield of its protection all classes of men, at all times, and under all circumstances. No doctrine, involving more pernicious consequences, was ever invented by the wit of man than that any of its provisions can be suspended during any of the great exigencies of government. Such a doctrine leads directly to anarchy or despotism, but the theory of necessity on which it is based is false; for the government, within the Constitution, has all the powers granted to it, which are necessary to preserve its existence; as has been happily proved by the result of the great effort to throw off its just authority.

Have any of the rights guaranteed by the Constitution been violated in the case of Milligan? and if so, what are they?

Every trial involves the exercise of judicial power; and from what source did the military commission that tried him derive their authority? Certainly no part of the judicial power of the country was conferred on them; because the Constitution expressly vests it "in one supreme court and such inferior courts as the Congress may from time to time ordain and establish," and it is not pretended that the commission was a court ordained and established by Congress. They cannot justify on the mandate of the President; because he is controlled by law, and has his appropriate sphere of duty, which is to execute, not to make, the laws; and there is "no unwritten criminal code to which resort can be had as a source of jurisdiction."

But it is said that the jurisdiction is complete under the "laws and usages of war."

It can serve no useful purpose to inquire what those laws and usages are, whence they originated, where found, and on whom they operate; they can never be applied to citizens in states which have upheld the authority of the government, and where the courts are open and their process unobstructed. This court has judicial knowledge that in Indiana the Federal authority was always unopposed, and its courts always open to hear criminal accusations and redress grievances; and no usage of war could sanction a military trial there for any offence whatever of a citizen in civil life, in nowise connected with the military service. Congress could grant no such power; and to the honor of our national legislature be it said, it has never been provoked by the state of the country even to attempt its exercise. One of the plainest constitutional provisions was, therefore, infringed when Milligan was tried by a court not ordained and established by Congress, and not composed of judges appointed during good behavior.

Why was he not delivered to the Circuit Court of Indiana to be proceeded against according to law? No reason of necessity could be urged against it; because Congress had declared penalties against the offences charged, provided for their punishment, and directed that court to hear and determine them. And soon after this military tribunal was ended, the Circuit Court met, peacefully transacted its business, and adjourned. It needed no bayonets to protect it, and required no military aid to execute its judgments. It was held in a state, eminently distinguished for patriotism, by judges commissioned during the Rebellion, who were provided with juries, upright, intelligent, and selected by a marshal appointed by the President. The government had no right to conclude that Milligan, if guilty, would not receive in that court merited punishment; for its records disclose that it was constantly engaged in the trial of similar offences, and was never interrupted in its administration of criminal justice. . . .

Another guarantee of freedom was broken when Milligan was denied a trial by jury. The great minds of the country have differed on the correct interpretation to be given to various provisions of the Federal Constitution; and judicial decision has been often invoked to settle their true meaning; but until recently no one ever doubted that the right of trial by jury was fortified in the organic law against the power of attack. It is *now* assailed; but if ideas can be expressed in words, and language has any meaning, *this right*—one of the most valuable in a free country—is preserved to every one accused of crime who is not attached to the army, or navy, or militia in actual service. . . .

It is claimed that martial law covers with its broad mantle the proceedings of this military commission. The proposition is this: that in a time of war the commander of an armed force (if in his opinion the exigencies of the country demand it, and of which he is to judge), has the power, within the lines of his military district, to suspend all civil rights and their remedies, and subject citizens as well as soldiers to the rule of *his will;* and in the exercise of his lawful authority cannot be restrained, except by his superior officer or the President of the United States.

If this position is sound to the extent claimed, then when war exists, foreign or domestic, and the country is subdivided into military departments for mere convenience, the commander of one of them can, if he chooses, within his limits, on the plea of necessity, with the approval of the Executive, substitute military force for and to the exclusion of the laws, and punish all persons, as he thinks right and proper, without fixed or certain rules.

The statement of this proposition shows its importance; for, if true, republican government is a failure, and there is an end of liberty regulated by law. Martial law, established on such a basis, destroys every guarantee of the Constitution, and effectually renders the "military independent of and superior to the civil power"—the attempt to do which by the King of Great Britain was deemed by our fathers such an offence, that they assigned it to the world as one of the causes which impelled them to declare their independence. Civil liberty and this kind of martial law cannot endure together; the antagonism is irreconcilable; and, in the conflict, one or the other must perish.

This nation, as experience has proved, cannot always remain at peace, and has no right to expect that it will always have wise and humane rulers, sincerely attached to the principles of the Constitution. Wicked men, ambitious of power, with hatred of liberty and contempt of law, may fill the place once occupied by Washington and Lincoln; and if this right is conceded, and the calamities of war again befall us, the dangers to human liberty are frightful to contemplate. If our fathers had failed to provide for just such a contingency, they would have been false to the trust reposed in them. They knew—the history of the world told them—the nation they were founding, be its existence short or long, would be involved in war; how often or how long continued, human foresight could not tell; and that unlimited power, wherever lodged at such a time, was especially hazardous to freemen. For this, and other equally weighty reasons, they secured the inheritance they had fought to maintain, by incorporating in a written constitution the safeguards which *time* had proved were essential to its preservation. Not one of these safeguards can the President, or Congress, or the Judiciary disturb, except the one concerning the writ of *habeas corpus.*

It is essential to the safety of every government that, in a great crisis, like the one we have just passed through, there should be a power somewhere of suspending the writ of *habeas corpus*. In every war, there are men of previously good character, wicked enough to counsel their fellow-citizens to resist the measures deemed necessary by a good government to sustain its just authority and overthrow its enemies; and their influence may lead to dangerous combinations. In the emergency of the times, an immediate public investigation according to law may not be possible; and yet, the peril to the country may be too imminent to suffer such persons to go at large. Unquestionably, there is then an exigency which demands that the government, if it should see fit in the exercise of a proper discretion to make arrests, should not be required to produce the persons arrested in answer to a writ of *habeas corpus*. The Constitution goes no further. It does not say after a writ of *habeas corpus* is denied a citizen, that he shall be tried otherwise than by the course of the common law; if it had intended this result, it was easy by the use of direct words to have accomplished it. The illustrious men who framed that instrument were guarding the foundations of civil liberty against the abuses of unlimited power; they were full of wisdom, and the lessons of history informed them that a trial by an established court, assisted by an impartial jury, was the only sure way of protecting the citizen against oppression and wrong. Knowing this, they limited the suspension to one great right, and left the rest to remain forever inviolable. But, it is insisted that the safety of the country in time of war demands that this broad claim for martial law shall be sustained. If this were true, it could be well said that a country, preserved at the sacrifice of all the cardinal principles of liberty, is not worth the cost of preservation. Happily, it is not so. . . .

❧ 16 ❧

Articles of Impeachment
against Andrew Johnson

(1868)

THE CONSTITUTION STIPULATES that the president "shall be removed from office on Impeachment for, and Conviction of, Treason, Bribery, or other high Crimes and Misdemeanors." The House of Representatives is charged to impeach the president, by majority vote; the Senate, with the chief justice of the Supreme Court presiding, then tries the president and decides whether to convict and remove. A two-thirds majority "of the Members present" is required to do so.

In all of American history, just one president has undergone the entire impeachment process: Andrew Johnson. A Jacksonian Democrat from Tennessee, Johnson had been the only southern senator who chose to remain in Congress after his state seceded from the Union in 1861. In 1864, at the request of President Abraham Lincoln, the National Union Party convention (the Republican convention had decided to change its name in an effort to attract unionist Democrats) nominated Johnson for vice president. Johnson succeeded to the presidency when Lincoln died of an assassin's bullet on April 15, 1865.

As president, Johnson was embroiled in a series of bitter controversies with the Radical Republicans, who took control of Congress in the 1866 elections, over Reconstruction of the South. The secretary of war, Edwin M. Stanton, sided more with Congress on these issues than with the president. Congress protected Stanton from being fired by passing the Tenure of Office Act and by overriding Johnson's veto of the bill on March 2, 1867. The act broke with the precedent established by the First Congress in 1789 by barring the president from removing any Senate-confirmed appointee from office until the Senate approved the nomination of a successor. (See Document 5, p. 34.)

After Congress went into recess in 1867, Johnson, taking advantage of a loophole in the Tenure of Office Act that allowed him to act temporarily when Congress was not in session, suspended Stanton as secretary of war and replaced him with Gen. Ulysses S. Grant. Reconvening in 1868, however, the Senate disapproved Johnson's action, and Grant turned the office back to Stanton. Johnson had thought he had Grant's promise to ignore the Senate vote and thus to force a confrontation with Congress and, ultimately, a decision by the Supreme Court about the constitutionality of the Tenure of Office Act. But Grant decided not to jeopardize his presidential ambitions by siding with the president and alienating congressional Republicans.

In February 1868, acting in explicit defiance of the act, Johnson fired

Stanton and appointed Gen. Lorenzo Thomas to replace him. While Thomas tried (unsuccessfully) to persuade Stanton to vacate the building, the House voted on February 21 to open an impeachment inquiry against the president.

The House took little time to act. The ardently radical Committee on Reconstruction quickly prepared an eleven-article impeachment resolution, which the House approved by a 126–47 vote on March 2 and 3, 1868, after only two days of debate. The first eight articles dealt with various aspects of Johnson's violation of the Tenure of Office Act. Article IX accused him of violating another recently enacted law when he bypassed the general of the army to give an order to a general in the field. Articles X and XI charged that Johnson's inflammatory speeches in the 1866 congressional election campaign had sought to bring Congress into "disgrace, ridicule, hatred, contempt, and reproach."

Seven members of the House were appointed to present the case for removal in the Senate trial. Johnson's lawyers argued that the president was entitled to violate a law he regarded as unconstitutional in order to bring the issue before the Supreme Court. The lawyers also argued, more narrowly, that the Tenure of Office Act did not bar Johnson from firing Stanton because Stanton had been appointed by a different president, Lincoln. They dismissed Articles IX, X, and XI as frivolous.

Thirty-six votes were needed for conviction in the fifty-four-member Senate. By most reckonings, twelve senators (nine of them Democrats) were counted as Johnson supporters and thirty as Johnson opponents. That left the decision in the hands of twelve undecided Republicans, some of whom dreaded the prospect that Senate president pro tempore and Reconstruction hardliner Benjamin Wade of Ohio would (under the law that prevailed at the time) succeed to the presidency if Johnson were removed. In votes taken on May 16 and May 26, 1868, seven of the twelve voted not to convict the president. As a result, the margin in favor of conviction was 35–19, one short of the required two-thirds.

Johnson completed his term as president on March 4, 1869. He returned to Tennessee where, after two unsuccessful attempts to win office, he was elected by the state legislature to the U.S. Senate in 1874. On July 31, 1875, five months after taking office, Johnson died.

※ ※ ※

IN THE HOUSE OF REPRESENTATIVES, UNITED STATES,

March 2, 1868

ARTICLES EXHIBITED BY THE HOUSE OF REPRESENTATIVES OF THE UNITED STATES, IN THE NAME OF THEMSELVES AND ALL THE PEOPLE OF THE UNITED STATES, AGAINST ANDREW JOHNSON, PRESIDENT OF THE UNITED STATES, IN MAINTENANCE AND SUPPORT OF THEIR IMPEACHMENT AGAINST HIM FOR HIGH CRIMES AND MISDEMEANORS IN OFFICE.

Article I

That said Andrew Johnson, President of the United States, on the 21st day of February, A.D. 1868, at Washington, in the District of Columbia, unmindful of the high duties of his office, of his oath of office, and of the requirement of the Constitution that he should take care that the laws be faithfully executed, did unlawfully and in violation of the Constitution and laws of the United States issue an order in writing for the removal of Edwin M. Stanton from the office of Secretary for the Department of War, said Edwin M. Stanton having been theretofore duly appointed and commissioned, by and with the advice and consent of the Senate of the United States, as such Secretary; and said Andrew Johnson, President of the United States, on the 12th day of August, A.D. 1867, and during the recess of said Senate, having suspended by his order Edwin M. Stanton from said office, and within twenty days after the first day of the next meeting of said Senate—that is to say, on the 12th day of December, in the year last aforesaid—having reported to said Senate such suspension, with the evidence and reasons for his action in the case and the name of the person designated to perform the duties of such office temporarily until the next meeting of the Senate; and said Senate thereafterwards, on the 13th day of January, A.D. 1868, having duly considered the evidence and reasons reported by said Andrew Johnson for said suspension, and having refused to concur in said suspension, whereby and by force of the provisions of an act entitled "An act regulating the tenure of certain civil offices," passed March 2, 1867, said Edwin M. Stanton did forthwith resume the functions of his office, whereof the said Andrew Johnson had then and there due notice; and said Edwin M. Stanton, by reason of the premises, on said 21st day of February, being lawfully entitled to hold said office of Secretary for the Department of War; which said order for the removal of said Edwin M. Stanton is in substance as follows; that is to say:

EXECUTIVE MANSION,
Washington, D.C., February 21, 1868.

HON. EDWIN M. STANTON,
Washington, D.C.

SIR: By virtue of the power and authority vested in me as President by the Constitution and laws of the United States, you are hereby removed from office as Secretary for the Department of War, and your functions as such will terminate upon the receipt of this communication.

You will transfer to Brevet Major-General Lorenzo Thomas, Adjutant-General of the Army, who has this day been authorized and empowered to act as secretary of War ad interim, all records, books, papers, and other public property now in your custody and charge.

Respectfully, yours,

ANDREW JOHNSON

Which order was unlawfully issued with intent then and there to violate the act entitled "An act regulating the tenure of certain civil offices," passed March 2, 1867, and with the further intent, contrary to the provisions of said act, in violation thereof, and contrary to the provisions of the Constitution of the United States, and without the advice and consent of the Senate of the United States, the said Senate then and there being in session, to remove said Edwin M. Stanton from the office of Secretary for the Department of War, the said Edwin M. Stanton being then and there Secretary for the Department of War, and being then and there in the due and unlawful execution and discharge of the duties of said office; whereby said Andrew Johnson, President of the United States, did then and there commit and was guilty of a high misdemeanor in office. . . .

Article IX

That said Andrew Johnson, President of the United States, on the 22d day of February, A.D. 1868, at Washington, in the District of Columbia, in disregard of the Constitution and the laws of the United States duly enacted, as Commander in Chief of the Army of the United States, did bring before himself then and there William H. Emory, a major-general by brevet in the Army of the United States, actually in command of the Department of Washington and the military forces thereof, and did then and there, as such Commander in Chief, declare to and instruct said Emory that part of a law of the United States, passed March 2, 1867, entitled "Act making appropriations for the support of the Army for the year ending June 30, 1868, and for other purposes," especially the second section thereof, which provides, among other things, that "all orders and instructions relating to military operations issued by the President or Secretary of War shall be issued through the General of the Army, and in case of his inability through the next in rank," was unconstitutional and in contravention of the commission of said Emory, and which said provision of law had been theretofore duly and legally promulgated by general order for the government and direction of the Army of the United States, as the said Andrew Johnson then and there well knew, with intent thereby to induce said Emory, in his official capacity as commander of the Department of Washington, to violate the provisions of said act and to take and receive, act upon, and obey such orders as he, the said Andrew Johnson, might make and give, and which should not be issued through the General of the Army of the United States, according to the provisions of said act, and with the further intent thereby to enable him, and said Andrew Johnson, to prevent the execution of the act entitled "An act regulating the tenure of certain civil offices," passed March 2, 1867, and to unlawfully prevent Edwin M. Stanton, then being Secretary for the Department of War, from holding said office and discharging the duties thereof; whereby said Andrew Johnson, President of the United States, did then and there commit and was guilty of a high misdemeanor in office.

And the House of Representatives, by protestation, saving to themselves the liberty of exhibiting at any time hereafter any further articles or other accusation or impeachment against the said Andrew Johnson, President of the United States, and also of replying to his answers which he shall make unto the articles herein preferred against him, and of offering proof to the same, and every part thereof, and to all and every other article, accusation, or impeachment which shall be exhibited by them, as the case shall require, do demand that the said Andrew Johnson may be put to answer the high crimes and misdemeanors in office here-in charged against him, and that such proceedings, examinations, trials, and judgments may be thereupon had and given as may be agreeable to law and justice.

SCHUYLER COLFAX,
Speaker of the House of Representatives
EDWARD MCPHERSON,
Clerk of the House of Representatives

Attest:

The following additional articles of impeachment were agreed to viz:

IN THE HOUSE OF REPRESENTATIVES, UNITED STATES
March 3, 1868

Article X

That said Andrew Johnson, President of the United States, unmindful of the high duties of his office and the dignity and proprieties thereof, and of the harmony and courtesies which ought to exist and be maintained between the executive and legislative branches of the Government of the United States, designing and intending to set aside the rightful authority and powers of Congress, did attempt to bring into disgrace, ridicule, hatred, contempt, and reproach the Congress of the United States and the several branches thereof, to impair and destroy the regard and respect of all the good people of the United States for the Congress and legislative power thereof (which all officers of the Government ought inviolably to preserve and maintain) and to excite the odium and resentment of all the good people of the United States against Congress and the laws by it duly and constitutionally enacted; and, in pursuance of his said design and intent, openly and pubicly, and before divers assemblages of the citizens of the United States, convened in divers parts thereof to meet and receive said Andrew Johnson as the Chief Magistrate of the United States, did, on the 18th day of August, A.D. 1866, and on divers other days and times, as well before as afterwards, make and deliver with a loud voice certain intemperate, inflammatory, and scandalouse harangues, and did therein utter loud threats and bitter menaces, as well against Congress as the laws of the United States, duly enacted thereby, amid the cries, jeers, and laughter of the multitudes then assembled and in hearing, which are set forth in the several specifications hereinafter written, in substance and effect, that is to say:

Specification first.—In this, that at Washington, in the District of Columbia in the Executive Mansion, to a committee of citizens who called upon the President of the United States, speaking of and concerning the Congress of the United States, said Andrew Johnson, President of the United States, heretofore, to wit, on the 18th day of August, in the year of our Lord 1866, did, in a loud voice, declare in substance and effect, among other things, that is to say:

"So far as the executive department of the Government is concerned, the effort has been made to restore the Union, to heal the breach, to pour oil into the wounds which were consequent upon the struggle, and (to speak in common phrase) to prepare, as the learned and wise physician would, a plaster healing in character and coextensive with the wound. We thought, and we think, that we had partially succeeded; but as the work progresses, as reconstruction seemed to be taking place and the country was becoming reunited, we found a disturbing and marring element opposing us. In alluding to that element, I shall go no further than your convention and the distinguished gentleman who had delivered to me the report of its proceedings. I shall make no reference to it that I do not believe the time and the occasion justify.

"We have witnessed in one department of the Government every endeavor to prevent the restoration of peace, harmony, and union. We have seen hanging upon the verge of the Government, as it were, a body called, or which assumes to be, the Congress of the United States, while in fact it is a Congress of only a part of the States. We have seen this Congress pretend to be for the Union when its every step and act tended to perpetrate disunion and make a disruption of the States inevitable. We have seen Congress gradually encroach step by step upon constitutional rights and violate, day after day and month after month, fundamental principles of the Government. We have seen a Congress that seemed to forget that there was a limit to the sphere and scope of legislation. We have seen a Congress in a minority assume to exercise power which, allowed to be consummated, would result in despotism or monarchy itself."

Specification second.—In this, that at Cleveland, in the State of Ohio, heretofore, to wit, on the 3d day of September, in the year of our Lord 1866, before a public assemblage of citizens and others, said Andrew Johnson, President of the United States, speaking of and concerning the Congress of the United States did, in a loud voice, declare in substance and effect among other things, that is to say:

"I will tell you what I did do. I called upon your Congress that is trying to break up the Government.

"In conclusion, beside that, Congress had taken much pains to poison their constituents against him. But what had a Congress done? Have they done anything to restore the Union of these States? No; on the contrary, they had done everything to prevent it; and because he stood now where he did when the rebellion commenced he had been denounced as a traitor. Who had run greater risks or made greater sacrifices than himself? But Congress, factious and domineering, had undertaken to poison the minds of the American people."

Specification third.—In this, that at St. Louis, in the State of Missouri, heretofore, to wit, on the 8th day of September, in the year of our Lord 1866, before a public assemblage of citizens and others, said Andrew Johnson, President of the United States, speaking of and concerning the Congress of the United States, did, in a loud voice, declare, in substance and effect, among other things, that is to say:

"Go on. Perhaps if you had a word or two on the subject of New Orleans, you might understand more about it than you do. And if you will go back—if you will go back and ascertain the cause of the riot at New Orleans, perhaps you will not be so prompt in calling out 'New Orleans.' If you will take up the riot at New Orleans and trace it back to its source or its immediate cause, you will find out who was responsible for the blood that was shed there. If you will take up the riot at New Orleans and trace it back to the Radical Congress, you will find that the riot at New Orleans was substantially planned. If you will take up the proceedings in their caucuses, you will understand that they there knew that a convention was to be called which was extinct by its power having expired; that it was said that the intention was that a new government was to be organized, and on the organization of that government the intention was to enfranchise one portion of the population, called the colored population, who had just been emancipated, and at the same time disenfranchise white men. When you design to talk about New Orleans you ought to understand what you are talking about. When you read the speeches that were made, and take up the facts on the Friday and Saturday before that convention sat, you will find that speeches were made incendiary in their character, exciting that portion of the population, the black population, to arm themselves and prepare for the shedding of blood. You will also find that that convention did assemble in violation of law, and the intention of that convention was to supersede the reorganized authorities in the State government of Louisiana, which had been recognized by the Government of the United States; and every man engaged in that rebellion in that convention, with the intention of superseding and upturning the civil government which had been recognized by the Government of the United States, I say that he was a traitor to the Constitution of the United States, and hence you find that another rebellion was commenced having its origin in the Radical Congress.

"So much for the New Orleans riot. And there was the cause and the origin of the blood that was shed; and every drop of blood that was shed is upon their skirts, and they are responsible for it. I could test this thing a little closer, but will not do it here tonight. But when you talk about the causes and consequences that resulted from proceedings of that kind, perhaps as I have been introduced here and you have provoked questions of this kind, though it does not provoke me, I will tell you a few wholesome things that have been done by this Radical Congress in connection with New Orleans and the extension of the elective franchise.

"I know that I have been traduced and abused. I know it has come in advance of me here, as elsewhere, that I have attempted to exercise an arbitrary power in resisting laws that were intended to be forced upon the Government; that I had abandoned the party that elected me, and that I was a traitor because I exercised the veto power in attempting and did arrest for a time a bill that was called a 'Freedman's Bureau' bill; yes, that I was a traitor. And I have been traduced, I have been slandered, I have been maligned, I have been called Judas Iscariot, and all that. Now, my countrymen here tonight, it is very easy to indulge in epithets; it is easy to call a man a Judas and cry out traitor; but when he is called upon to give arguments and facts it is very easy to indulge in epithets; it is easy to call a man a Judas and he was one of the twelve apostles. Oh yes, the twelve apostles had a Christ. The twelve apostles had a Christ, and he never could have had a Judas unless he had had twelve apostles. If I have played the Judas, who has been my Christ that I have played the Judas with? Was it Thad. Stevens? Was it Wendell Philips? Was it Charles Sumner? These are the men that stop and compare themselves with the Saviour; and everybody that differs with them in opinion, and to try and stay and arrest the diabolical and nefarious policy, is to be denounced as a Judas.

"Well, let me say to you, if you will stand by me in this action; if you will stand by me in trying to give the people a fair chance, soldiers and citizens, to participate in these offices, God being willing, I will kick them out, I will kick them out just as fast as I can.

"Let me say to you, in concluding that what I have said I intended to say. I was not provoked into this, and I care not for their menaces, the taunts, and the jeers, I care not for threats, I do not intend to be bullied by my enemies nor overawed by my friends. But, God willing, with your help I will veto their measures whenever any of them come to me."

Which said utterances, declarations, threats, and harangues, highly censurable in any, are peculiarly indecent and unbecoming in the Chief Magistrate of the United States, by means whereof said Andrew Johnson has brought the high office of the President of the United States into contempt, ridicule, and disgrace, to the great scandal of all good citizens, whereby said Andrew Johnson, President of the United States, did commit, and was then and there guilty of, a high misdemeanor in office.

Article XI

That said Andrew Johnson, President of the United States, unmindful of the high duties of his office and of his oath of office, and in disregard of the Constitution and laws of the United States, did heretofore, to wit, on the 18th day of August, A.D. 1866, at the city of Washington, in the District of Columbia, by public speech, declare and affirm in substance that the Thirty-ninth Congress of the United States was not a Congress of the United States authorized by the Constitution to exercise legislative power under the same, but, on the contrary, was a Congress of only part of the States; thereby denying and intending to deny that the legislation of said Congress was valid or obligatory upon him, the said Andrew Johnson, except in so far as he saw fit to approve the same, and also thereby denying and intending to deny the power of the said Thirty-ninth Congress to propose amendments to the Constitution of the United States; and in pursuance of said declaration the said Andrew Johnson, President of the United States, afterwards, to wit, on the 21st day February, A.D. 1868, at the city of Washington, in the District of Columbia, did unlawfully, and in disregard of the requirement of the Constitution that he should take care that the laws be faithfully executed, attempt to prevent the execution of an act entitled "An act regulating the tenure of certain civil offices," passed March 2, 1867, by unlawfully devising and contriving, and attempting to devise and contrive, means by which he should prevent Edwin M. Stanton from forthwith resuming the functions of the office of Secretary for the Department of War, notwithstanding the refusal of the Senate to concur in the suspension theretofore made by said Andrew Johnson of said Edwin M. Stanton from said office of Secretary for the Department of War, and also by further unlawfully devising and contriving, and attempting to devise and contrive, means then and there to prevent the execution of an act entitled "An act making appropriations for the support of the Army for the fiscal year ending June 30, 1868 and for other purposes," approved March 2, 1867, and also to prevent the execution of an act entitled "An act to provide for the more efficient government of the rebel States," passed March 2, 1867, whereby the said Andrew Johnson, President of the United States, did then, to wit, on the 21st day of February, A.D. 1868, at the city of Washington, commit and was guilty of a high misdemeanor in office.

SCHUYLER COLFAX,
Speaker of the House of Representatives

EDWARD MCPHERSON,
Clerk of the House of Representatives

Theodore Roosevelt's and William Howard Taft's Theories of Presidential Power

(1913, 1916)

THEODORE ROOSEVELT, who was elected vice president in 1900, succeeded to the presidency when President William McKinley was assassinated on September 15, 1901, and won a full term as president in the 1904 election. Roosevelt invigorated the office with an energy and initiative not seen since the Lincoln administration, but declined to seek reelection in 1908, retiring in favor of his close friend and secretary of war, William Howard Taft. Although Taft was elected president, Roosevelt came to regard him as an overly cautious and conservative leader and challenged him for the 1912 Republican presidential nomination. After Taft was nominated, Roosevelt reentered the race as the candidate of the Progressive (or "Bull Moose") Party. They split the Republican vote in November and were defeated by Democrat Woodrow Wilson.

Soon after their administrations were over, former presidents Roosevelt and Taft produced a classic exchange on the proper nature of presidential power. Roosevelt articulated his "stewardship" theory of the presidency in *The Autobiography of Theodore Roosevelt,* published in 1913. Taft expounded his "literalist" theory in a 1916 book called *Our Chief Magistrate and His Powers.* The exchange is significant not only because of the light it sheds on the conflict that developed between the two former friends and political allies, especially on conservation policy, but also because it offers a striking comparison of the way most presidents regarded the presidency in the nineteenth century (Taft's view) and in the twentieth (Roosevelt's view).

Like Pacificus and Helvidius—that is, Alexander Hamilton and James Madison—before them, Roosevelt and Taft took the Constitution as their point of departure. (See Document 6, p. 39.) But they differed radically on how to interpret that document. In a nutshell, Roosevelt believed that the president could do anything that the Constitution or laws did not expressly forbid, while Taft felt that the president could not do anything that the Constitution or laws did not expressly permit.

Roosevelt claimed that "I acted for the public welfare, I acted for the common well-being of all our people, whenever and in whatever manner was necessary, unless prevented by direct constitutional or legislative prohibition." He regarded the president as "a steward of the people bound actively and affirmatively to do all he could for the people, and not to content himself with the negative merit of keeping his talents undamaged in a napkin."

Taft, on the other hand, believed that "the President can exercise no power which cannot be fairly and reasonably traced to some specific grant of power or justly implied and included within such express grant as proper and necessary to its exercise." He added: "There is no undefined residuum of power which he can exercise because it seems to him to be in the public interest."

Each president's philosophy of the presidency helps to explain his actions in office. Taft seldom spoke out publicly in defense of his policies. He neglected the press and, although willing to recommend legislation, stood by as Congress worked its will. When Congress resisted Roosevelt's legislative agenda, however, he broke precedent by making a speechmaking tour of the country, "appealing over the heads of the Senate and House leaders to the people, who were the masters of both of us." He used the press to personalize both his administration and his agenda. Roosevelt was "TR" (the first president to be known by his initials), and his program was the "Square Deal" (which foreshadowed labels such as "New Deal," "New Frontier," and "Great Society"). In foreign policy, Roosevelt was active and, on occasion, defiant toward Congress.

Theodore Roosevelt

The most important factor in getting the right spirit in my Administration, next to insistence upon courage, honesty, and a genuine democracy of desire to serve the plain people, was my insistence upon the theory that the executive power was limited only by specific restrictions and prohibitions appearing in the Constitution or imposed by Congress under its constitutional powers.

My view was that every executive officer, and above all every executive officer in high position, was a steward of the people bound actively and affirmatively to do all he could for the people, and not to content himself with the negative merit of keeping his talents undamaged in a napkin. I declined to adopt the view that what was imperatively necessary for the nation could not be done by the President unless he could find some specific authorization to do it. My belief was that it was not only his right but his duty to do anything that the needs of the nation demanded unless such action was forbidden by the Constitution or by the laws. Under this interpretation of executive power I did and caused to be done many things not previously done by the President and the heads of the departments. I did not usurp power, but I did greatly broaden the use of executive power. In other words, I acted for the public welfare, I acted for the common well-being of all our people, whenever and in whatever manner was necessary, unless prevented by direct constitutional or legislative prohibition. . . .

The course I followed, of regarding the Executive as subject only to the people, and, under the Constitution, bound to serve the people affirmatively in cases where the Constitution does not explicitly forbid him to render the service, was substantially the course followed by both Andrew Jackson and Abraham Lincoln. Other honorable and well-meaning Presidents, such as James Buchanan, took the opposite and, as it seems to me, narrowly legalistic view that the President is the servant of Congress rather than of the people, and can do nothing, no matter how necessary it be to act, unless the Constitution explicitly commands the action. Most able lawyers who are past middle age take this view, and so do large numbers of well-meaning, respectable citizens. My successor in office [William Howard Taft] took this, the Buchanan, view of the President's powers and duties.

For example, under my administration we found that one of the favorite methods adopted by the men desirous of stealing the public domain was to carry the decision of the secretary of the interior into court. By vigorously opposing such action, and only by so doing, we were able to carry out the policy of properly protecting the public domain. My successor not only took the opposite view, but recommended to Congress the passage of a bill which would have given the courts direct appellate power over the secretary of the interior in these land matters. . . . Fortunately, Congress declined to pass the bill. Its passage would have been a veritable calamity.

I acted on the theory that the President could at any time in his discretion withdraw from entry any of the public lands of the United States and reserve the same for forestry, for water-power sites, for irrigation, and other public purposes. Without such action it would have been impossible to stop the activity of the land-thieves. No one ventured to test its legality by lawsuit. My successor, however, himself questioned it, and referred the matter to Congress. Again Congress showed its wisdom by passing a law which gave the President the power which he had long exercised, and of which my successor had shorn himself.

Perhaps the sharp difference between what may be called the Lincoln-Jackson and the Buchanan-Taft schools, in their views of the power and duties of the President, may be best illustrated by comparing the attitude of my successor toward his Secretary of the Interior, Mr. [Richard A.] Ballinger, when the latter was accused of gross misconduct in office, with my attitude toward my chiefs of department and other subordinate officers. More than once while I was President my officials were attacked by Congress, generally because these officials did their duty well and fearlessly. In every such case I stood by the official and refused to recognize the right of Congress to interfere with me excepting by impeachment or in other constitutional manner. On the other hand, wherever I found the officer unfit for his position, I promptly removed him, even although the most influential men in Congress fought for his retention. The Jackson-Lincoln view is that a President who is fit to do good work should be able to form his own judgment as to his own subordinates, and, above all, of the subordinates standing highest and in closest and most intimate touch with him. My secretaries and their subordinates were responsible to me, and I accepted the responsibility for all their deeds. As long as they were satisfactory to me I stood by them against every critic or assailant, within or without Congress; and as for getting Congress to make up my mind for me about them, the thought would have been inconceivable to me. My successor took the opposite, or Buchanan, view when he permitted and requested Congress to pass judgment on the charges made against Mr. Ballinger as an executive officer. These charges were made to the President; the President had the facts before him and could get at them at any time, and he alone had power to act if the charges were true. However, he permitted and requested Congress to investigate Mr. Ballinger. The party minority of the committee that investigated him, and one member of the majority, declared that the charges were well-founded and that Mr. Ballinger should be removed. The other members of the majority declared the charges ill-founded. The President abode by the view of the majority. Of course believers in the Jackson-Lincoln theory of the presidency would not be content with this town meeting majority and minority method of determining by another branch of the government what it seems the especial duty of the President himself to determine for himself in dealing with his own subordinate in his own department. . . .

William Howard Taft

While it is important to mark out the exclusive field of jurisdiction of each branch of the government, Legislative, Executive and Judicial, it should be said that in the proper working of the government there must be cooperation of all branches, and without a willingness of each branch to perform its function, there will follow a hopeless obstruction to the progress of the whole government. Neither branch can compel the other to affirmative action, and each branch can greatly hinder the other in the attainment of the object of its activities and the exercise of its discretion.

The true view of the Executive functions is, as I conceive it, that the President can exercise no power which cannot be fairly and reasonably traced to some specific grant of power or justly implied and included within such express grant as proper and necessary to its exercise. Such specific grant must be either in the Federal Constitution or in an act of Congress passed in pursuance thereof. There is no undefined residuum of power which he can exercise because it seems to him to be in the public interest, and there is nothing in the Neagle case [*In re Neagle* (1890)] and its definition of a law of the United States, or in other precedents, warranting such an inference. The grants of Executive power are necessarily in general terms in order not to embarrass the Executive within the field of action plainly marked for him, but his jurisdiction must be justified and vindicated by affirmative constitutional or statutory provision, or it does not exist. There have not been wanting, however, eminent men in high public office holding a different view and who have insisted upon the necessity for an undefined residuum of Executive power in the public interest. They have not been confined to the present generation. We may learn this from the complaint of a Virginia statesman, Abel P. Upshur, a strict constructionist of the old school, who succeeded Daniel Webster as Secretary of State under President [John] Tyler. He was aroused by Story's commentaries on the Constitution to write a monograph answering and criticizing them, and in the course of this he comments as follows on the Executive power under the Constitution:

The most defective part of the Constitution beyond all question, is that which related to the Executive Department. It is impossible to read that instrument, without being struck with the loose and unguarded terms in which the powers and duties of the President are pointed out. So far as the legislature is concerned, the limitations of the Constitution, are, perhaps, as precise and strict as they could safely have been made; but in regard to the Executive, the Convention appears to have studiously selected such loose and general expressions, as would enable the President, by implication and construction either to neglect his duties or to enlarge his powers. *We have heard it gravely asserted in Congress that whatever power is neither legislative nor judiciary, is of course executive, and, as such, belongs to the President under the Constitution.* How far a majority of that body would have sustained a doctrine so monstrous, and so utterly at war with the whole genius of our government, it is impossible to say, but this, at least, we know, that it met with no rebuke from those who supported the particular act of Executive power, in defense of which it was urged. Be this as it may, it is a reproach to the Constitution that the Executive trust is so ill-defined, as to leave any plausible pretense even to the insane zeal of party devotion, for attributing to the President of the United States the power of a despot; powers which are wholly unknown in any limited monarchy in the world.

The view that he takes as a result of the loose language defining the Executive powers seems exaggerated. But one must agree with him in his condemnation of the view of the Executive power which he says was advanced in Congress. In recent years there has been put forward a similar view by executive officials and to some extent acted on. Men who are not such strict constructionists of the Constitution as Mr. Upshur may well feel real concern if such views are to receive the general acquiescence. Mr. [James R.] Garfield, when Secretary of the Interior, under Mr. Roosevelt, in his final report to Congress in reference to the power of the Executive over the public domain, said:

Full power under the Constitution was vested in the Executive Branch of the Government and the extent to which that power may be exercised is governed wholly by the discretion of the Executive unless any specific act has been prohibited either by the Constitution or by legislation.

In pursuance of this principle, Mr. Garfield, under an act for the reclamation of arid land by irrigation, which authorized him to make contracts for irrigation works and incur liability equal to the amount on deposit in the Reclamation Fund, made contracts with associations of settlers by which it was agreed that if these settlers would advance money and work, they might receive certificates from the government engineers of the labor and money furnished by them, and that such certificates might be received in the future in the discharge of their legal obligations to the government for water rent and other things under the statute. It became necessary for the succeeding [Taft] administration to pass on the validity of these government certificates. They were held by Attorney-General [George] Wickersham to be illegal, on the ground that no authority existed for their issuance. . . .

My judgment is that the view of Mr. Garfield and Mr. Roosevelt, ascribing an undefined residuum of power to the President is an unsafe doctrine and that it might lead under emergencies to results of an arbitrary character, doing irremediable injustice to private right. The mainspring of such a view is that the Executive is charged with responsibility for the welfare of all the people in a general way, that he is to play the part of a Universal Providence and set all things right, and that anything that in his judgment will help the people he ought to do, unless he is expressly forbidden not to do it. The wide field of action that this would give to the Executive one can hardly limit.

❧ 18 ❧

Woodrow Wilson's First State of the Union Address

(1913)

WOODROW WILSON was the only professional political scientist ever to be able to implement his theories as president. Wilson, who earned his doctorate at Johns Hopkins University and later became a professor and president of Princeton University, had argued since his student days that the relationship between the president and Congress should be marked by cooperation rather than conflict. In his 1885 book, *Congressional Government,* Wilson urged that the executive departments should effectively be made part of Congress so that the legislative branch could take the lead. By the early 1900s, however, Wilson regarded interbranch cooperation as more likely to occur if the presidency were strengthened so that the president could lead Congress.

Wilson's popularity as president of Princeton made him a prime candidate for governor of New Jersey in 1910. He was elected and, two years later, was nominated for president by the Democratic National Convention on the forty-sixth ballot. The beneficiary of a split in the Republican Party that prompted both President William Howard Taft and former president Theodore Roosevelt to run in 1912, Wilson was elected overwhelmingly. (See Document 17, p. 93.)

Wilson led a newly invigorated Democratic Party. Only the second Democrat to be elected president since the Civil War, Wilson brought in a Democratic Congress on his coattails and expected it to cooperate with him on an explicitly partisan basis. Perhaps most important, he committed the party to his "New Freedom" agenda, which proposed to use the power of the federal government to reduce the power of big business.

Wilson also ushered in the "rhetorical presidency," believing that the president could lead Congress by leading public opinion. With few exceptions, Wilson's nineteenth-century predecessors had eschewed rhetorical leadership, deferring to the broad political consensus that such an approach was unseemly. Andrew Johnson was impeached and nearly removed from office, in part because of speeches he had made attacking Congress. (See Document 16, p. 82.) Earlier, Thomas Jefferson had set a precedent by electing to fulfill his constitutional duty to "from time to time give to the Congress Information of the State of the Union" with annual written messages instead of speeches to the assembled legislators, such as those George Washington and John Adams had given. Jefferson claimed that the State of the Union address was too reminiscent of the British king's speech from the throne. The written messages sent by Jefferson's successors usually consisted of a long recitation of the activities of the various executive departments.

Wilson, in his effort to rouse public support, used oratory effectively and created the practice of regular press conferences. His most dramatic innovation, however, was to restore the practice of appearing personally before a joint session of Congress in the chamber of the House of Representatives to deliver the State of the Union address. Equally important, Wilson used the address to tell Congress what he hoped it would do in the coming year, not just to report on what had happened during the preceding year.

Standing in the well of the House on April 8, 1913, Wilson began by saying, "I am very glad indeed to have this opportunity to address the two Houses directly and to verify for myself the impression that the President of the United States is a person, not a mere department of the Government hailing Congress from some isolated island of jealous power, sending messages, not speaking naturally and with his own voice— that he is a human being trying to co-operate with other human beings in a common service."

Wilson focused his address on a call for tariff reform, which Congress heeded by passing reductions of 15 percent and by removing tariffs entirely from some one hundred items. In an unprecedented display of peacetime presidential leadership, Wilson also persuaded Congress during his first term to establish a graduated income tax; to regulate banking and unfair business competition by creating the Federal Reserve System and Federal Trade Commission, respectively; to crack down on the trusts by passing the Clayton Antitrust Act; and to aid agriculture with the Smith-Lever Act and the Federal Farm Loan Act.

❧ ❧ ❧

Gentlemen of the Congress:

I am very glad indeed to have this opportunity to address the two Houses directly and to verify for myself the impression that the President of the United States is a person, not a mere department of the Government hailing Congress from some isolated island of jealous power, sending messages, not speaking naturally and with his own voice—that he is a human being trying to co-operate with other human beings in a common service. After this pleasant experience I shall feel quite normal in all our dealings with one another.

I have called the Congress together in extraordinary session because a duty was laid upon the party now in power at the recent elections which it ought to perform promptly, in order that the burden carried by the people under existing law may be lightened as soon as possible, and in order, also, that the business interests of the country may not be kept too long in suspense as to what the fiscal changes are to be to which they will be required to adjust themselves. It is clear to the whole country that the tariff duties must be altered. They must be changed to meet the radical alteration in the conditions of our economic life which the country has witnessed within the last generation. While the whole face and method of our industrial and commercial life were being changed beyond recognition the tariff schedules have remained what they were before the change began, or have moved in the direction they were given when no large circumstance of our industrial development was what it is to-day. Our task is to square them with the actual facts. The sooner that is done the sooner our men of business will be free to thrive by the law of nature—the nature of free business—instead of by the law of legislation and artificial arrangement.

We have seen tariff legislation wander very far afield in our day—very far indeed from the field in which our prosperity might have had a normal growth and stimulation. No one who looks the facts squarely in the face or knows anything that lies beneath the surface of action can fail to perceive the principles upon which recent tariff legislation has been based. We long ago passed beyond the modest notion of "protecting" the industries of the country and moved boldly forward to the idea that they were entitled to the direct patronage of the Government. For a long time—a time so long that the men now active in public policy hardly remember the conditions that preceded it—we have sought in our tariff schedules to give each group of manufacturers or producers what they themselves thought that they needed in order to maintain a practically exclusive market as against the rest of the world. Consciously or unconsciously, we have built up a set of privileges and exemptions from competition behind which it was easy by any, even the crudest, forms of combination to organize monopoly; until at last nothing is normal, nothing is obliged to stand the tests of efficiency and economy, in our world of big business, but everything thrives by concerted arrangement. Only new principles of action will save us from a final hard crystallization of monopoly and a complete loss of the influences that quicken enterprise and keep independent energy alive.

It is plain what those principles must be. We must abolish everything that bears even the semblance of privilege or of any kind of artificial advantage, and put our business men and producers under the stimulation of a constant necessity to be efficient, economical, and enterprising, masters of competitive supremacy, better workers and merchants than any in the world. Aside from the duties laid upon articles which we do not, and probably can not, produce, therefore, and the duties laid upon luxuries and merely for the sake of the revenues they yield, the object of the tariff duties henceforth laid must be effective competition, the whetting of American wits by contest with the wits of the rest of the world.

It would be unwise to move toward this end headlong, with reckless haste, or with strokes that cut at the very roots of what has grown up amongst us by long process and at our own invitation. It does not alter a thing to upset it and break it and deprive it of a chance to change. It destroys it. We must make changes in our fiscal laws, in our fiscal system, whose object is development, a more free and wholesome development, not revolution or upset or confusion. We must build up trade, especially foreign trade. We need the outlet and the enlarged field of energy more than we ever did before. We must build up industry as well, and must adopt freedom in the place of artificial stimulation only so far as it will build, not pull down. In dealing with the tariff the method by which this may be done will be a matter of judgment exercised item by item. To some not accustomed to the excitements and responsibilities of greater freedom our methods may in some respects and at some points seem heroic but remedies may be heroic and yet be remedies. It is our business to be sure that they are genuine remedies. Our object is clear. If our motive is above just challenge and only an occasional error of judgment is chargeable against us, we shall be fortunate.

We are called upon to render the country a great service in more matters than one. Our responsibility should be met and our methods should be thorough, as thorough as moderate and well considered, based upon the facts as they are, and not worked out as if we were beginners. We are to deal with the facts of our own day, with the facts of no other and to make laws which square with those facts. It is best, indeed it is necessary, to begin with the tariff. I will urge nothing upon you now at the opening of your session which can obscure that first object or divert our energies from that clearly defined duty. At a later time I may take the liberty of calling your attention to reforms which should press close upon the heels of the tariff changes, if not accompany them, of which the chief is the reform of our banking and currency laws; but just now I refrain. For the present, I put these matters on one side and think only of this one thing—of the changes in our fiscal system which may best serve to open once more the free channels of prosperity to a great people whom we would serve to the utmost and throughout both rank and file.

I sincerely thank you for your courtesy.

⟨ 19 ⟩

The Teapot Dome Resolution

(1924)

THE ELECTION OF WARREN G. HARDING as president in 1920 marked the beginning of a lull in the period of presidential activism and progressive politics that began with presidents Theodore Roosevelt and Woodrow Wilson in the 1900s and 1910s and resumed with Franklin D. Roosevelt in the 1930s. In May 1920, Senator Harding of Ohio had expressed the nation's weariness with change and upheaval in a speech to the Home Market Club in Boston: "America's present need is not heroics but healing; not nostrums but normalcy; not revolution but restoration . . . ; not surgery but serenity." That summer the leaders of the deadlocked Republican National Convention gathered in the legendary "smoke-filled room" at Chicago's Blackstone Hotel and decided to anoint Harding as the party's nominee for president.

The undistinguished but attractive senator, they believed, would be an appealing candidate and an easily controllable president.

The Republican leaders were correct on both counts. Harding and his vice-presidential running mate, Gov. Calvin Coolidge of Massachusetts, were elected by a landslide. In office, Harding offered few legislative initiatives and allowed his party-picked cabinet members relatively free rein over their departments.

Harding died, probably of a heart attack, on August 2, 1923, while on a speaking tour of the West. The combination of Harding's personal popularity and the growing prominence of the presidency evoked an extraordinary outpouring of national grief. But not long after Harding's death, it became apparent that, as an inattentive president, he had unwittingly presided over one of the most corrupt administrations in history.

The most notorious scandal of the Harding administration involved the naval oil reserves at Teapot Dome, Wyoming, and Elk Hill, California. In 1921 Secretary of the Interior Albert B. Fall persuaded Secretary of the Navy Edwin Denby to transfer these oil fields to the Interior Department, with Harding's offhand approval. Fall then leased the fields without competitive bidding—Teapot Dome to Harry F. Sinclair's Mammoth Oil Co. and Elk Hill to Edward L. Doheny's Pan-American Co.—in return for several hundred thousand dollars in bribes. In October 1923, after an eighteen-month investigation and two months after Harding's death, the Senate Committee on Public Lands and Surveys exposed the scandal in public hearings.

Teapot Dome eventually led to the resignation of Denby; the cancellation of the oil leases; the firing of Attorney General Harry M. Daugherty, who had refused to cooperate with the Senate investigation and had ordered federal agents to spy on certain senators; and the imprisonment of Sinclair and Fall. (Incredibly, a jury acquitted Doheny.) Coolidge, who succeeded Harding as president, steered clear of the scandal by heeding Congress's call to investigate and prosecute vigorously.

Teapot Dome was neither the first major presidential scandal—the tax-evading "Whiskey Ring," for example, nearly brought down Ulysses S. Grant in the 1870s—nor the last: the Watergate scandal drove Richard Nixon to resign in 1974. (See Documents 35–38, pp. 190–211.) But Teapot Dome, like most other presidential scandals, demonstrated dramatically that the congressional power of investigation is a strong weapon in the ongoing struggle between the president and Congress.

※ ※ ※

A joint resolution directing the President to institute and prosecute suits to cancel certain leases of oil lands and incidental contracts, and for other purposes.

Whereas it appears from evidence taken by the Committee on Public Lands and Surveys of the United States Senate that certain lease of naval reserve No. 3, in the State of Wyoming, bearing date April 7, 1922, made in form by the Government of the United States, through Albert B. Fall, Secretary of the Interior, and Edwin Denby, Secretary of the Navy, as lessor, to the Mammoth Oil Co., as lessee, and that certain contract between the Government of the United States and the Pan American Petroleum & Transport Co., dated April 25, 1922, signed by Edward C. Finney, Acting Secretary of the Interior, and Edwin Denby, Secretary of the Navy, relating among other things to the construction of oil tanks at Pearl Harbor, Territory of Hawaii, and that certain lease of naval reserve No. 1, in the State of California, bearing date December 11, 1922, made in form by the Government of the United States through Albert B. Fall, Secretary of the Interior, and Edwin Denby, Secretary of the Navy, as lessor, to the Pan American Petroleum Co., as lessee, were executed under circumstances indicating fraud and corruption; and

Whereas the said leases and contract were entered into without authority on the part of the officers purporting to act in the execution of the same for the United States and in violation of the laws of Congress; and

Whereas such leases and contract were made in defiance of the settled policy of the Government adhered to through three successive administrations, to maintain in the ground a great reserve supply of oil adequate to the needs of the Navy in any emergency threatening the national security: Therefore be it

Resolved, etc., That the said leases and contract are against the public interest and that the lands embraced therein should be recovered and held for the purpose to which they were dedicated; and

Resolved further, That the President of the United States be, and he hereby is, authorized and directed immediately to cause suit to be instituted and prosecuted for the annulment and cancellation of the said leases and contract and all contracts incidental or supplemental thereto, to enjoin further extraction of oil from the said reserves under said leases or from the territory covered by the same, to secure any further appropriate incidental relief, and to prosecute such other actions or proceedings, civil and criminal, as may be warranted by the facts in relation to the making of the said leases and contract.

And the President is further authorized and directed to appoint, by and with the advice and consent of the Senate, special counsel who shall have charge and control of the prosecution of such litigation, anything in the statutes touching the powers of the Attorney General of the Department of Justice to the contrary notwithstanding.

❦ 20 ❦

Franklin D. Roosevelt's First Inaugural Address*

(1933)

FRANKLIN D. ROOSEVELT was the last president to be inaugurated on March 4; the Twentieth Amendment (1933) advanced the start of the president's term to January 20. During the long winter between Roosevelt's landslide election against President Herbert C. Hoover in November 1932 and his inauguration the following March, the Great Depression that had sunk the nation into economic inactivity worsened. Factories for producing goods and land for growing crops were abundant, but they had fallen into disuse. On February 14 Roosevelt was the target of an assassination attempt in Miami by an unemployed bricklayer, the only president-elect ever to be almost killed.

Roosevelt saw one of his main challenges as restoring the people's confidence in government and raising their personal morale. It was a challenge to which he was well suited, despite his privileged upbringing on a family estate in Hyde Park, New York. Always self-confident and infectiously optimistic, Roosevelt had nonetheless developed empathy with those who suffer during his bout with polio in the early 1920s. (The disease left him disabled for the rest of his life.) In the best-remembered line of his 1933 inaugural address, one of the first

*Go to *http://www.cc.columbia.edu/acis/bartleby/inaugural/pres49.html*

to be broadcast nationally by radio, Roosevelt proclaimed that "the only thing we have to fear is fear itself—nameless, unreasoning, unjustified terror which paralyzes needed efforts to convert retreat into advance."

Roosevelt also used his address to make clear his contempt for the probusiness policies of the Harding, Coolidge, and Hoover administrations. "The money changers have fled from their high seats in the temple of our civilization," he said. "We may now restore that temple to the ancient truths. The measure of that restoration lies in the extent to which we apply social values more noble than mere monetary profit."

Finally, Roosevelt pledged to "act, and act quickly" to combat the depression, using and perhaps extending the full powers of the presidency to do so. "It is to be hoped," Roosevelt said, "that the normal balance of executive and legislative authority may be wholly adequate to meet the unprecedented task before us. . . . But in the event that . . . the national emergency is still critical . . . I shall ask the Congress for the one remaining instrument to meet the crisis—broad executive power to wage a war against the emergency as great as the power that would be given me if we were in fact invaded by a foreign foe."

Roosevelt's cousin, former president Theodore Roosevelt, was the first to describe the presidency as a "bully pulpit" for moral leadership. Franklin Roosevelt made full use of the pulpit in 1933 and afterward. Responding to his inaugural address, around 500,000 people wrote to express their thanks and support in an unprecedented outpouring of mail. A week later, on March 13, Roosevelt delivered the first of twenty-seven informal radio addresses, called "fireside chats," which marked a revolutionary change in presidential communications. (See Document 23, p. 123.)

In his acceptance speech at the 1932 Democratic Convention, Roosevelt had pledged "a new deal for the American people." The vague phrase became the catchword for his presidency. More than anything else, "New Deal" came to mean presidentially sponsored government programs to support both the general goal of economic prosperity and the particular needs of people who were suffering economic distress.

President Hoover, Mr. Chief Justice, my friends:

This is a day of national consecration, and I am certain that my fellow-Americans expect that on my induction into the Presidency I will address them with a candor and a decision which the present situation of our nation impels.

This is pre-eminently the time to speak the truth, the whole truth, frankly and boldly. Nor need we shrink from honestly facing conditions in our country today. This great nation will endure as it has endured, will revive and will prosper.

So first of all let me assert my firm belief that the only thing we have to fear is fear itself—nameless, unreasoning, unjustified terror which paralyzes needed efforts to convert retreat into advance.

In every dark hour of our national life a leadership of frankness and vigor has met with that understanding and support of the people themselves which is essential to victory. I am convinced that you will again give that support to leadership in these critical days.

In such a spirit on my part and on yours we face our common difficulties. They concern, thank God, only material things. Values have shrunken to fantastic levels; taxes have risen; our ability to pay has fallen; government of all kinds is faced by serious curtailment of income; the means of exchange are frozen in the currents of trade; the withered leaves of industrial enterprise lie on every side; farmers find no markets for their produce; the savings of many years in thousands of families are gone.

More important, a host of unemployed citizens face the grim problem of existence, and an equally great number toil with little return. Only a foolish optimist can deny the dark realities of the moment.

Yet our distress comes from no failure of substance. We are stricken by no plague of locusts. Compared with the perils which our forefathers conquered because they believed and were not afraid, we have still much to be thankful for. Nature still offers her bounty and human efforts have multiplied it. Plenty is at our doorstep, but a generous use of it languishes in the very sight of the supply.

Primarily, this is because the rulers of the exchange of mankind's goods have failed through their own stubbornness and their own incompetence, have admitted their failure and abdicated. Practices of the unscrupulous money changers stand indicted in the court of public opinion, rejected by the hearts and minds of men. True, they have tried, but their efforts have been cast in the pattern of an outworn tradition. Faced by failure of credit, they have proposed only the lending of more money.

Stripped of the lure of profit by which to induce our people to follow their false leadership, they have resorted to exhortations, pleading tearfully for restored confidence. They know only the rules of a generation of self-seekers.

They have no vision, and when there is no vision the people perish.

The money changers have fled from their high seats in the temple of our civilization. We may now restore that temple to the ancient truths.

The measure of the restoration lies in the extent to which we apply social values more noble than mere monetary profit.

Happiness lies not in the mere possession of money; it lies in the joy of achievement, in the thrill of creative effort.

The joy and moral stimulation of work no longer must be forgotten in the mad chase of evanescent profits. These dark days will be worth all they cost us if they teach us that our true destiny is not to be ministered unto but to minister to ourselves and to our fellow-men.

Recognition of the falsity of material wealth as the standard of success goes hand in hand with the abandonment of the false belief that public office and high political position are to be valued only by the standards of pride of place and personal profit; and there must be an end to a conduct in banking and in business which too often has given to a sacred trust the likeness of callous and selfish wrongdoing.

Small wonder that confidence languishes, for it thrives only on honesty, on honor, on the sacredness of obligations, on faithful protection, on unselfish performance. Without them it cannot live.

Restoration calls, however, not for changes in ethics alone. This nation asks for action, and action now.

Our greatest primary task is to put people to work. This is no unsolvable problem if we face it wisely and courageously.

It can be accomplished in part by direct recruiting by the government itself, treating the task as we would treat the emergency of a war, but at the same time, through this employment accomplishing greatly needed projects to stimulate and reorganize the use of our natural resources.

Hand in hand with this, we must frankly recognize the overbalance of population in our industrial centers and, by engaging on a national scale in the redistribution, endeavor to provide a better use of the land for those best fitted for the land.

The task can be helped by definite efforts to raise the values of agricultural products and with this the power to purchase the output of our cities.

It can be helped by preventing realistically the tragedy of the growing loss, through foreclosure, of our small homes and our farms.

It can be helped by insistence that the Federal, State and local governments act forthwith on the demand that their cost be drastically reduced.

It can be helped by the unifying of relief activities which today are often scattered, uneconomical and unequal. It can be helped by national planning for and supervision of all forms of transportation and of communications and other utilities which have a definitely public character.

There are many ways in which it can be helped, but it can never be helped merely by talking about it. We must act, and act quickly.

Finally, in our progress toward a resumption of work we require two safeguards against a return of the evils of the old order; there must be a strict supervision of all banking and credits and investments; there must be an end to speculation with other people's money, and there must be provision for an adequate but sound currency.

These are the lines of attack. I shall presently urge upon a new Congress in special session detailed measures for their fulfillment, and I shall seek the immediate assistance of the several States.

Through this program of action we address ourselves to putting our own national house in order and making income balance outgo.

Our international trade relations, though vastly important, are, in point of time and necessity, secondary to the establishment of a sound national economy.

I favor as a practical policy the putting of first things first. I shall spare no effort to restore world trade by international economic readjustment, but the emergency at home cannot wait on that accomplishment.

The basic thought that guides these specific means of national recovery is not narrowly nationalistic.

It is the insistence, as a first consideration, upon the interdependence of the various elements in, and parts of, the United States—a recognition of the old and permanently important manifestation of the American spirit of the pioneer.

It is the way to recovery. It is the immediate way. It is the strongest assurance that the recovery will endure.

In the field of world policy I would dedicate this nation to the policy of the good neighbor—the neighbor who resolutely respects himself and, because he does so, respects the rights of others—the neighbor who respects his obligations and respects the sanctity of his agreements in and with a world of neighbors.

If I read the temper of our people correctly, we now realize as we have never before, our interdependence on each other; that we cannot merely take, but we must give as well; that if we are to go forward we must move as a trained and loyal army willing to sacrifice for the good of a common discipline, because, without such discipline, no progress is made, no leadership becomes effective.

We are, I know, ready and willing to submit our lives and property to such discipline because it makes possible a leadership which aims at a larger good.

This I propose to offer, pledging that the larger purposes will bind upon us all as a sacred obligation with a unity of duty hitherto evoked only in time of armed strife.

With this pledge taken, I assume unhesitatingly the leadership of this great army of our people, dedicated to a disciplined attack upon our common problems.

Action in this image and to this end is feasible under the form of government which we have inherited from our ancestors.

Our Constitution is so simple and practical that it is possible always to meet extraordinary needs by changes in emphasis and arrangement without loss of essential form.

That is why our constitutional system has proved itself the most superbly enduring political mechanism the modern world has produced. It has met every stress of vast expansion of territory, of foreign wars, of bitter internal strife, of world relations.

It is to be hoped that the normal balance of executive and legislative authority may be wholly adequate to meet the unprecedented task before us. But it may be that an unprecedented demand and need for undelayed action may call for temporary departure from that normal balance of public procedure.

I am prepared under my constitutional duty to recommend the measures that a stricken nation in the midst of a stricken world may require.

These measures, or such other measures as the Congress may build out of its experience and wisdom, I shall seek, within my constitutional authority, to bring to speedy adoption.

But in the event that the Congress shall fail to take one of these two courses, and in the event that the national emergency is still critical, I shall not evade the clear course of duty that will then confront me.

I shall ask the Congress for the one remaining instrument to meet the crisis—broad executive power to wage a war against the emergency as great as the power that would be given me if we were in fact invaded by a foreign foe.

For the trust reposed in me I will return the courage and the devotion that befit the time. I can do no less.

We face the arduous days that lie before us in the warm courage of national unity; with the clear consciousness of seeking old and precious moral values;

with the clean satisfaction that comes from the stern performance of duty by old and young alike.

We aim at the assurance of a rounded and permanent national life.

We do not distrust the future of essential democracy. The people of the United States have not failed. In their need they have registered a mandate that they want direct, vigorous action.

They have asked for discipline and direction under leadership. They have made me the present instrument of their wishes. In the spirit of the gift I take it.

In this dedication of a nation we humbly ask the blessing of God. May He protect each and every one of us! May He guide me in the days to come!

❦ 21 ❧

Humphrey's Executor v. United States*

(1935)

FOR NEARLY A CENTURY AND A HALF, issues concerning the president's removal power vexed the political system. The Constitution, so clear in stating that presidential appointments to the executive branch must obtain "the Advice and Consent of the Senate," was silent about the Senate's role, if any, in removing appointees from office. In 1789, the First Congress had acknowledged the president's exclusive power of removal. (See Document 5, p. 34.) But in 1867, Congress passed the Tenure of Office Act, which required that the president obtain the consent of the Senate before removing any Senate-confirmed appointee. (See Document 16, p. 82.)

After the tenure act's target, President Andrew Johnson, left office, Congress gradually softened the removal requirement but did not fully eliminate it. In 1926, the Supreme Court weighed in, strengthening the president's power by declaring in *Myers v. United States* that a law re-

---

*Go to *http://www.findlaw.com*, click on "U.S. Supreme Court Cases," then type in "Humphrey's Ex'r" in the box called "Party Name Search"

quiring the Senate's consent before the president could fire a postmaster was unconstitutional. Former president (now Chief Justice) William Howard Taft wrote the opinion of the Court: "The power of removal is incident to the [president's] power of appointment, not to the [Senate's] power of advising and consenting."

Taft's opinion was so sweeping in its defense of the president's removal power as to suggest that no government official (other than legislators and judges) was immune from a presidential firing for any reason. By implication, members of an independent regulatory agency such as the Interstate Commerce Commission or the Federal Trade Commission (FTC) served at the president's sufferance, even though Congress had assigned to these members terms of fixed duration that, by law, could be abridged only for "inefficiency, neglect of duty, or malfeasance in office."

In 1933 President Franklin D. Roosevelt wrote a series of letters to William E. Humphrey, an outspoken administration critic who had been appointed to a seven-year term on the FTC by President Herbert C. Hoover in 1931. Roosevelt's first letter asked Humphrey to resign as commissioner so that "the aims and purposes of the Administration with respect to the work of the Commission can be carried out most effectively with personnel of my own choosing." (The FTC had jurisdiction over many New Deal programs.) When Humphrey refused to resign, Roosevelt notified him on October 7 that he was fired.

Humphrey died in early 1934, never having accepted the propriety of his removal. The executor of his estate sued the government for the salary Humphrey was not paid after being forced from office. The executor argued that Roosevelt had fired Humphrey for avowedly political, and thus legally impermissible, reasons.

The case reached the Supreme Court, which sided with Humphrey's executor by a unanimous 9–0 vote. Writing for the court, Justice George Sutherland argued that the *Myers* ruling did not apply to Humphrey's situation. Because Frank Myers, a postmaster, had been employed by a federal agency that clearly was "an arm or an eye of the Executive," the president's constitutional responsibility as chief executive included the power to remove him, unfettered by Congress. But the FTC, like other independent regulatory agencies, was "an administrative body created by Congress to carry into effect legislative policies."

Thus, Congress had the constitutional right to legislate its own guide-lines for removing Humphrey or any other employee.

The Supreme Court's decision in *Humphrey's Executor* was announced on May 27, 1935. It was one of a historically unprecedented series of de-cisions in 1935 and 1936 that overturned presidential actions and ad-ministration-supported laws. Yet *Humphrey's Executor* reportedly infuri-ated Roosevelt more than any other case—he took it as a personal insult by the justices—and, in the opinion of some of his aides, provoked the president to try to "pack" the Court. (See Document 23, p. 123.)

※ ※ ※

MR. JUSTICE SUTHERLAND delivered the opinion of the Court. . . .

First. The question first to be considered is whether, by the provisions of §1 of the Federal Trade Commission Act already quoted, the President's power is limited to removal for the specific causes enumerated therein. . . .

The commission is to be non-partisan; and it must, from the very nature of its duties, act with entire impartiality. It is charged with the enforcement of no policy except the policy of the law. Its duties are neither political nor execu-tive, but predominantly quasi-judicial and quasi-legislative. Like the Inter-state Commerce Commission, its members are called upon to exercise the trained judgment of a body of experts "appointed by law and informed by ex-perience." *Illinois Central R. Co. v. Interstate Commerce Comm'n,* 206 U.S. 441, 454; *Standard Oil Co. v. United States,* 283 U.S. 235, 238–239.

The legislative reports in both houses of Congress clearly reflect the view that a fixed term was necessary to the effective and fair administration of the law. . . .

The debates in both houses demonstrate that the prevailing view was that the commission was not to be "subject to anybody in the government but . . . only to the people of the United States"; free from "political domination or control" or the "probability or possibility of such a thing"; to be "separate and apart from any existing department of the government—not subject to the or-ders of the President."

More to the same effect appears in the debates, which were long and thor-ough and contain nothing to the contrary. While the general rule precludes the use of these debates to explain the meaning of the words of the statute, they may be considered as reflecting light upon its general purposes and the evils which it sought to remedy. *Federal Trade Comm'n v. Raladam Co.,* 283 U.S. 643, 650.

Thus, the language of the act, the legislative reports, and the general purposes of the legislation as reflected by the debates, all combine to demonstrate the Congressional intent to create a body of experts who shall gain experience by length of service—a body which shall be independent of executive authority, *except in its selection,* and free to exercise its judgment without the leave or hindrance of any other official or any department of the government. To the accomplishment of these purposes, it is clear that Congress was of opinion that length and certainty of tenure would vitally contribute. And to hold that, nevertheless, the members of the commission continue in office at the mere will of the President, might be to thwart, in large measure, the very ends which Congress sought to realize by definitely fixing the term of office.

We conclude that the intent of the act is to limit the executive power of removal to the causes enumerated, the existence of none of which is claimed here; and we pass to the second question.

Second. To support its contention that the removal provision of § 1, as we have just construed it, is an unconstitutional interference with the executive power of the President, the government's chief reliance is *Myers v. United States,* 272 U.S. 52. That case has been so recently decided, and the prevailing and dissenting opinions so fully review the general subject of the power of executive removal, that further discussion would add little of value to the wealth of material there collected. These opinions examine at length the historical, legislative and judicial data bearing upon the question, beginning with what is called "the decision of 1789" in the first Congress and coming down almost to the day when the opinions were delivered. They occupy 243 pages of the volume in which they are printed. Nevertheless, the narrow point actually decided was only that the President had power to remove a postmaster of the first class, without the advice and consent of the Senate as required by act of Congress. In the course of the opinion of the court, expressions occur which tend to sustain the government's contention, but these are beyond the point involved and, therefore, do not come within the rule of *stare decisis.* In so far as they are out of harmony with the views here set forth, these expressions are disapproved. . . .

The office of a postmaster is so essentially unlike the office now involved that the decision in the *Myers* case cannot be accepted as controlling our decision here. A postmaster is an executive officer restricted to the performance of executive functions. He is charged with no duty at all related to either the legislative or judicial power. The actual decision in the *Myers* case finds support in the theory that such an officer is merely one of the units in the executive department and, hence, inherently subject to the exclusive and illimitable power of removal by the Chief Executive, whose subordinate and aid he is. Putting aside *dicta,* which may be followed if sufficiently persuasive but which are not controlling, the necessary reach of the decision goes far enough to include all purely executive officers. It goes no farther;—much less does it include an officer who occupies no place in the executive department and who exercises no part of the executive power vested by the Constitution in the President.

The Federal Trade Commission is an administrative body created by Congress to carry into effect legislative policies embodied in the statute in accordance with the legislative standard therein prescribed, and to perform other specified duties as a legislative or as a judicial aid. Such a body cannot in any proper sense be characterized as an arm or an eye of the executive. Its duties are performed without executive leave and, in the contemplation of the statute, must be free from executive control. In administering the provisions of the statute in respect of "unfair methods of competition"—that is to say in filling in and administering the details embodied by that general standard—the commission acts in part quasi-legislatively and in part quasi-judicially. In making investigations and reports thereon for the information of Congress under § 6, in aid of the legislative power, it acts as a legislative agency. Under § 7, which authorizes the commission to act as a master in chancery under rules prescribed by the court, it acts as an agency of the judiciary. To the extent that it exercises any executive function—as distinguished from executive power in the constitutional sense—it does so in the discharge and effectuation of its quasi-legislative or quasi-judicial powers, or as an agency of the legislative or judicial departments of the government.[1]

If Congress is without authority to prescribe causes for removal of members of the trade commission and limit executive power of removal accordingly, that power at once becomes practically all-inclusive in respect of civil officers with the exception of the judiciary provided for by the Constitution. The Solicitor General, at the bar, apparently recognizing this to be true, with commendable candor, agreed that his view in respect of the removability of members of the Federal Trade Commission necessitated a like view in respect of the Interstate Commerce Commission and the Court of Claims. We are thus confronted with the serious question whether not only the members of these quasi-legislative and quasi-judicial bodies, but the judges of the legislative Court of Claims, exercising judicial power (*Williams v. United States,* 289 U.S. 553, 565-567), continue in office only at the pleasure of the President.

We think it plain under the Constitution that illimitable power of removal is not possessed by the President in respect of officers of the character of those just named. The authority of Congress, in creating quasi-legislative or quasi-judicial agencies, to require them to act in discharge of their duties indepen-

dently of executive control cannot well be doubted; and that authority includes, as an appropriate incident, power to fix the period during which they
shall continue in office, and to forbid their removal except for cause in the
meantime. For it is quite evident that one who holds his office only during the
pleasure of another, cannot be depended upon to maintain an attitude of independence against the latter's will.

The fundamental necessity of maintaining each of the three general departments of government entirely free from the control or coercive influence, direct
or indirect, of either of the others, has often been stressed and is hardly open to
serious question. So much is implied in the very fact of the separation of the
powers of these departments by the Constitution; and in the rule which recog-
nizes their essential co-equality. The sound application of a principle that
makes one master in his own house precludes him from imposing his control
in the house of another who is master there. James Wilson, one of the framers
of the Constitution and a former justice of this court, said that the independence of each department required that its proceedings "should be free from
the remotest influence, direct or indirect, of either of the other two powers."
Andrews, The Works of James Wilson (1896), vol. 1, p. 367. And Mr. Justice
Story in the first volume of his work on the Constitution, 4th ed., § 530, citing
No. 48 of the Federalist, said that neither of the departments in reference to
each other "ought to possess, directly or indirectly, an overruling influence in
the administration of their respective powers." And see *O'Donoghue v. United
States, supra,* at pp. 530–531.

The power of removal here claimed for the President falls within this principle, since its coercive influence threatens the independence of a commission,
which is not only wholly disconnected from the executive department, but
which, as already fully appears, was created by Congress as a means of carrying
into operation legislative and judicial powers, and as an agency of the legislative and judicial departments. . . .

The result of what we now have said is this: Whether the power of the President to remove an officer shall prevail over the authority of Congress to condition the power by fixing a definite term and precluding a removal except for
cause, will depend upon the character of the office; the *Myers* decision, affirming the power of the President alone to make the removal is confined to purely
executive officers; and as to officers of the kind here under consideration, we
hold that no removal can be made during the prescribed term for which the
officer is appointed, except for one or more of the causes named in the applicable statute.

To the extent that, between the decision in the *Myers* case, which sustains the unrestrictable power of the President to remove purely executive officers, and our present decision that such power does not extend to an office such as that here involved, there shall remain a field of doubt, we leave such cases as may fall within it for future consideration and determination as they may arise. . . .

NOTE

1. The provision of § 6 (d) of the act which authorizes the President to direct an investigation and report by the commission in relation to alleged violations of the anti-trust acts, is so obviously collateral to the main design of the act as not to detract from the force of this general statement as to the character of that body.

<hr>

❧ 22 ❧

United States v. Curtiss-Wright Export Corp.*

(1936)

UNITED STATES V. CURTISS-WRIGHT EXPORT CORP. is perhaps the most important Supreme Court decision in history concerning the president's constitutional powers in foreign affairs. The expansive view of presidential authority that the decision endorsed is all the more remarkable because in 1935 and 1936 the Court had been unusually hostile to the New Deal domestic policies of President Franklin D. Roosevelt. (See Document 21, p. 112, and Document 23, p. 123.) Indeed, the author of the Court's opinion in the case, Justice George Sutherland, was one of the most ardent judicial foes of the New Deal. Yet, in *United States v. Curtiss-Wright,* Sutherland and his fellow justices promulgated a constitutional theory that echoed Alexander Hamilton as Pacificus in describing "the President as the sole organ of the federal government in the field of international relations," even though the Constitution had not explicitly conferred such a role. (See Document 6, p. 39.)

*Go to *http://www.findlaw.com*, click on "U.S. Supreme Court Cases," then type "Curtiss-Wright Export Corp." in the box called "Party Name Search"

The *Curtiss-Wright* case was triggered by the government's effort to limit the so-called Chaco War between Bolivia and Paraguay, which had taken 100,000 lives and jeopardized the peace of all of South America. On May 28, 1934, Congress passed a joint resolution that granted the president the power to prohibit, at his discretion, the sale of any or all American-made arms to the two nations. Later that day, Roosevelt issued an order that banned all such sales.

In 1936 the Curtiss-Wright Export Corporation was indicted for conspiring to sell machine guns to Bolivia in violation of the president's order. The corporation and its officers responded in federal court by challenging the constitutionality of the law under which the president acted. They claimed that Congress had made an unconstitutional delegation of power to the president.

In favoring the president's position in the case, the Court could simply have decided that Congress's delegation of power was constitutional. But in several recent rulings that had overturned Roosevelt's New Deal domestic programs, Sutherland and his conservative colleagues had accused Congress of delegating power to the president indiscriminately and improperly. Thus, a new constitutional theory was needed if the Court were to justify the actions of the president and Congress in the *Curtiss-Wright* case.

Sutherland found his theory in the concept of sovereignty. The United States had been formed as a nation, he noted, by thirteen previously separate states. These states had domestic powers at the time they united and, in writing the Constitution, they had described which of these powers would be granted to the national government. But, Sullivan argued, because the states had never had power to deal in international relations, the national government that was formed by the Constitution did not have to rely for its foreign affairs powers on any explicit constitutional authorization. Instead, as the plan of government for a nation, the Constitution implicitly granted the national government all the traditional sovereign powers that any nation wields, except as specifically limited by the document itself.

The sovereign powers of the United States in international affairs, Sutherland continued, obviously reside in the president: "he, not Congress, has the better opportunity of knowing the conditions which prevail in foreign countries, and especially is this true in time of war. He has his confidential sources of information. He has his agents in the form of diplomatic, consular, and other officials." Indeed, Sutherland and the Court suggested, Roosevelt may not even have needed Congress's permission to ban the sale of arms to Bolivia and Paraguay.

※ ※ ※

MR. JUSTICE SUTHERLAND delivered the opinion of the Court. . . .

Whether, if the Joint Resolution had related solely to internal affairs it would be open to the challenge that it constituted an unlawful delegation of legislative power to the Executive, we find it unnecessary to determine. The whole aim of the resolution is to affect a situation entirely external to the United States, and falling within the category of foreign affairs. The determination which we are called to make, therefore, is whether the Joint Resolution, as applied to that situation, is vulnerable to attack under the rule that forbids a delegation of the law-making power. In other words, assuming (but not deciding) that the challenged delegation, if it were confined to internal affairs, would be invalid, may it nevertheless be sustained on the ground that its exclusive aim is to afford a remedy for a hurtful condition within foreign territory?

It will contribute to the elucidation of the question if we first consider the differences between the powers of the federal government in respect of foreign or external affairs and those in respect of domestic or internal affairs. That there are differences between them, and that these differences are fundamental, may not be doubted.

The two classes of powers are different, both in respect of their origin and their nature. The broad statement that the federal government can exercise no powers except those specifically enumerated in the Constitution, and such implied powers as are necessary and proper to carry into effect the enumerated powers, is categorically true only in respect of our internal affairs. In that field, the primary purpose of the Constitution was to carve from the general mass of legislative powers *then possessed by the states* such portions as it was thought desirable to vest in the federal government, leaving those not included in the enumeration still in the states. *Carter v. Carter Coal Co.,* 298 U.S. 238, 294. That this doctrine applies only to powers which the states had, is self evident. And since the states severally never possessed international powers, such powers could not have been carved from the mass of state powers but obviously were transmitted to the United States from some other source. During the colonial period, those powers were possessed exclusively by and were entirely under the control of the Crown. By the Declaration of Independence, "the Representatives of the United States of America" declared the United [not the several] Colonies to be free and independent states, and as such to have "full Power to levy War, conclude Peace, contract Alliances, establish Commerce and to do all other Acts and Things which Independent States may of right do."

As a result of the separation from Great Britain by the colonies acting as a unit, the powers of external sovereignty passed from the Crown not to the colonies severally, but to the colonies in their collective and corporate capacity as the United States of America. Even before the declaration, the colonies were a unit in foreign affairs, acting through a common agency—namely the Continental Congress, composed of delegates from the thirteen colonies. That agency exercised the powers of war and peace, raised an army, created a navy, and finally adopted the Declaration of Independence. Rulers come and go; governments end and forms of government change; but sovereignty survives. A political society cannot endure without a supreme will somewhere. Sovereignty is never held in suspense. When, therefore, the external sovereignty of Great Britain in respect of the colonies ceased, it immediately passed to the Union. *See Penhallow v. Doane,* 3 Dall. 54, 80–81. That fact was given practical application almost at once. The treaty of peace, made on September 23, 1783, was concluded between his Brittanic Majesty and the "United States of America." 8 Stat.—European Treaties—80. . . .

It results that the investment of the federal government with the powers of external sovereignty did not depend upon the affirmative grants of the Constitution. The powers to declare and wage war, to conclude peace, to make treaties, to maintain diplomatic relations with other sovereignties, if they had never been mentioned in the Constitution, would have vested in the federal government as necessary concomitants of nationality. . . .

Not only, as we have shown, is the federal power over external affairs in origin and essential character different from that over internal affairs, but participation in the exercise of the power is significantly limited. In this vast external realm, with its important, complicated, delicate and manifold problems, the President alone has the power to speak or listen as a representative of the nation. He *makes* treaties with the advice and consent of the Senate; but he alone negotiates. Into the field of negotiation the Senate cannot intrude; and Congress itself is powerless to invade it. As [John] Marshall said in his great argument of March 7, 1800, in the House of Representatives, "The President is the sole organ of the nation in its external relations, and its sole representative with foreign nations." Annals, 6th Cong., col. 613. . . .

It is important to bear in mind that we are here dealing not alone with an authority vested in the President by an exertion of legislative power, but with such an authority plus the very delicate, plenary and exclusive power of the President as the sole organ of the federal government in the field of international relations—a power which does not require as a basis for its exercise an act of Congress, but which, of course, like every other governmental power, must be exercised in subordination to the applicable provisions of the Constitution. It is quite apparent that if, in the maintenance of our international relations, embarrassment—perhaps serious embarrassment—is to be avoided and success for our aims achieved, congressional legislation which is to be made effective through negotiation and inquiry within the international field must often accord to the President a degree of discretion and freedom from statutory restriction which would not be admissible were domestic affairs alone involved. Moreover, he, not Congress, has the better opportunity of knowing the conditions which prevail in foreign countries, and especially is this true in time of war. He has his confidential sources of information. He has his agents in the form of diplomatic, consular and other officials. Secrecy in respect of information gathered by them may be highly necessary, and the premature disclosure of it productive by harmful results. Indeed, so clearly is this true that the first President refused to accede to a request to lay before the House of Representatives the instructions, correspondence and documents relating to the negotiation of the Jay Treaty—a refusal the wisdom of which was recognized by the House itself and has never since been doubted. . . .

The marked difference between foreign affairs and domestic affairs in this respect is recognized by both houses of Congress in the very form of their requisitions for information from the executive departments. In the case of every department except the Department of State, the resolution *directs* the official to furnish the information. In the case of the State Department, dealing with foreign affairs, the President is *requested* to furnish the information "if not incompatible with the public interest." A statement that to furnish the information is not compatible with the public interest rarely, if ever, is questioned.

When the President is to be authorized by legislation to act in respect of a matter intended to affect a situation in foreign territory, the legislator properly bears in mind the important consideration that the form of the President's action—or, indeed, whether he shall act at all—may well depend, among other things, upon the nature of the confidential information which he has or may thereafter receive, or upon the effect which his action may have upon our foreign relations. This consideration, in connection with what we have already said on the subject, discloses the unwisdom of requiring Congress in this field of governmental power to lay down narrowly definite standards by which the President is to be governed. . . .

We deem it unnecessary to consider, *seriatim,* the several clauses which are said to evidence the unconstitutionality of the Joint Resolution as involving an unlawful delegation of legislative power. It is enough to summarize by saying that, both upon principle and in accordance with precedent, we conclude there is sufficient warrant for the broad discretion vested in the President to determine whether the enforcement of the statute will have a beneficial effect upon the reestablishment of peace in the affected countries; whether he shall make proclamation to bring the resolution into operation; whether and when the resolution shall cease to operate and to make proclamation accordingly; and to prescribe limitations and exceptions to which the enforcement of the resolution shall be subject. . . .

⋆⋖ 23 ⋗⋆

Franklin D. Roosevelt's "Court-packing" Address

(1937)

O N FEBRUARY 5, 1937, President Franklin D. Roosevelt, reacting to a long string of Supreme Court decisions that were hostile to the New Deal, asked Congress to add as many as six new positions to the Court, one for every sitting justice seventy years or older who refused to retire.

Roosevelt's frustration with the Supreme Court was long-standing. When he became president in 1933, the Court was dominated by conservatives. In 1935 and 1936, the Court overturned an unprecedented number of important federal laws that Roosevelt and Congress had enacted to combat the depression, including the National Industrial Recovery Act, the Agricultural Adjustment Act, and the Railway Pension Act. Other significant New Deal legislation, such as the Social Security Act and the National Labor Relations Act, seemed doomed to a similar fate as soon as they came before the Court.

Privately, Roosevelt raged against the Court; publicly, he was relatively quiet, fearing an adverse political reaction to any assault he might launch against the widely respected judicial branch. In 1936 Roosevelt ran a cautious campaign for reelection and was returned to office by the largest electoral vote plurality in history, 523–8. Scarcely two weeks after his inauguration on January 20, 1937, however, the president revealed to a startled cabinet, Congress, and nation his proposal to expand the number of Supreme Court justices from nine to fifteen, which would enable him to appoint six New Deal sympathizers to the Court immediately.

In a severe political miscalculation, Roosevelt initially defended the Court-packing plan as an effort to relieve the workload of the justices, six of whom (including most of the conservatives) were in their seventies. Not only was this rationale inaccurate—Chief Justice Charles Evans Hughes was able to demonstrate easily to Congress that the Court had never been more efficient in handling its caseload—but it was transparently implausible. Critics attacked the president for disguising his real intention, which was to dilute the conservatives' influence on the Court.

On March 9, Roosevelt gave one of his celebrated "fireside chats" to a national radio audience. In it, he changed tactics and spoke frankly of his concern that "the Court has been acting not as a judicial body, but as a policy-making body." He conceded his intention of "'packing the Court' . . . [i]f by that phrase [is meant] . . . that I would appoint Justices who will not undertake to override the judgment of the Congress on legislative policy."

Politically, Roosevelt's speech was too little, too late: the Court-packing plan was dead. But in a series of decisions beginning later in March, Justice Owen Roberts, previously an ally of the Court's four hard-core conservatives, began voting to uphold New Deal laws. Several other justices retired within a few years, and Roosevelt eventually appointed nine justices. Although his later claim that he had lost the Court-packing battle but won the war was too facile (the battle was a major defeat in its own right, and it marked the birth of the conservative coalition of Republicans and southern Democrats that would dominate Congress for decades), Roosevelt never encountered another problem with the Supreme Court.

※ ※ ※

Tonight, sitting at my desk in the White House, I make my first radio report to the people in my second term of office.

I am reminded of that evening in March, four years ago, when I made my first radio report to you. We were then in the midst of the great banking crisis.

Soon after, with the authority of the Congress, we asked the Nation to turn over all of its privately held gold, dollar for dollar, to the Government of the United States.

Today's recovery proves how right that policy was.

But when, almost two years later, it came before the Supreme Court its constitutionality was upheld only by a five-to-four vote. The change of one vote would have thrown all the affairs of this great Nation back into hopeless chaos. In effect, four Justices ruled that the right under a private contract to exact a pound of flesh was more sacred than the main objectives of the Constitution to establish an enduring Nation.

In 1933 you and I knew that we must never let our economic system get completely out of joint again—that we could not afford to take the risk of another great depression.

We also became convinced that the only way to avoid a repetition of those dark days was to have a government with power to prevent and to cure the abuses and the inequalities which had thrown that system out of joint.

We then began a program of remedying those abuses and inequalities—to give balance and stability to our economic system—to make it bombproof against the causes of 1929.

Today we are only part-way through that program—and recovery is speeding up to a point where the dangers of 1929 are again becoming possible, not this week or month perhaps, but within a year or two.

National laws are needed to complete that program. Individual or local or state effort alone cannot protect us in 1937 any better than ten years ago. . . .

The American people have learned from the depression. For in the last three national elections an overwhelming majority of them voted a mandate that the Congress and the President begin the task of providing that protection—not after long years of debate, but now.

The Courts, however, have cast doubts on the ability of the elected Congress to protect us against catastrophe by meeting squarely our modern social and economic conditions. . . .

Last Thursday I described the American form of Government as a three horse team provided by the Constitution to the American people so that their field might be plowed. The three horses are, of course, the three branches of government—the Congress, the Executive and the Courts. Two of the horses are pulling in unison today; the third is not. Those who have intimated that the President of the United States is trying to drive that team, overlook the simple fact that the President, as Chief Executive, is himself one of the three horses.

It is the American people themselves who are in the driver's seat.

It is the American people themselves who want the furrow plowed.

It is the American people themselves who expect the third horse to pull in unison with the other two.

I hope that you have re-read the Constitution of the United States in these past few weeks. Like the Bible, it ought to be read again and again.

It is an easy document to understand when you remember that it was called into being because the Articles of Confederation under which the original thirteen States tried to operate after the Revolution showed the need of a National Government with power enough to handle national problems. In its Preamble, the Constitution states that it was intended to form a more perfect Union and promote the general welfare; and the powers given to the Congress to carry out those purposes can be best described by saying that they were all the powers needed to meet each and every problem which then had a national character and which could not be met by merely local action.

But the framers went further. Having in mind that in succeeding generations many other problems then undreamed of would become national problems, they gave to the Congress the ample broad powers "to levy taxes . . . and provide for the common defense and general welfare of the United States."

That, my friends, is what I honestly believe to have been the clear and underlying purpose of the patriots who wrote a Federal Constitution to create a National Government with national power, intended as they said, "to form a more perfect union . . . for ourselves and our posterity."

For nearly twenty years there was no conflict between the Congress and the Court. Then Congress passed a statute which, in 1803, the Court said violated an express provision of the Constitution. The Court claimed the power to declare it unconstitutional and did so declare it. But a little later the Court itself admitted that it was an extraordinary power to exercise and through Mr. Justice Washington laid down this limitation upon it: "It is but a decent respect due to the wisdom, the integrity and the patriotism of the legislative body, by which any law is passed, to presume in favor of its validity until its violation of the Constitution is proved beyond all reasonable doubt."

But since the rise of the modern movement for social and economic progress through legislation, the Court has more and more often and more and more boldly asserted a power to veto laws passed by the Congress and State Legislatures in complete disregard of this original limitation.

In the last four years the sound rule of giving statutes the benefit of all reasonable doubt has been cast aside. The Court has been acting not as a judicial body, but as a policy-making body. . . .—a super-legislature, as one of the justices has called it—reading into the Constitution words and implications which are not there, and which were never intended to be there. . . .

I want—as all Americans want—an independent judiciary as proposed by the framers of the Constitution. That means a Supreme Court that will enforce the Constitution as written—that will refuse to amend the Constitution by the arbitrary exercise of judicial power—amendment by judicial say-so. It does not mean a judiciary so independent that it can deny the existence of facts universally recognized.

How then could we proceed to perform the mandate given us? It was said in last year's Democratic platform, "If these problems cannot be effectively solved within the Constitution, we shall seek such clarifying amendment as will assure the power to enact those laws, adequately to regulate commerce, protect public health and safety, and safeguard economic security." In other words, we said we would seek an amendment only if every other possible means by legislation were to fail.

When I commenced to review the situation with the problem squarely before me, I came by a process of elimination to the conclusion that, short of amendments, the only method which was clearly constitutional, and would at the same time carry out other much needed reforms, was to infuse new blood into all our Courts. We must have men worthy and equipped to carry out impartial justice. But, at the same time, we must have Judges who will bring to the Courts a present-day sense of the Constitution—Judges who will retain in the Courts the judicial functions of a court, and reject the legislative powers which the courts have today assumed.

In forty-five out of the forty-eight States of the Union, Judges are chosen not for life but for a period of years. In many States Judges must retire at the age of seventy. Congress has provided financial security by offering life pensions at full pay for Federal Judges on all Courts who are willing to retire at seventy. In the case of Supreme Court Justices, that pension is $20,000 a year. But all Federal Judges, once appointed, can, if they choose, hold office for life, no matter how old they may get to be.

What is my proposal? It is simply this: whenever a Judge or Justice of any Federal Court has reached the age of seventy and does not avail himself of the opportunity to retire on a pension, a new member shall be appointed by the President then in office, with the approval, as required by the Constitution, of the Senate of the United States.

The plan has two chief purposes. By bringing into the judicial system a steady and continuing stream of new and younger blood, I hope, first, to make the administration of all Federal justice speedier and, therefore, less costly; secondly, to bring to the decision of social and economic problems younger men who have had personal experience and contact with modern facts and circumstances under which average men have to live and work. This plan will save our national Constitution from hardening of the judicial arteries.

The number of Judges to be appointed would depend wholly on the decision of present Judges now over seventy, or those who would subsequently reach the age of seventy.

If, for instance, any one of the six Justices of the Supreme Court now over the age of seventy should retire as provided under the plan, no additional place would be created. Consequently, although there never can be more than fifteen, there may be only fourteen, or thirteen, or twelve. And there may be only nine. . . .

Those opposing this plan have sought to arouse prejudice and fear by crying that I am seeking to "pack" the Supreme Court and that a baneful precedent will be established.

What do they mean by the words "packing the Court"?

Let me answer this question with a bluntness that will end all *honest* misunderstanding of my purposes.

If by that phrase "packing the Court" it is charged that I wish to place on the bench spineless puppets who would disregard the law and would decide specific cases as I wished them to be decided, I make this answer: that no President fit for his office would appoint, and no Senate of honorable men fit for their office would confirm, that kind of appointees to the Supreme Court.

But if by that phrase the charge is made that I would appoint and the Senate would confirm Justices worthy to sit beside present members of the Court who understand those modern conditions, that I will appoint Justices who will not undertake to override the judgment of the Congress on legislative policy, that I will appoint Justices who will act as Justices and not as legislators—if the appointment of such Justices can be called "packing the Courts," then I say that I and with me the vast majority of the American people favor doing just that thing—now.

Is it a dangerous precedent for the Congress to change the number of the Justices? The Congress has always had, and will have, that power. The number of Justices has been changed several times before, in the Administrations of John Adams and Thomas Jefferson—both signers of the Declaration of Independence—Andrew Jackson, Abraham Lincoln and Ulysses S. Grant. . . .

It is the clear intention of our public policy to provide for a constant flow of new and younger blood into the Judiciary. Normally every President appoints a large number of District and Circuit Judges and a few members of the

Supreme Court. Until my first term practically every President of the United States had appointed at least one member of the Supreme Court. President [William Howard] Taft appointed five members and named a Chief Justice; President [Woodrow] Wilson, three; President [Warren G.] Harding, four, including a Chief Justice.

Such a succession of appointments should have provided a Court well-balanced as to age. But chance and the disinclination of individuals to leave the Supreme bench have now given us a Court in which five Justices will be over seventy-five years of age before next June and one over seventy. Thus a sound public policy has been defeated. . . .

I have thus explained to you the reasons that lie behind our efforts to secure results by legislation within the Constitution. I hope that thereby the difficult process of constitutional amendment may be rendered unnecessary. . . .

And remember one thing more. Even if an amendment were passed, and even if in the years to come it were to be ratified, its meaning would depend upon the kind of Justices who would be sitting on the Supreme Court bench. An amendment, like the rest of the Constitution, is what the Justices say it is rather than what its framers or you might hope it is. . . .

I am in favor of action through legislation:

First, because I believe that it can be passed at this session of the Congress.

Second, because it will provide a reinvigorated, liberal-minded Judiciary necessary to furnish quicker and cheaper justice from bottom to top.

Third, because it will provide a series of Federal Courts willing to enforce the Constitution as written, and unwilling to assert legislative powers by writing into it their own political and economic policies.

During the past half century the balance of power between the three great branches of the Federal Government, has been tipped out of balance by the Courts in direct contradiction of the high purposes of the framers of the Constitution. It is my purpose to restore that balance. You who know me will accept my solemn assurance that in a world in which democracy is under attack, I seek to make American democracy succeed. You and I will do our part.

24

Report of the Brownlow Committee

(1937)

THE FIRST INAUGURATION of Franklin D. Roosevelt as president on March 4, 1933, was followed by an explosion of legislative activity aimed at combating the depression. During Roosevelt's fabled "first hundred days," Congress passed more than a dozen pieces of major administration-sponsored legislation. After the 1934 midterm elections, in which the president's party broke historical precedent by gaining seats in the House and Senate, Congress passed additional legislation. Cumulatively, these laws created a large and active role for the federal government in the nation's economy.

Because Roosevelt doubted the loyalty and ability of most of the existing departments and agencies, which had been created in less active times and were staffed mainly by Republican appointees, he persuaded Congress to authorize new agencies to carry out his new programs. By adding so many components to the executive branch, however, Roosevelt created an administrative nightmare. He was frustrated by his inability to get the information he needed from the bureaucracy or to communicate to it effectively his desires for action.

On March 20, 1936, Roosevelt appointed the Committee on Administrative Management, better known as the Brownlow Committee after its chair, Louis D. Brownlow. (The two other members were the political scientists Charles E. Merriam and Luther Gulick.) The commission's charge was to design and recommend an overhaul of the executive branch that would make it more efficient and responsive to the president. On January 8, 1937, Brownlow and his colleagues issued their report, which Roosevelt accepted wholeheartedly.

Arguing that "the president needs help," the Brownlow Committee recommended that the president be authorized to hire six personal assistants "possessed of high competence, great physical vigor, and a passion for anonymity." Their task would be to help the president "in obtaining quickly and without delay all pertinent information possessed by any of the executive departments so as to guide him in making his responsible decisions; and then when decisions have been made, to assist him in seeing to it that every administrative department and agency affected is promptly informed."

In addition to the personal staff positions, the Brownlow Committee recommended that the Executive Office of the President (EOP) be created to serve the long-term interests of the presidency as an institution. The main components of the EOP were to be the Bureau of the Budget, then housed in the Treasury Department, and the Civil Service Commission, an independent agency.

After receiving the Brownlow Committee's report, Roosevelt immediately asked Congress for authorization to implement its recommendations. Angry over the president's effort to "pack" the Supreme Court, however (see Document 23, p. 123), Congress did not approve the president's request until April 1939. (Even then, the Civil Service Commission was left independent.) On September 8, 1939, Roosevelt issued Executive Order 8248, and the Brownlow Committee's major proposals took effect.

⁂ ⁂ ⁂

. . . Our Presidency unites at least three important functions. From one point of view the President is a political leader—leader of a party, leader of the Congress, leader of a people. From another point of view he is head of the Nation in the ceremonial sense of the term, the symbol of our American national solidarity. From still another point of view the President is the Chief Executive and administrator within the Federal system and service. In many types of government these duties are divided or only in part combined, but in the United States they have always been united in one and the same person whose duty it is to perform all of these tasks.

Your Committee on Administrative Management has been asked to investigate and report particularly upon the last function; namely, that of administrative management—the organization for the performance of the duties imposed upon the President in exercising the executive power vested in him by the Constitution of the United States. . . .

Since the Civil War, as the tasks and responsibilities of our Government have grown with the growth of the Nation in sweep and power, some notable attempts have been made to keep our administrative system abreast of the new times. The assassination of President [James] Garfield by a disappointed office seeker aroused the Nation against the spoils system and led to the enactment of the civil-service law of 1883. We have struggled to make the principle of this law effective for half a century. The confusion in fiscal management led to the establishment of the Bureau of the Budget and the budgetary system in 1921. We still strive to realize the goal set for the Nation at that time. And, indeed, many other important forward steps have been taken.

Now we face again the problem of governmental readjustment, in part as the result of the activities of the Nation during the desperate years of the industrial depression, in part because of the very growth of the Nation, and in part because of the vexing social problems of our times. There is room for vast increase in our national productivity and there is much bitter wrong to set right in neglected ways of human life. There is need for improvement of our governmental machinery to meet new conditions and to make us ready for the problems just ahead. . . .

Fortunately the foundations of effective management in public affairs, no less than in private, are well known. They have emerged universally wherever men have worked together for some common purpose, whether through the state, the church, the private association, or the commercial enterprise. They have been written into constitutions, charters, and articles of incorporation, and exist as habits of work in the daily life of all organized peoples. Stated in simple terms these canons of efficiency require the establishment of a responsible and effective chief executive as the center of energy, direction, and administrative management; the systematic organization of all activities in the hands of qualified personnel under the direction of the chief executive; and to aid him in this, the establishment of appropriate managerial and staff agencies. There must also be provision for planning, a complete fiscal system, and means for holding the Executive accountable for his program. . . .

While in general principle our organization of the Presidency challenges the admiration of the world, yet in equipment for administrative management our Executive Office is not fully abreast of the trend of our American times, either in business or in government. Where, for example, can there be found an executive in any way comparable upon whom so much petty work is thrown? Or who is forced to see so many persons on unrelated matters and to make so many decisions on the basis of what may be, because of the very press of work, incomplete information? How is it humanly possible to know fully the affairs and problems of over 100 separate major agencies, to say nothing of being responsible for their general direction and coordination?

These facts have been known for many years and are so well appreciated that it is not necessary for us to prove again that the President's administrative equipment is far less developed than his responsibilities, and that a major task before the American Government is to remedy this dangerous situation. What we need is not a new principle, but a modernizing of our managerial equipment. . . .

In this broad program of administrative reorganization the White House itself is involved. The President needs help. His immediate staff assistance is entirely inadequate. He should be given a small number of executive assistants who would be his direct aides in dealing with the managerial agencies and administrative departments of the Government. These assistants, probably not exceeding six in number, would be in addition to his present secretaries, who deal with the public, with the Congress, and with the press and the radio. These aides would have no power to make decisions or issue instructions in their own right. They would not be interposed between the President and the heads of his departments. They would not be assistant presidents in any sense. Their function would be, when any matter was presented to the President for action affecting any part of the administrative work of the Government, to assist him in obtaining quickly and without delay all pertinent information possessed by any of the executive departments so as to guide him in making his responsible decisions; and then when decisions have been made, to assist him in seeing to it that every administrative department and agency affected is promptly informed. Their effectiveness in assisting the President will, we think, be directly proportional to their ability to discharge their functions with restraint. They would remain in the background, issue no orders, make no decisions, emit no public statements. Men for these positions should be carefully chosen by the President from within and without the Government. They should be men in whom the President has personal confidence and whose character and attitude is such that they would not attempt to exercise power on their own account. They should be possessed of high competence, great physical vigor, and a passion for anonymity. They should be installed in the

White House itself, directly accessible to the President. In the selection of these aides the President should be free to call on departments from time to time for the assignment of persons who, after a tour of duty as his aides, might be restored to their old positions.

This recommendation arises from the growing complexity and magnitude of the work of the President's office. Special assistance is needed to insure that all matters coming to the attention of the President have been examined from the over-all managerial point of view, as well as from all standpoints that would bear on policy and operation. It also would facilitate the flow upward to the President of information upon which he is to base his decisions and the flow downward from the President of the decisions once taken for execution by the department or departments affected. Thus such a staff would not only aid the President but would also be of great assistance to the several executive departments and to the managerial agencies in simplifying executive contacts, clearance, and guidance.

The President should also have at his command a contingent fund to enable him to bring in from time to time particular persons possessed of particular competency for a particular purpose and whose services he might usefully employ for short periods of time.

The President in his regular office staff should be given a greater number of positions so that he will not be compelled, as he has been compelled in the past, to use for his own necessary work persons carried on the payrolls of other departments.

If the President be thus equipped he will have but the ordinary assistance that any executive of a large establishment is afforded as a matter of course.

In addition to this assistance in his own office the President must be given direct control over and be charged with immediate responsibility for the great managerial functions of the Government which affect all of the administrative departments. . . . These functions are personnel management, fiscal and organizational management, and planning management. Within these three groups may be comprehended all of the essential elements of business management.

The development of administrative management in the Federal Government requires the improvement of the administration of these managerial activities, not only by the central agencies in charge, but also by the departments and bureaus. The central agencies need to be strengthened and developed as managerial arms of the Chief Executive, better equipped to perform their central responsibilities and to provide the necessary leadership in bringing about improved practices throughout the Government.

The three managerial agencies, the Civil Service Administration, the Bureau of the Budget, and the national Resources Board should be a part and parcel of the Executive Office. Thus the President would have reporting to him directly the three managerial institutions whose work and activities would affect all of the administrative departments.

The budgets for the managerial agencies should be submitted to the Congress by the President as a part of the budget for the Executive Office. This would distinguish these agencies from the operating administrative departments of the Government, which should report to the President through the heads of departments who collectively compose his Cabinet. Such an arrangement would materially aid the President in his work of supervising the administrative agencies and would enable the Congress and the people to hold him to strict accountability for their conduct. . . .

[In addition to these recommendations concerning

1) the White House staff and
2) the three managerial agencies,]

. . . 3. The merit system should be extended upward, outward, and downward to cover all non–policy-determining posts, and the civil service system should be reorganized and opportunities established for a career system attractive to the talent of the Nation.

4. The whole Executive Branch of Government should be overhauled and the present 100 agencies reorganized under a few large departments in which every executive activity would find its place.

5. The fiscal system should be extensively revised in the light of the best governmental and private practice, particularly with reference to financial records, audit, and accountability of the Executive to the Congress. . . .

25

Youngstown Sheet and Tube Co. v. Sawyer*

(1952)

IN JUNE 1950, troops from Communist North Korea invaded South
Korea, a U.S. ally. At the behest of the United States, the Security
Council of the recently formed United Nations (UN) passed a resolution
condemning the invasion and asking UN member nations to "render
every assistance" to South Korea. President Harry S. Truman, relying on
the resolution and on his constitutional authority as commander in
chief, committed American men and materiel to South Korea's defense
without asking Congress to declare war.

The fighting did not go as well as Truman had hoped, and the longer
the war lasted, the more unpopular it and the president became. On
April 8, 1952, when a labor dispute in the steel industry made the situation even more uncertain, Truman ordered Secretary of Commerce
Charles Sawyer "to take possession of and operate the plants and facilities of certain steel companies," including the Youngstown Sheet and
Tube Co. in Youngstown, Ohio. Truman acted partly out of the fear that
an impending strike for higher wages (a goal he supported) by the United Steel Workers union would jeopardize the ability of the United
States to maintain both its military effort in the Korean War and its
commitment to supply arms to Western Europe. He was not alone in
this belief. Robert Lovett, the secretary of defense, and Dean Acheson,
the secretary of state, agreed with the president.

Truman had authority under the Labor-Management Relations Act
of 1947 (better known as the Taft-Hartley Act) to impose a court-
ordered, sixty-day "cooling-off" period on both labor and management
whenever the nation's health or safety was imperiled. But for political
reasons—Truman had opposed the act and sought its repeal—he was
unwilling to do so. Instead, he grounded his authority to seize the mills
in the existence of a wartime emergency and in his authority "as Presi-

*Go to *http://www.findlaw.com*, click on "U.S. Supreme Court Cases," then type
"Youngstown Sheet and Tube" in the box called "Party Name Search"

dent of the United States and Commander in Chief of the Armed Forces." Truman was aware that previous presidents, including Abraham Lincoln and Franklin D. Roosevelt, had seized private property without prior congressional authorization. He also knew that only once—and never against a sitting president—had the Supreme Court declared a presidential action unconstitutional during a war. (See Document 15, p. 77.)

Truman conceded in an April 9, 1952, report that Congress had the power to countermand his steel seizure order, confident that it would not do so. In this assessment he was correct. Although certain that the steel companies would sue to have the Supreme Court declare the order unconstitutional, Truman expected the Court's support as well, not just because of the long history of judicial deference to the president in foreign and military matters but also because he had appointed three of the nine justices and believed that three others were either pro-union or pro-presidential prerogative. In this assessment Truman was wrong.

On June 2, 1952, ruling in the case of *Youngstown Sheet and Tube Co. v. Sawyer* (also known as the Steel Seizure Case), the Supreme Court declared Truman's order to Secretary Sawyer unconstitutional by a 6–3 vote. Because seven of the nine justices, including all six in the majority, wrote separate opinions and only three endorsed Justice Hugo L. Black's opinion of the Court in its entirety, the full implications of this ruling for presidential power were (and are) unclear. But one thing a majority of justices could agree on was that Congress had foreclosed the president from seizing industries during national emergencies by rejecting a proposed amendment to the Taft-Hartley Act that would have conferred such authority.

Although Truman lost the case, his constitutional claim that the president has an inherent, unstated constitutional power to act in times of national emergency was accepted, to one degree or another, by a majority of the justices. Black rejected this argument, but Robert H. Jackson's concurring opinion has turned out to be of more enduring influence. Jackson argued that presidential power is variable: strong when supported by Congress, moderate when Congress is silent, and "at its lowest ebb" when exercised in opposition to Congress.

༖ ༖ ༖

MR. JUSTICE BLACK delivered the opinion of the Court.

We are asked to decide whether the President was acting within his constitutional power when he issued an order directing the Secretary of Commerce [Charles Sawyer] to take possession of and operate most of the Nation's steel mills. The mill owners argue that the President's order amounts to lawmaking, a legislative function which the Constitution has expressly confided to the Congress and not to the President. The Government's position is that the order was made on findings of the President that his action was necessary to avert a national catastrophe which would inevitably result from a stoppage of steel production, and that in meeting this grave emergency the President was acting within the aggregate of his constitutional powers as the Nation's Chief Executive and the Commander in Chief of the Armed Forces of the United States. . . .

The President's power, if any, to issue the order must stem either from an act of Congress or from the Constitution itself. There is no statute that expressly authorizes the President to take possession of property as he did here. Nor is there any act of Congress to which our attention has been directed from which such a power can fairly be implied. Indeed, we do not understand the Government to rely on statutory authorization for this seizure. There are two statutes which do authorize the President to take both personal and real property under certain conditions. However, the Government admits that these conditions were not met and that the President's order was not rooted in either of the statutes. The Government refers to the seizure provisions of one of these statutes (§ 201 (b) of the Defense Production Act) as "much too cumbersome, involved, and time-consuming for the crisis which was at hand."

Moreover, the use of the seizure technique to solve labor disputes in order to prevent work stoppages was not only unauthorized by any congressional enactment; prior to this controversy, Congress had refused to adopt that method of settling labor disputes. When the Taft-Hartley Act was under consideration in 1947, Congress rejected an amendment which would have authorized such governmental seizures in cases of emergency. . . .

It is clear that if the President had authority to issue the order he did, it must be found in some provision of the Constitution. And it is not claimed that express constitutional language grants this power to the President. The contention is that presidential power should be implied from the aggregate of his powers under the Constitution. Particular reliance is placed on provisions in Article II which says that "The executive Power shall be vested in a President . . ."; that "he shall take Care that the Laws be faithfully executed"; and that he "shall be Commander in Chief of the Army and Navy of the United States."

The order cannot properly be sustained as an exercise of the President's military power as Commander in Chief of the Armed Forces. The Government attempts to do so by citing a number of cases upholding broad powers in military commanders engaged in day-to-day fighting in a theater of war. Such cases need not concern us here. Even though "theater of war" be an expanding concept, we cannot with faithfulness to our constitutional system hold that the Commander in Chief of the Armed Forces has the ultimate power as such to take possession of private property in order to keep labor disputes from stopping production. This is a job for the Nation's lawmakers, not for its military authorities.

Nor can the seizure order be sustained because of the several constitutional provisions that grant executive power to the President. In the framework of our Constitution, the President's power to see that the laws are faithfully executed refutes the idea that he is to be a lawmaker. The Constitution limits his functions in the lawmaking process to the recommending of laws he thinks wise and the vetoing of laws he thinks bad. And the Constitution is neither silent nor equivocal about who shall make laws which the President is to execute. The first section of the first article says that "All legislative Powers herein granted shall be vested in a Congress of the United States. . . ." After granting many powers to the Congress, Article I goes on to provide that Congress may "make all Laws which shall be necessary and proper for carrying into Execution the foregoing Powers, and all other Powers vested by this Constitution in the Government of the United States, or in any Department or Officer thereof."

The President's order does not direct that a congressional policy be executed in a manner prescribed by Congress—it directs that a presidential policy be executed in a manner prescribed by the President. . . .

It is said that other Presidents without congressional authority have taken possession of private business enterprises in order to settle labor disputes. But even if this be true, Congress has not thereby lost its exclusive constitutional authority to make laws necessary and proper to carry out the powers vested by the Constitution "in the Government of the United States, or any Department or Officer thereof."

The Founders of this Nation entrusted the lawmaking power to the Congress alone in both good and bad times. It would do no good to recall the historical events, the fears of power and the hopes for freedom that lay behind their choice. Such a review would but confirm our holding that this seizure order cannot stand.

The judgment of the District Court is Affirmed.

MR. JUSTICE JACKSON, concurring in the judgment and opinion of the Court. . . .

A judge, like an executive adviser, may be surprised at the poverty of really useful and unambiguous authority applicable to concrete problems of executive power as they actually present themselves. Just what our forefathers did envision, or would have envisioned had they foreseen modern conditions, must be divined from materials almost as enigmatic as the dreams Joseph was called upon to interpret for Pharaoh. A century and a half of partisan debate and scholarly speculation yields no net result but only supplies more or less apt quotations from respected sources on each side of any question. They largely cancel each other. And court decisions are indecisive because of the judicial practice of dealing with the largest questions in the most narrow way.

The actual art of governing under our Constitution does not and cannot conform to judicial definitions of the power of any of its branches based on isolated clauses or even single Articles torn from context. While the Constitution diffuses power the better to secure liberty, it also contemplates that practice will integrate the dispersed powers into a workable government. It enjoins upon its branches separateness but interdependence, autonomy but reciprocity. Presidential powers are not fixed but fluctuate, depending upon their disjunction or conjunction with those of Congress. We may well begin by a somewhat over-simplified grouping of practical situations in which a President may doubt, or others may challenge, his powers, and by distinguishing roughly the legal consequences of this factor of relativity.

1. When the President acts pursuant to an express or implied authorization of Congress, his authority is at its maximum, for it includes all that he possesses in his own right plus all that Congress can delegate. In these circumstances, and in these only, may he be said (for what it may be worth) to personify federal sovereignty. If his act is held unconstitutional under these circumstances, it usually means that the Federal Government as an undivided whole lacks power. A seizure executed by the President pursuant to an Act of Congress would be supported by the strongest of presumptions and the widest latitude of judicial interpretation, and the burden of persuasion would rest heavily upon any who might attack it.

2. When the President acts in absence of either a congressional grant or denial of authority, he can only rely upon his own independent powers, but there is a zone of twilight in which he and Congress may have concurrent authority, or in which its distribution is uncertain. Therefore, congressional inertia, indifference or quiescence may sometimes, at least as a practical matter, enable, if not invite, measures on independent presidential responsibility. In this area,

any actual test of power is likely to depend on the imperatives of events and contemporary imponderables rather than on abstract theories of law.

3. When the President takes measures incompatible with the expressed or implied will of Congress, his power is at its lowest ebb, for then he can rely only upon his own constitutional powers minus any constitutional powers of Congress over the matter. Courts can sustain exclusive presidential control in such a case only by disabling the Congress from acting upon the subject. Presidential claim to a power at once so conclusive and preclusive must be scrutinized with caution, for what is at stake is the equilibrium established by our constitutional system.

Into which of these classifications does this executive seizure of the steel industry fit? It is eliminated from the first by admission, for it is conceded that no congressional authorization exists for this seizure. That takes away also the support of the many precedents and declarations which were made in relation, and must be confined, to this category.

Can it then be defended under flexible tests available to the second category? It seems clearly eliminated from that class because Congress has not left seizure of private property an open field but has covered it by three statutory policies inconsistent with this seizure. In cases where the purpose is to supply needs of the Government itself, two courses are provided: one, seizure of a plant which fails to comply with obligatory orders placed by the Government; another, condemnation of facilities, including temporary use under the power of eminent domain. The third is applicable where it is the general economy of the country that is to be protected rather than exclusive governmental interests. None of these were invoked. In choosing a different and inconsistent way of his own, the President cannot claim that it is necessitated or invited by failure of Congress to legislate upon the occasions, grounds and methods for seizure of industrial properties.

This leaves the current seizure to be justified only by the severe tests under the third grouping, where it can be supported only by any reminder of executive power after subtraction of such powers as Congress may have over the subject. In short, we can sustain the President only by holding that seizure of such strike-bound industries is within his domain and beyond control by Congress. Thus, this Court's first review of such seizures occurs under circumstances which leave presidential power most vulnerable to attack and in the least favorable of possible constitutional postures. . . .

The Solicitor General seeks the power of seizure in three clauses of the Executive Article, the first reading, "The executive Power shall be vested in a President of the United States of America." Lest I be thought to exaggerate, I quote the interpretation which his brief puts upon it: "In our view, this clause constitutes a grant of all the executive powers of which the Government is capable." If that be true, it is difficult to see why the forefathers bothered to add several specific items, including some trifling ones. . . .

The clause on which the Government next relies is that "The President shall be Commander in Chief of the Army and Navy of the United States. . . ." These cryptic words have given rise to some of the most persistent controversies in our constitutional history. Of course, they imply something more than an empty title. But just what authority goes with the name has plagued presidential advisers who would not waive or narrow it by nonassertion yet cannot say where it begins or ends. It undoubtedly puts the Nation's armed forces under presidential command. Hence, this loose appellation is sometimes advanced as support for any presidential action, internal or external, involving use of force, the idea being that it vests power to do anything, anywhere, that can be done with an army or navy.

That seems to be the logic of an argument tendered at our bar—that the President having, on his own responsibility, sent American troops abroad derives from that act "affirmative power" to seize the means of producing a supply of steel for them. To quote, "Perhaps the most forceful illustration of the scope of Presidential power in this connection is the fact that American troops in Korea, whose safety and effectiveness are so directly involved here, were sent to the field by an exercise of the President's constitutional powers." Thus, it is said, he has invested himself with "war powers."

I cannot foresee all that it might entail if the Court should indorse this argument. Nothing in our Constitution is plainer than that declaration of a war is entrusted only to Congress. . . .

There are indications that the Constitution did not contemplate that the title Commander in Chief *of the Army and Navy* will constitute him also Commander in Chief of the country, its industries and its inhabitants. He has no monopoly of "war powers," whatever they are. While Congress cannot deprive the President of the command of the army and navy, only Congress can provide him an army or navy to command. It is also empowered to make rules for the "Government and Regulation of land and naval Forces," by which it may to some unknown extent impinge upon even command functions. . . .

We should not use this occasion to circumscribe, much less to contract, the lawful role of the President as Commander in Chief. I should indulge the widest latitude of interpretation to sustain his exclusive function to command the instruments of national force, at least when turned against the outside world for the security of our society. But, when it is turned inward, not because of rebellion but because of a lawful economic struggle between industry and labor, it should have no such indulgence. His command power is not such an absolute as might be implied from that office in militaristic system but is subject to limitations consistent with a constitutional Republic whose law and policy-making branch is a representative Congress. The purpose of lodging dual titles in one man was to insure that the civilian would control the military, not to enable the military to subordinate the presidential office. No penance would ever expiate the sin against free government of holding that a President can escape control of executive powers by law through assuming his military role. What the power of command may include I do not try to envision, but I think it is not a military prerogative, without support of law, to seize persons or property because they are important or even essential for the military and naval establishment.

The third clause in which the Solicitor General finds seizure powers is that "he shall take Care that the Laws be faithfully executed. . . ." That authority must be matched against words of the Fifth Amendment that "No person shall be . . . deprived of life, liberty or property, without due process of law. . . ." One gives a governmental authority that reaches so far as there is law, the other gives a private right that authority shall go no farther. These signify about all there is of the principle that ours is a government of laws, not of men, and that we submit ourselves to rulers only if under rules.

The Solicitor General lastly grounds support of the seizure upon nebulous, inherent powers never expressly granted but said to have accrued to the office from the customs and claims of preceding administrations. The plea is for a resulting power to deal with a crisis or an emergency according to the necessities of the case, the unarticulated assumption being that necessity knows no law. . . .

In the practical working of our Government we already have evolved a technique within the framework of the Constitution by which normal executive powers may be considerably expanded to meet an emergency. Congress may and has granted extraordinary authorities which lie dormant in normal times but may be called into play by the Executive in war or upon proclamation of a national emergency. In 1939, upon congressional request, the Attorney General listed ninety-nine such separate statutory grants by Congress of emergency or wartime executive powers. They were invoked from time to time as need appeared. Under this procedure we retain Government by law—special, temporary law, perhaps, but law nonetheless. The public may know the extent and limitations of the powers that can be asserted, and persons affected may be informed from the statute of their rights and duties.

In view of the ease, expedition and safety with which Congress can grant and has granted large emergency powers, certainly ample to embrace this crisis, I am quite unimpressed with the argument that we should affirm possession of them without statute. Such power either has no beginning or it has no end. If it exists, it need submit to no legal restraint. I am not alarmed that it would plunge us straightway into dictatorship, but it is at least a step in that wrong direction.

As to whether there is imperative necessity for such powers, it is relevant to note the gap that exists between the President's paper powers and his real powers. The Constitution does not disclose the measure of the actual controls wielded by the modern presidential office. That instrument must be understood as an Eighteenth-Century sketch of a government hoped for, not as a blueprint of the Government that is. Vast accretions of federal power, eroded from that reserved by the States, have magnified the scope of presidential activity. Subtle shifts take place in the centers of real power that do not show on the face of the Constitution.

Executive power has the advantage of concentration in a single head in whose choice the whole Nation has a part, making him the focus of public hopes and expectations. In drama, magnitude and finality his decisions so far overshadow any others that almost alone he fills the public eye and ear. No other personality in public life can begin to compete with him in access to the public mind through modern methods of communications. By his prestige as head of state and his influence upon public opinion he exerts a leverage upon those who are supposed to check and balance his power which often cancels their effectiveness.

Moreover, [the] rise of the party system has made a significant extraconstitutional supplement to real executive power. No appraisal of his necessities is realistic which overlooks that he heads a political system as well as a legal system. Party loyalties and interests, sometimes more binding than law, extend his effective control into branches of government other than his own and he often may win, as a political leader, what he cannot command under the Constitution. Indeed, Woodrow Wilson, commenting on the President as leader both of his party and of the Nation, observed, "If he rightly interpret the national thought and boldly insist upon it, he is irresistible. . . . His office is anything he has the sagacity and force to make it." I cannot be brought to believe that this country will suffer if the Court refuses further to aggrandize the presidential office, already so potent and so relatively immune from judicial review, at the expense of Congress.

But I have no illusion that any decision by this Court can keep power in the hands of Congress if it is not wise and timely in meeting its problems. A crisis that challenges the President equally, or perhaps primarily, challenges Congress. If not good law, there was worldly wisdom in the maxim attributed to Napoleon that "The tools belong to the man who can use them." We may say that power to legislate for emergencies belongs in the hands of Congress, but only Congress itself can prevent power from slipping through its fingers.

The essence of our free Government is "leave to live by no man's leave, underneath the law"—to be governed by those impersonal forces which we call law. Our Government is fashioned to fulfill this concept so far as humanly possible. The Executive, except for recommendation and veto, has no legislative power. The executive action we have here originates in the individual will of the President and represents an exercise of authority without law. No one, perhaps not even the President, knows the limits of the power he may seek to exert in this instance and the parties affected cannot learn the limit of their rights. We do not know today what powers over labor or property would be claimed to flow from Government possession if we should legalize it, what rights to compensation would be claimed or recognized, or on what contingency it would end. With all its defects, delays and inconveniences, men have discovered no technique for long preserving free government except that the Executive be under the law, and that the law be made by parliamentary deliberations.

Such institutions may be destined to pass away. But it is the duty of the Court to be last, not first, to give them up.

✥ 26 ✥

Dwight D. Eisenhower's Little Rock Executive Order

(1957)

T HE CONSTITUTION VESTS the "executive Power" in the "President of the United States of America"; it also charges the president to "take Care that the laws be faithfully executed." Taken in combination, these constitutional clauses have given rise to a presidential power that is not mentioned in the Constitution: the power to issue executive orders. Nearly fourteen thousand executive orders have been issued by presidents from George Washington to Bill Clinton, all but around a thousand of them in the twentieth century. The legal authority for each of these orders has been grounded either in statutes enacted by Congress or in the president's constitutional authority. In most cases, the orders have established executive agencies, changed executive decision-making procedures, modified bureaucratic rules and practices, or given substance and force to statutes.

The train of events that led to President Dwight D. Eisenhower's issuance of Executive Order 10730 began with the Supreme Court's declaration in *Brown v. Board of Education* (1954) that legally segregated public schools violate the Constitution. The southern states, taking heart from Eisenhower's refusal to endorse the wisdom of the Court's decision, responded by strenuously resisting school integration. When the school board of Little Rock, Arkansas, decided to inaugurate a six-year plan of integration by admitting a small number of African-American students to the all-white Central High School in September 1957, Gov. Orval Faubus forcefully intervened. On September 2 Faubus, in defiance of an order of the federal district court for the Eastern District of Arkansas, deployed the Arkansas national guard to prevent the nine black students designated by the school board from enrolling at Central High. Mobs of angry, sometimes violent whites surrounded the school.

Eisenhower may have had doubts about mandatory school integration, but he had none about defiance of the law. He was also concerned about the Soviet Union's use of the crisis to portray the United States as racist to the newly independent countries of Africa and Asia. After an unsuccessful September 14 meeting with Faubus at the president's summer home in Newport, Rhode Island, Eisenhower issued a proclamation on September 23 "to command all persons engaged in obstruction of justice to cease and desist therefrom, and to disperse forthwith." The next day, after Faubus and the mob ignored the proclamation, Eisenhower issued an executive order directing Secretary of Defense Charles Wilson to federalize the Arkansas national guard and to deploy approximately one thousand armed paratroopers from the army's 101st Airborne Division to Little Rock. That night, Eisenhower addressed the nation on television, having returned to Washington from Newport for the stated purpose of buttressing the "firmness" of his remarks by "speaking from the House of Lincoln, of Jackson and of Wilson."

Eisenhower grounded his authority to issue Executive Order 10730 in "the authority vested in me by the Constitution and statutes of the United States," including several Civil War–era laws concerning "unlawful obstruction," "rebellion," and "interference with state and Federal law." He explained that he had issued the proclamation the previous day because one of the laws required that he do so before deploying the armed forces in a domestic situation.

Once the paratroopers arrived, the mob dispersed and Central High was integrated, at least on a token basis. But Faubus, who was seeking reelection in 1958 (he won overwhelmingly), remained defiant and even closed the schools in Little Rock for academic year 1958–1959. School integration only became widespread in the South in the early 1970s.

Eisenhower was not the first president to issue an executive order on behalf of civil rights. During World War II, Franklin D. Roosevelt ordered an easing of segregation in defense plants and, in 1948, Harry S. Truman integrated the armed forces with an executive order. Nor would Eisenhower be the last. Lyndon B. Johnson, for example, used an executive order to direct businesses contracting with the federal government to create affirmative action hiring programs after Congress refused to do so in the Civil Rights Act of 1964.

᳐ ᳐ ᳐

Executive Order 10730

The White House
U.S. Naval Base
Newport, R.I.

PROVIDING ASSISTANCE FOR THE REMOVAL OF AN OBSTRUCTION OF JUSTICE WITHIN THE STATE OF ARKANSAS

Whereas, on Sept. 23, 1957, I issued proclamation No. 3204 reading in part as follows:

"Whereas, certain persons in the State of Arkansas, individually and in unlawful assemblages, combinations, and conspiracies, have wilfully obstructed the enforcement of orders of the United States District Court for the Eastern

District of Arkansas with respect to matters relating to enrollment and attendance at public schools, particularly at Central High School, located in Little Rock School District, Little Rock, Ark., and

"Whereas, such wilful obstruction of justice hinders the execution of the laws of that state and of the United States, and makes it impracticable to enforce such laws by the ordinary course of judicial proceedings, and

"Whereas, such obstruction of justice constitutes a denial of the equal protection of the laws secured by the Constitution of the United States and impedes the court of justice under those laws;

"Now, therefore, I, Dwight D. Eisenhower, President of the United States, under and by the virtue of the authority vested in me by the Constitution and statutes of the United States, including Chapter 15 of Title 10, of the United States Code, particularly Sections 332, 333 and 334 thereof, do command all persons engaged in such obstruction of justice to cease and desist therefrom, and to disperse forthwith" and

Whereas, the command contained in that proclamation has not been obeyed and wilful obstruction of enforcement of said court order still exists and threatens to continue;

Now, therefore, by virtue of the authority vested in me by the Constitution and statutes of the United States, including Chapter 15 and Title 10, particularly Sections 332, 333 and 334 thereof, and Section 301 of Title Three, of the United States Code, is hereby ordered as follows:

"Section 1. I hereby authorize and direct the Secretary of Defense to order into the active military service of the United States, as he may deem appropriate to carry out the purposes of this order, any or all of the units of the National Guard of the United States and of the Air National Guard of the United States within the State of Arkansas to serve in the active military service of the United States for an indefinite period and until relieved by appropriate order.

"Section 2. The Secretary of Defense is authorized and directed to take all appropriate steps to enforce any order of the United States District Court for the Eastern District of Arkansas for the removal of an obstruction of justice in the State of Arkansas with respect to matters relating to enrollment and attendance at public schools in the Little Rock School District, Little Rock, Arkansas. In carrying out the provisions of this section, the Secretary of Defense is authorized to use the units and members thereof, ordered into active military service of the United States pursuant to section 1 of this order.

"Section 3. In furtherance of the enforcement of the aforementioned order of the United States District Court for the Eastern District of Arkansas, the Secretary of Defense is authorized to use such forces of the armed forces of the United States as he may deem necessary.

"Section 4. The Secretary of Defense is authorized to delegate to the Secretary of the Army or the Secretary of the Air Force, or both, any of the authority conferred upon him by this order."

❧ 27 ❧
The First Kennedy-Nixon Debate*
(1960)

UNTIL 1960 PRESIDENTIAL CANDIDATES never debated each other. The famous debates between Abraham Lincoln and Stephen A. Douglas took place during the Illinois Senate campaign of 1858. Even with the coming of television in the 1950s, debates were effectively forestalled by a federal law that required stations to give all minor as well as major party candidates equal time on the air.

In 1960, however, the Democratically controlled Congress voted to suspend the equal-time provision in order to force Vice President Richard Nixon, the Republican presidential nominee, to debate the lesser-known Democratic candidate, Sen. John F. Kennedy of Massachusetts. Nixon, confident of his debating skills, readily agreed to debate Kennedy on four live prime-time broadcasts during late September and October.

The first Kennedy-Nixon debate, held in a television studio in Chicago on the evening of September 26, turned out to be politically crucial. Eighty million people watched, setting a new record for the largest television audience in history. The format was less that of a classic debate than of a joint press conference—a panel of four reporters asked each candidate questions, with the veteran broadcast journalist Howard K. Smith serving as moderator.

As their opening statements indicate, Nixon and Kennedy differed little from each other on substantive issues. Consequently, the political outcome of the debate turned on matters of appearance and style.

*For the text of all four debates, go to *http://www.netcapitol.com/Debates/60*

Kennedy won handily on both counts. He was tanned and rested, and his dark blue suit stood out well against the gray studio background. (Television showed only black-and-white pictures at the time.) Nixon, who had recently been ill, eschewed professional makeup and wore a light gray suit that blended into the background. He looked pale skinned, hollow eyed, and dark bearded.

As to style, Kennedy spoke directly to the camera and, regardless of the questions, gave answers that sounded the campaign themes he wanted to emphasize. For example, his opening statement, which was supposed to be about domestic policy, began by stressing the decline of American prestige in the world. In contrast, Nixon mostly responded to Kennedy's points, often disagreeing but sometimes agreeing with them. Nixon's first words of the evening were, "The things that Senator Kennedy has said, many of us can agree with."

The first debate gave the Kennedy campaign a boost in enthusiasm and public support that helped carry it to a narrow victory on election day. Kennedy's popular-vote majority was only two-tenths of one percent.

The lesson many political leaders learned from the Kennedy-Nixon experience was that the better-known candidate in a presidential election has more to lose in debates and should avoid them. Thus, the next round of presidential debates did not take place until 1976, when President Gerald R. Ford, trailing badly in the polls, felt he had no choice but to face his opponent, former Georgia governor Jimmy Carter. In 1980 President Carter had similar political reasons to debate Ronald Reagan, the ex-governor of California.

In contrast to 1960, the Ford-Carter and Carter-Reagan debates established a precedent that subsequent presidential candidates have been loath to ignore for fear of alienating voters. Debates have become a regular feature of presidential elections.

Kennedy's election both reflected and encouraged other democratizing trends in national politics. He broke down the barriers of prejudice that had prevented Roman Catholics from becoming president. Perhaps more important, he was the first candidate to win his party's nomination through a series of primary victories. Party leaders still controlled the nominating process in 1960, as in the past. But Kennedy was able to use the primaries to convince influential Democrats that his Catholicism would not repel more voters than it would attract. (See Document 33, p. 177.)

(See Document 33, p. 177.)

※ ※ ※

HOWARD K. SMITH (MODERATOR): Good evening. The television and radio stations of the United States and their affiliated stations are proud to provide facilities for a discussion of issues in the current political campaign by the two major candidates for the Presidency. The candidates need no introduction. The Republican candidate, Vice President Richard M. Nixon, and the Democratic candidate, Senator John F. Kennedy. According to the rules set by the candidates themselves each man shall make an opening statement of approximately eight minutes duration and a closing statement of approximately three minutes duration. In between the candidates will answer or comment upon answers to questions put by a panel of correspondents. In this, the first discussion in the series of four joint appearances, the subject matter as has been agreed will be restricted to internal or domestic American matters. And now for the first opening statement by Senator John F. Kennedy.

KENNEDY: Mr. Smith, Mr. Nixon, in the election of 1860, Abraham Lincoln said the question was whether this nation could exist half slave or half free. In the election of 1960 and with the world around us the question is whether the world will exist half slave or half free, whether it will move in the direction of freedom, in the direction of the road that we are taking or whether it will move in the direction of slavery.

I think it will depend in great measure upon what we do here in the United States, on the kind of society that we build, on the kind of strength that we maintain.

We discuss tonight domestic issues but I would not want there to be any implication to be given that this does not involve directly our struggle with [Soviet leader Nikita] Khrushchev for survival. Mr. Khrushchev is in New York and he maintains the Communist offensive throughout the world because of the productive power of the Soviet Union itself.

The Chinese Communists have always had a large population but they are important and dangerous now because they are mounting a major effort within their own country. The kind of country we have here, the kind of society we have, the kind of strength we build in the United States will be the defense of freedom.

If we do well here, if we meet our obligations, if we are moving ahead, then I think freedom will be secure around the world. If we fail, then freedom fails.

Therefore, I think the question before the American people is, are we doing as much as we can do? Are we as strong as we should be? Are we as strong as we must be if we are going to maintain our independence and if we are going to maintain and hold out the hand of friendship to those who look to us for assistance, to those who look to us for survival?

I should make it very clear that I do not think we are doing enough, that I am not satisfied as an American with the progress that we are making. This is a great country but I think it could be a more powerful country.

I'm not satisfied to have fifty percent of our steel mill capacity unused. I'm not satisfied when the United States had last year the lowest rate of economic growth of any major industrialized society in the world—because economic growth means strength and vitality. It means we are able to sustain our defenses. It means we are able to meet our commitments abroad.

I'm not satisfied when we have over $9 billion worth of food, some of it rotting, even though there is a hungry world and even though four million Americans wait every month for a food package from the government which averages five cents a day per individual. I saw cases in West Virginia, here in the United States, where children took home part of their school lunch in order to feed their families. Because of this I don't think we are meeting our obligations towards these Americans.

I'm not satisfied when the Soviet Union is turning out twice as many scientists and engineers as we are.

I'm not satisfied when many of our teachers are inadequately paid or when our children go to school in part-time shifts. I think we should have an educational system second to none. I'm not satisfied when I see men like [Teamsters union president] Jimmy Hoffa, in charge of the largest union in the United States, still free.

I'm not satisfied when we are failing to develop the natural resources of the United States to the fullest. Here is the United States which developed the Tennessee Valley and which built the Grand Coulee and the other dams in the northwest United States. At the present rate of hydro power production, and that is the hallmark of an industrialized society, the Soviet Union by 1975 will be producing more power than we are.

These are all the things I think in this country that can make our society strong or can mean that it stands still.

I'm not satisfied until every American enjoys his full Constitutional rights. If a Negro baby is born, and this is true also of Puerto Ricans and Mexicans in some of our cities, he has about one half as much chance to get through high school as a white baby. He has one third as much chance to get through college as a white student. He has about a third as much chance to be a professional man, about half as much chance to own a house. He has about four times as much chance that he will be out of work in his life as the white baby. I think we can do better. I don't want the talents of any American to go to waste.

I know that there are those who say that we want to turn everything over to the Government. I don't at all. I want the individuals to meet their responsibilities and I want the states to meet their responsibilities but I think there is also a national responsibility.

The argument has been used against every piece of social legislation in the last 25 years. The people of the United States individually could not have developed the Tennessee Valley. Collectively they could have.

A cotton farmer in Georgia or a peanut farmer, or a dairy farmer in Wisconsin or Minnesota, he cannot protect himself against the forces of supply and demand in the market place but working together in effective governmental programs he can do so.

Seventeen million Americans who live over 65 on an average Social Security check of about $78.00 a month, they are not able to sustain themselves individually but they can sustain themselves through the Social Security system.

I don't believe in big government, but I believe in effective governmental action. And I think that is the only way that the United States is going to maintain its freedom. It is the only way we are going to move ahead. I think we can do a better job. I think we are going to have to do a better job if we are going to meet the responsibilities which time and events have placed upon us.

We cannot turn the job over to anyone else. If the United States fails, then the whole cause of freedom fails and I think it depends in great measure on what we do here in this country.

The reason Franklin Roosevelt was a good neighbor in Latin America was because he was a good neighbor in the United States, because they felt that American society was moving again. I want us to recapture that image. I want people in Latin America and Africa and Asia to start to look to America to see how we are doing things, to wonder what the President of the United States is doing and not to look at Khrushchev or look at the Chinese Communists. That is the obligation upon our generation.

In 1933, Franklin Roosevelt said in his inaugural that this generation of Americans has a rendezvous with destiny. I think our generation of Americans has the same rendezvous. The question now is: can freedom be maintained under the most severe attack it has ever known? I think it can be, and I think in the final analysis it depends upon what we do here. I think it is time America started moving again.

SMITH: And now the opening statement by Vice President Richard M. Nixon.

NIXON: Mr. Smith, Senator Kennedy. The things that Senator Kennedy has said, many of us can agree with. There is no question but that we cannot discuss our internal affairs in the United States without recognizing that they have a tremendous bearing on our international position. There is no question but that this nation cannot stand still because we are in a deadly competition, a competition not only with the men in the Kremlin, but the men in Peking. We are ahead in this competition as Senator Kennedy I think has implied, but when you are in a race the only way to stay ahead is to move ahead. And I subscribe completely to the spirit that Senator Kennedy has expressed tonight, the spirit that the United States should move ahead.

Where then do we disagree?

I think we disagree on the implication of his remarks tonight, and on the statements that he has made on many occasions during his campaign to the effect that the United States has been standing still. We heard tonight for example, the statement made that our growth in national product last year was the lowest of any industrial nation in the world.

Now, last year, of course, was 1958. That happened to be a recession year, but when we look at the growth of GNP this year, a year of recovery, we find that it is six and nine tenths percent and one of the highest in the world today. More about that later.

Looking, then, to this problem of how the United States should move ahead and where the United States is moving, I think it is well that we take the advice of a very famous campaigner: Let's look at the record.

Is the United States standing still?

Is it true that this administration, as Senator Kennedy has charged, has been an administration of retreat, of defeat, of stagnation?

Is it true that as far as this country is concerned in the field of electric power, in all of the fields that he has mentioned, we have not been moving ahead?

Well, we have a comparison that we can make. We have the record of the Truman Administration of seven and one-half years and the seven and one-half years of the Eisenhower Administration.

When we compare these two records in the areas that Senator Kennedy has discussed tonight, I think we find that America has been moving ahead.

Let's take the schools. We have built more schools in this seven and one-half years than we have in the previous seven and one-half, for that matter in the previous twenty years.

Let's take hydroelectric power. We have developed more hydroelectric power in these seven and one-half years than was developed in any previous administration in history.

Let us take hospitals. We find more have been built in this administration than in the previous administration. The same is true of highways.

Let's put it in terms that all of us can understand.

We often hear gross national product discussed. And in that respect may I say that when we compare the growth in this administration with that of the previous administration that then there was a total growth of 11 percent over seven years. In this administration there has been a total growth of 19 percent over seven years.

That shows that there has been more growth in this administration than in its predecessor, but let's not put it there. Let's put it in terms of the average family.

What has happened to you?

We find that your wages have gone up five times as much in the Eisenhower Administration as they did in the Truman Administration.

What about the prices you pay?

We find that the prices you pay went up five times as much in the Truman Administration as they did in the Eisenhower Administration.

What is the net result of this?

This means that the average family income went up fifteen percent in the Eisenhower years as against two percent in the Truman years.

Now, this is not standing still, but good as this record is, may I emphasize it isn't enough. A record is never something to stand on. It is something to build on. And in building on this record I believe we have the secret for progress; we know the way to progress and I think first of all our own record proves that we know the way.

Senator Kennedy has suggested that he believes he knows the way.

I respect the sincerity with which he makes that suggestion but, on the one hand, when we look at the various programs that he offers, they do not seem to be new, they seem to be simply retreads of the programs of the Truman Administration which preceded it, and I would suggest that during the course of the evening he might indicate those areas in which his programs are new, where they will mean more progress than we had then.

What kind of programs are we for?

We are for programs that will expand educational opportunities, that will give to all Americans their equal chance for education, for all of the things which are necessary and dear to the hearts of our people.

We are for programs in addition which will see that our medical care for the aged is much better handled than it is at the present time.

Here again may I indicate that Senator Kennedy and I are not in disagreement as to the aim. We want to see that they do have adequate medical care. The question is the means.

I think that the means that I advocate will reach that goal better than the means that he advocates.

I could give better examples but for whatever it is, whether it's in the field of housing or health or medical care or schools or the development of electric power, we have programs which we believe will move America, move her forward and build on the wonderful record that we have made over these past seven and one-half years.

Now, when we look at these programs, might I suggest that in evaluating them, we often have a tendency to say that the test of a program is how much you are spending. I will concede that in all the areas to which I have referred, Senator Kennedy would have the federal government spend more than I would have it spend.

I figured out the cost of the Democratic platform. It runs a minimum of $13.2 billion a year more than we are presently spending to a maximum of $18 billion a year more than we are presently spending.

Now, the Republican platform will cost more too. It will cost a minimum of $4 billion a year more, a maximum of $4.9 billion a year more than we are presently spending.

Now, does this mean that his program is better than ours?

Not at all, because it isn't a question of how much the federal government spends, it isn't a question of which Government does the most, it's a question of which administration does the right things, and in our case I do believe that our programs will stimulate the creative energies of 180 million free Americans.

I believe the programs that Senator Kennedy advocates will have a tendency to stifle those creative energies.

I believe, in other words, that his programs would lead to the stagnation of the motive power that we need in this country to get progress.

The final point that I would like to make is this: Senator Kennedy has suggested in his speeches that we lack compassion for the poor, for the old, and for others that are unfortunate. Let us understand throughout this campaign that his motives and mine are sincere. I know what it means to be poor. I know what it means to see people who are unemployed. I know Senator Kennedy feels as deeply about these problems as I do but our disagreement is not about the goals for America but only about the means to reach those goals.

SMITH: Thank you, Mr. Nixon.

That completes the opening statements and now the candidates will answer questions or comment upon one another's answers to questions put by correspondents of the networks.

The correspondents.

VANOCUR: I am Sander Vanocur, *NBC News.*

WARREN: I am Charles Warren, *Mutual News.*

NOVINS: I am Stuart Novins, *CBS News.*

FLEMING: Bob Fleming, the *ABC News.*

SMITH: The first question, to Senator Kennedy, from Mr. Fleming.

FLEMING: Senator, the Vice President in his campaign has said that you were naive and at times immature. He has raised the question of leadership. On this issue why do you think people should vote for you rather than the Vice President?

KENNEDY: The Vice President and I came to the Congress together in 1946. We both served on the Labor Committee. I have been there now for 14 years, the same time that he has, so that our experience in government is comparable.

Secondly, I think the question is: what are the programs that we advocate? What is the party record that we lead?

I come out of the Democratic Party which in this century has produced Woodrow Wilson and Franklin Roosevelt and Harry Truman and which supported and sustained these programs which I have discussed tonight.

Mr. Nixon comes out of the Republican Party. He was nominated by it. And it is a fact that through most of these last 25 years the Republican leadership has opposed federal aid for education, medical care for the aged, development of the Tennessee Valley, development of our natural resources. I think Mr. Nixon is an effective leader of his party. I hope he would grant me the same. The question before us is which point of view and which party do we want to lead the United States.

SMITH: Mr. Nixon, would you like to comment on the statement?

NIXON: I have no comment.

SMITH: The next question, Mr. Novins.

NOVINS: Mr. Vice President, your campaign stresses the value of your 8-year experience and the question arises as to whether that experience was as an observer or as a participant or as an initiator of policy making. Would you tell us, please, specifically, what major proposals you have made in the last eight years that have been adopted by the administration?

NIXON: It would be rather difficult to cover them in eight—in two and one-half minutes. I would suggest that these proposals could be mentioned: First, after each of my foreign trips, I have made recommendations that have been adopted. For example, after my first trip abroad, I strongly recommended that we increase our exchange programs particularly as they related to exchange of persons, of leaders in the labor field and in the information field. After my trip to South America, I made recommendations that a separate inter-American lending agency be set up which the South American nations would like much better than to participate in the lending agencies which treated all the countries of the world the same.

I have made other recommendations after each of the other trips. For example, after my trip abroad to Hungary, I made some recommendations with regard to the Hungarian refugee situation which were adopted not only by the President but some of them were enacted into law by the Congress.

Within the Administration as Chairman of the President's Committee on Price Stability and Economic Growth, I have had the opportunity to make recommendations which have been adopted within the Administration and which I think have been reasonably effective.

I know Senator Kennedy suggested in his speech at Cleveland that the Committee had not been particularly effective. I would only suggest that while we do not take credit for it, I would not presume to, that since the Committee has been formed, the price line has been held very well within the United States.

KENNEDY: Well, I would say, in the latter, that the—and that's what I found somewhat unsatisfactory about the figures, Mr. Nixon, that you used in your previous speech, when you talked about the Truman Administration. Mr. Truman came to office in 1944 and at the end of the war and difficulties that were facing the United States during that period of transition, 1946, when price controls were lifted. So it is rather difficult using an over-all figure, taking those seven and one-half years and comparing them to the last eight years. I prefer to take the over-all percentage record of the last twenty years of the Democrats and the eight years of the Republicans to show an over-all period of growth.

In regard to price stability, I am not aware that the Committee did produce recommendations that ever were certainly before the Congress from the point of view of legislation in regard to controlling prices.

In regard to the exchange of students of labor unions, I am chairman of the Subcommittee on Africa. I think that one of the most unfortunate phases of our policy towards that country was the very minute number of exchanges that we had.

I think it is true of Latin America also. We did come forward with a program of students for the Congo of over three hundred, which was more than the federal government had for all of Africa the previous year. So that I don't think that we have moved, at least in those two areas, with sufficient vigor. . . .

❧ 28 ❧

John F. Kennedy's Inaugural Address*

(1961)

ON JANUARY 20, 1961, as on every presidential inauguration day, the nation was governed by one president until noon and by another one afterward. The contrast between the outgoing president, Dwight D. Eisenhower, and his incoming successor, John F. Kennedy, was dramatic and visible: the youngest man ever to be elected president (Kennedy was forty-three) was replacing the oldest man yet to leave the office (Eisenhower was seventy); a Democrat was replacing a Republican; a celebrated World War II combat hero was replacing a celebrated World War II commander; and a professional politician who had served three terms in the House of Representatives and two terms as the junior senator from Massachusetts was replacing a career military leader whose first and only elective office was the presidency. Most important, perhaps, Kennedy's election replaced a defender of caution, prudence, and restraint with an advocate of change and energetic leadership.

The new president's inaugural address, delivered outdoors from the East Front of the Capitol on a bright but bitterly cold day, accentuated most of these contrasts. Kennedy emphasized his youth by noting that "the torch has been passed to a new generation of Americans—born in this century." He reached out to the Soviet Union: "Let us never negotiate out of fear. But let us never fear to negotiate." But he also pledged that "we shall pay any price, bear any burden, meet any hardship, support any friend, oppose any foe to assure the survival and the success of liberty." Finally, in the best-remembered phrase of his presidency, Kennedy summoned the idealism of the American people: "ask not what your country can do for you—ask what you can do for your country."

Kennedy's foreign policy was prefigured by his inaugural address. He negotiated an important nuclear test ban treaty with the Soviet Union.

*Go to *http://www.cc.columbia.edu/acis/bartleby/inaugural/pres56.html*

But he also resisted Communist aggression in a number of global settings, including Berlin, Cuba, and Vietnam. Scholars continue to debate whether Kennedy, having sent 16,500 American soldiers to help
defend South Vietnam, would have escalated the war had he lived to
serve a second term.

As it happened, Kennedy did not live to complete even his first term.
During the fall of 1963, the president made several trips around the
country to build support for his 1964 reelection bid. While riding
through Dallas, Texas, in an open car on November 22, Kennedy was
shot in the head and neck. Shortly afterward, he died at a nearby hospi-
tal without having regained consciousness. Although police quickly apprehended his assassin, ex-Marine and Communist sympathizer Lee
Harvey Oswald, Oswald's own murder while in police custody by Dallas nightclub owner Jack Ruby fostered speculation that the Kennedy
assassination may have been the product of a conspiracy. Nonetheless, a
special presidential commission headed by Chief Justice Earl Warren
concluded in 1964 that Oswald had acted alone.

The combination of Kennedy's youth and glamour and his sudden,
violent death has given the late president a special place in the consciousness of the American people. Polls often find that the public re-
gards Kennedy as the greatest president in history, a verdict not shared
even by admiring historians.

⁂ ⁂ ⁂

We observe today not a victory of party but a celebration of freedom—sym-
bolizing an end as well as a beginning—signifying renewal as well as change.
For I have sworn before you and Almighty God the same solemn oath our forebears prescribed nearly a century and three quarters ago.

The world is very different now. For man holds in his mortal hands the
power to abolish all forms of human poverty and all forms of human life. And
yet the same revolutionary beliefs for which our forebears fought are still at issue around the globe—the belief that the rights of man come not from the
generosity of the state but from the hand of God.

We dare not forget today that we are the heirs of that first revolution. Let
the word go forth from this time and place, to friend and foe alike, that the
torch has been passed to a new generation of Americans—born in this century,
tempered by war, disciplined by a hard and bitter peace, proud of our ancient
heritage—and unwilling to witness or permit the slow undoing of those hu-

man rights to which this nation has always been committed, and to which we are committed today at home and around the world.

Let every nation know, whether it wishes us well or ill, that we shall pay any price, bear any burden, meet any hardship, support any friend, oppose any foe to assure the survival and the success of liberty.

This much we pledge—and more.

To those old allies whose cultural and spiritual origins we share, we pledge the loyalty of faithful friends. United, there is little we cannot do in a host of cooperative ventures. Divided, there is little we can do—for we dare not meet a powerful challenge at odds and split asunder.

To those new states whom we welcome to the ranks of the free, we pledge our word that one form of colonial control shall not have passed away merely to be replaced by a far more iron tyranny. We shall not always expect to find them supporting our view. But we shall always hope to find them strongly support-ing their own freedom—and to remember that, in the past, those who foolish-ly sought power by riding the back of the tiger ended up inside.

To those peoples in the huts and villages of half the globe struggling to break the bonds of mass misery, we pledge our best efforts to help them help themselves, for whatever period is required—not because the communists may be doing it, not because we seek their votes, but because it is right. If a free society cannot help the many who are poor, it cannot save the few who are rich.

To our sister republics south of our border, we offer a special pledge—to convert our good words into good deeds—in a new alliance for progress—to assist free men and free governments in casting off the chains of poverty. But this peaceful revolution of hope cannot become the prey of hostile powers. Let all our neighbors know that we shall join with them to oppose aggression or subversion anywhere in the Americas. And let every other power know that this Hemisphere intends to remain the master of its own house.

To that world assembly of sovereign states, the United Nations, our last best hope in an age where the instruments of war have far outpaced the instru-ments of peace, we renew our pledge of support—to prevent it from becoming merely a forum for invective—to strengthen its shield of the new and the weak—and to enlarge the area in which its writ may run.

Finally, to those nations who would make themselves our adversary, we offer not a pledge but a request: that both sides begin anew the quest for peace, be-fore the dark powers of destruction unleashed by science engulf all humanity in planned or accidental self-destruction.

We dare not tempt them with weakness. For only when our arms are sufficient beyond doubt can we be certain beyond doubt that they will never be employed.

But neither can two great and powerful groups of nations take comfort from our present course—both sides overburdened by the cost of modern weapons, both rightly alarmed by the steady spread of the deadly atom, yet both racing to alter that uncertain balance of terror that stays the hand of mankind's final war.

So let us begin anew—remembering on both sides that civility is not a sign of weakness, and sincerity is always subject to proof. Let us never negotiate out of fear. But let us never fear to negotiate.

Let both sides explore what problems unite us instead of belaboring those problems which divide us.

Let both sides, for the first time, formulate serious and precise proposals for the inspection and control of arms—and bring the absolute power to destroy other nations under the absolute control of all nations.

Let both sides seek to invoke the wonders of science instead of its terrors. Together let us explore the stars, conquer the deserts, eradicate disease, tap the ocean depths and encourage the arts and commerce.

Let both sides unite to heed in all corners of the earth the command of Isaiah—to "undo the heavy burdens . . . (and) let the oppressed go free."

And if a beach-head of cooperation may push back the jungle of suspicion, let both sides join in creating a new endeavor, not a new balance of power, but a new world of law, where the strong are just and the weak secure and the peace preserved.

All this will not be finished in the first one hundred days. Nor will it be finished in the first one thousand days, nor in the life of this Administration, nor even perhaps in our lifetime on this planet. But let us begin.

In your hands, my fellow citizens, more than mine, will rest the final success or failure of our course. Since this country was founded, each generation of Americans has been summoned to give testimony to its national loyalty. The graves of young Americans who answered the call to service surround the globe.

Now the trumpet summons us again—not as a call to bear arms, though arms we need—not as a call to battle, though embattled we are—but a call to bear the burden of a long twilight struggle, year in and year out, "rejoicing in hope, patient in tribulation"—a struggle against the common enemies of man: tyranny, poverty, disease and war itself.

Can we forge against these enemies a grand and global alliance, North and South, East and West, that can assure a more fruitful life for all mankind? Will you join in that historic effort?

In the long history of the world, only a few generations have been granted the role of defending freedom in its hours of maximum danger. I do not shrink from this responsibility—I welcome it. I do not believe that any of us would exchange places with any other people or any other generation. The energy, the faith, the devotion which we bring to this endeavor will light our country and all who serve it—and the glow from that fire can truly light the world.

And so, my fellow Americans: ask not what your country can do for you— ask what you can do for your country.

My fellow citizens of the world: ask not what America will do for you, but what together we can do for the freedom of man.

Finally, whether you are citizens of America or citizens of the world, ask of us here the same high standards of strength and sacrifice which we ask of you. With a good conscience our only sure reward, with history the final judge of our deeds, let us go forth to lead the land we love, asking His blessing and His help, but knowing that here on earth God's work must truly be our own.

⋠ 29 ⋗

The Cuban Missile Crisis

John F. Kennedy's Letter to Soviet Premier Nikita Khrushchev

(1962)

SOON AFTER BECOMING PRESIDENT IN 1961, President John F. Kennedy endorsed a plan developed by the Central Intelligence Agency (CIA) during the Eisenhower administration to arm, train, and land approximately 1,400 Cuban exiles in Cuba in an attempt to overthrow the Communist government of Fidel Castro. The April 17, 1961, operation, known as the Bay of Pigs invasion after the location in Cuba where the exile forces landed, was a complete failure. All but two hundred of the invading Cubans were captured, and the United States was embarrassed before the world. Soon afterward, speaking at a press conference, Kennedy accepted full blame for the failure.

Both Castro and his patron, Soviet leader Nikita Khrushchev, were convinced that the United States would launch a subsequent full-scale invasion of Cuba. For this reason and one other—the Soviet Union's desire to add to the twenty nuclear missiles it already had aimed directly at the United States—Khrushchev secretly placed sixty-six intermediate-range missiles in Cuba.

On October 15, 1962, Kennedy received photographic evidence of the Soviet nuclear presence in Cuba. He secretly formed an "executive committee" (ExCom) of high administration officials to prepare the American response. ExCom included Secretary of State Dean Rusk, Secretary of Defense Robert S. McNamara, Attorney General Robert F. Kennedy, CIA director John McCone, and a number of military leaders, among others. Publicly, the president carried on business as usual, even appearing at a rally for Democratic congressional candidates in Chicago.

ExCom's initial judgment was that the United States should launch an air strike against the missile sites. Taking a more cautious and less overtly aggressive approach, Kennedy decided instead to impose a naval blockade around Cuba to prevent Soviet ships from bringing in supplies. Through diplomatic channels and in a televised address to the nation on October 22 (the first public report of what had been happening), Kennedy then demanded that the Soviet missiles be withdrawn. Nuclear war between the United States and the Soviet Union seemed more likely than at any time before or since.

Soviet reaction to the blockade and to the president's demand was hard to ascertain. A conciliatory message from Khrushchev was received on October 26; a harsh one followed on October 27. Kennedy decided to ignore the latter and reply to the former. Kennedy's October 27 letter to Khrushchev laid out part of the basis for the agreement that ended the crisis: the Soviet missiles would be removed in return for the president's pledge not to invade Cuba. (Khrushchev responded favorably the following day.) In 1989, at a conference of officials who had participated in their respective nations' decision making during the Cuban missile crisis, it was confirmed that Kennedy also had promised to remove obsolete American nuclear missiles from near the Soviet border in Turkey.

※ ※ ※

Dear Mr. Chairman:

I have read your letter of October 26th with great care and welcomed the statement of your desire to seek a prompt solution to the problem. The first thing that needs to be done, however, is for work to cease on offensive missile bases in Cuba and for all weapons systems in Cuba capable of offensive use to be rendered inoperable, under effective United Nations arrangements.

Assuming this is done promptly, I have given my representatives in New York instructions that will permit them to work out this weekend—in cooperation with the Acting Secretary General and your representative—an arrangement for a permanent solution to the Cuban problem along the lines suggested in your letter of October 26th. As I read your letter, the key elements of your proposals—which seem generally acceptable as I understand them—are as follows:

1) You would agree to remove these weapons systems from Cuba under appropriate United Nations observation and supervision; and undertake, with suitable safeguards, to halt the further introduction of such weapons systems into Cuba.

2) We, on our part, would agree—upon the establishment of adequate arrangements through the United Nations to ensure the carrying out and continuation of these commitments—(a) to remove promptly the quarantine measures now in effect and (b) to give assurances against an invasion of Cuba. I am confident that other nations of the Western Hemisphere would be prepared to do likewise.

If you will give your representative similar instructions, there is no reason why we should not be able to complete these arrangements and announce them to the world within a couple of days. The effect of such a settlement on easing world tensions would enable us to work toward a more general arrangement regarding "other armaments," as proposed in your second letter which you made public. I would like to say again that the United States is very much interested in reducing tensions and halting the arms race; and if your letter signifies that you are prepared to discuss a detente affecting NATO and the Warsaw Pact, we are quite prepared to consider with our allies any useful proposals.

But the first ingredient, let me emphasize, is the cessation of work on missile sites in Cuba and measures to render such weapons inoperable, under effective international guarantees. The continuation of this threat, or a prolonging of this discussion concerning Cuba by linking these problems to the broader questions of European and world security, would surely lead to an intensification of the Cuban crisis and a grave risk to the peace of the world. For this reason I hope we can quickly agree along the lines outlined in this letter and in your letter of October 26th.

Lyndon B. Johnson's "Great Society" Speech*
(1964)

VICE PRESIDENT LYNDON B. JOHNSON succeeded to the
presidency when President John F. Kennedy was assassinated in
Dallas, Texas, on November 22, 1963. Arriving that evening in Washington, Johnson pledged to a national television audience that the
watchword of his administration would be, "Let us continue." Capitalizing on the public disposition to support virtually anything the slain
president had proposed, Johnson persuaded Congress to enact most of
the unfinished business of Kennedy's "New Frontier" agenda in 1964,
including the most sweeping civil rights act in history and a large reduction in federal income taxes.

Johnson, who had served as Senate majority leader during the 1950s
and unsuccessfully challenged Kennedy for the 1960 Democratic presidential nomination, also wanted to make his own mark on history.
Within a few months, he chose the phrase "Great Society" as the theme
for his administration. In a May 22, 1964, commencement address at
the University of Michigan, Johnson developed the Great Society theme
in detail.

According to Johnson, the United States already had become "the
rich society and the powerful society" and now was challenged to reach
"upward." The effort to build a Great Society would have two main
goals. The first was "an end to poverty and racial injustice." The other
was "to advance the quality of our American civilization." As Johnson
described it, "the Great Society is a place where every child can find
knowledge to enrich his mind and to enlarge his talents. It is a place
where leisure is a welcome chance to build and reflect, not a feared cause
of boredom and restlessness. It is a place where the city of man serves
not only the needs of the body and the demands of commerce, but the
desire for beauty and the hunger for community."

*Go to *http://hs1.hst.msu.edu/~hst306/documents/great.html*

Johnson ran for president in 1964 against Republican senator Barry Goldwater of Arizona, an ardent conservative whom many viewed as a dangerous extremist. In addition to winning a personal landslide victory, Johnson brought in on his coattails a Congress that was two-thirds Democratic. In 1965 and 1966, the Eighty-ninth Congress passed a long list of Great Society initiatives: the Voting Rights Act, the Older Americans Act, the Freedom of Information Act, and legislation to establish Medicare and Medicaid, the National Endowment of the Arts and Humanities, the Department of Transportation, the Department of Housing and Urban Development, highway beautification, and urban mass transit.

Yet these accomplishments, although substantial, did not fulfill Johnson's vision of the Great Society. Problems developed in the implementation of many of the programs, and poverty proved to be more intractable than had been imagined. In addition, the war in Vietnam diverted attention and funding from the president's domestic agenda.

🐜 🐜 🐜

. . . The purpose of protecting the life of our Nation and preserving the liberty of our citizens is to pursue the happiness of our people. Our success in that pursuit is the test of our success as a nation. For a century we labored to settle and to subdue a continent. For half a century, we called upon unbounded invention and untiring industry to create an order of plenty for all of our people. The challenge of the next half century is whether we have the wisdom to use that wealth to enrich and elevate our national life, and to advance the quality of our American civilization.

Your imagination, your initiative and your indignation will determine whether we build a society where progress is the servant of our needs, or a society where old values and new visions are buried under unbridled growth.

For in your time we have the opportunity to move not only toward the rich society and the powerful society, but upward to the Great Society. The Great Society rests on abundance and liberty for all. It demands an end to poverty and racial injustice, to which we are totally committed in our time. But that is just the beginning.

The Great Society is a place where every child can find knowledge to enrich his mind and to enlarge his talents. It is a place where leisure is a welcome chance to build and reflect, not a feared cause of boredom and restlessness. It is a place where the city of man serves not only the needs of the body and the demands of commerce, but the desire for beauty and the hunger for community.

It is a place where man can renew contact with nature. It is a place which honors creation for its own sake and for what it adds to the understanding of the race. It is a place where men are more concerned with the quality of their goals than the quantity of their goods. But most of all, the great society is not a safe harbor, a resting place, a final objective, a finished work. It is a challenge constantly renewed, beckoning us toward a destiny where the meaning of our lives matches the marvelous products of our labor.

So I want to talk to you today about three places where we begin to build the Great Society—in our cities, in our countryside, and in our classrooms. . . .

Aristotle said, "Men come together in cities in order to live, but they remain together in order to live the good life."

It is harder and harder to live the good life in American cities today. The catalogue of ills is long: There is the decay of the centers and the despoiling of the suburbs. There is not enough housing for our people or transportation for our traffic. Open land is vanishing and old landmarks are violated. Worst of all, expansion is eroding the precious and time-honored values of community with neighbors and communion with nature. The loss of these values breeds loneliness and boredom and indifference. Our society will never be great until our cities are great. Today the frontier of imagination and innovation is inside those cities, and not beyond their borders. . . .

A second place where we begin to build the Great Society is in our countryside. We have always prided ourselves on being not only America the strong and America the free, but America the beautiful. Today that beauty is in danger. The water we drink, the food we eat, the very air that we breathe, are threatened with pollution. Our parks are overcrowded. Our seashores overburdened. Green fields and dense forests are disappearing.

A few years ago we were greatly concerned about the Ugly American. Today we must act to prevent an Ugly America.

For once the battle is lost, once our natural splendor is destroyed, it can never be recaptured. And once man can no longer walk with beauty or wonder at nature, his spirit will wither and his sustenance be wasted.

A third place to build the Great Society is in the classrooms of America. There your children's lives will be shaped. Our society will not be great until every young mind is set free to scan the farthest reaches of thought and imagination. We are still far from that goal. . . . In many places, classrooms are overcrowded and curricula are outdated. Most of our qualified teachers are underpaid, and many of our paid teachers are unqualified.

So we must give every child a place to sit and a teacher to learn from.

Poverty must not be a bar to learning, and learning must offer an escape from poverty.

But more classrooms and more teachers are not enough. We must seek an educational system which grows in excellence as it grows in size. This means better training for our teachers. It means preparing youth to enjoy their hours of leisure as well as their hours of labor. It means exploring new techniques of teaching, to find new ways to stimulate the love of learning and the capacity for creation.

These are three of the central issues of the Great Society. While our government has many programs directed at those issues, I do not pretend that we have the full answer to those problems. But I do promise this: We are going to assemble the best thought and the broadest knowledge from all over the world to find those answers for America. . . .

There are those timid souls who say this battle cannot be won, that we are condemned to a soulless wealth. I do not agree. We have the power to shape the civilization that we want. But we need your will, your labor, your hearts, if we are to build that kind of society.

Those who came to this land sought to build more than just a new country. They sought a free world.

So I have come here today to your campus to say that you can make their vision our reality. Let us from this moment begin our work so that in the future men will look back and say: It was then, after a long and weary way, that man turned the exploits of his genius to the full enrichment of his life.

Thank you. Goodbye.

❧ 31 ❧
Lyndon B. Johnson's Gulf of Tonkin Message*
(1964)

T WO THEMES DOMINATED the five-and-one-half-year presidency of Lyndon B. Johnson: the Great Society (see Document 30, p.

*Go to *http://www.luminet.net/~tgort/johnson.htm*

For the text of the Gulf of Tonkin Resolution passed by Congress, go to *http://hs1.hst. msu.edu/~hst306/documents/tonkin.html*

166) and the war in Vietnam. Much to Johnson's distress, the latter gradually overshadowed the former.

Since winning its independence from France on the battlefield in 1954, Vietnam had been divided into two countries: Communist North Vietnam (headed by the hero of the revolution, Ho Chi Minh) and anti-Communist South Vietnam. Unsatisfied with this arrangement, North Vietnam and the Vietcong guerrillas in the South had been fighting the South Vietnamese government in an effort to reunify the country under Communist rule. President Dwight D. Eisenhower had sent weapons and economic aid to South Vietnam during the 1950s. His successor, John F. Kennedy, added 16,500 U.S. military advisers to the war effort.

In early 1964 aides to Johnson privately drafted a congressional resolution that would give the president a virtual blank check to conduct the Vietnam War as he saw fit. Johnson feared that such a proposal would generate too much controversy. But on August 2 and 4, 1964, reports reached Washington that two American naval destroyers, the *Maddox* and the *C. Turner Joy,* had been attacked by North Vietnamese patrol boats in the Gulf of Tonkin near North Vietnam. The attack was described as unprovoked. In truth, at the time of the attack the *Maddox* was gathering sensitive intelligence information and the South Vietnamese navy was assaulting North Vietnam, but these facts became public only when the Senate Foreign Relations Committee uncovered them in 1968.

On August 5, 1964, Johnson sent what became known as the "Gulf of Tonkin message" to Congress, urging it to pass a resolution of support for his leadership. The resolution stated that "Congress approves and supports the determination of the President, as Commander-in-Chief, to take all necessary measures to repel any armed attack against the forces of the United States and to prevent further aggression." It also declared that the United States was "prepared, as the President determines, to take all necessary steps, including the use of armed force, to assist any member or protocol state of the Southeast Asia Collective Defense Treaty requesting assistance in defense of its freedom."

On August 7, the Gulf of Tonkin Resolution passed unanimously in the House of Representatives. The Senate approved it the same day by a vote of 88–2.

In later years, as the American military commitment became much larger and more controversial, Johnson claimed that the Gulf of Tonkin Resolution provided ample authority for his administration's policies, which included assigning more than 500,000 American soldiers to active combat in Vietnam. Publicly, Under Secretary of State Nicholas Katzenbach told Congress in 1967 that the resolution, in conjunction with American treaty obligations, was the "functional equivalent" of a declaration of war, giving rise to charges of an "imperial presidency." Privately, Johnson compared the resolution to "grandma's nightshirt—it covered everything."

Despite the American military effort, the Vietcong and North Vietnamese continued their assault on the government of South Vietnam. The war became increasingly unpopular in the United States, first on college campuses, then nationwide. In a largely symbolic act, Congress repealed the Gulf of Tonkin Resolution on December 31, 1970. By then, Johnson had withdrawn from politics and Richard Nixon, a Republican, had been elected.

In 1973, after four years in office, the Nixon administration concluded an agreement with North Vietnam that ended direct U.S. participation in the war in exchange for the return of American prisoners. Nixon secretly promised South Vietnamese president Nguyen Van Thieu that the United States would not allow his government to be overthrown by the Communists. But Nixon resigned as president in 1974 (see Document 37, p. 201), and when South Vietnam was unable to defend itself against a North Vietnamese offensive in 1975, Congress refused to allow President Gerald R. Ford to reinvolve the United States in the fighting.

🏮 🏮 🏮

To the Congress of the United States:

Last night I announced to the American people that the North Vietnamese regime had conducted further deliberate attacks against U.S. naval vessels operating in international waters, and that I had therefore directed air action against gun boats and supporting facilities used in these hostile operations. This air action has now been carried out with substantial damage to the boats and facilities. Two U.S. aircraft were lost in the action.

After consultation with the leaders of both parties in the Congress, I further announced a decision to ask the Congress for a Resolution expressing the unity and determination of the United States in supporting freedom and in protecting peace in Southeast Asia.

These latest actions of the North Vietnamese regime have given a new and grave turn to the already serious situation in Southeast Asia. Our commitments in that area are well known to the Congress. They were first made in 1954 by President Eisenhower. They were further defined in the Southeast Asia Collective Defense Treaty approved by the Senate in February 1955.

This Treaty with its accompanying protocol obligates the United States and other members to act in accordance with their Constitutional processes to meet Communist aggression against any of the parties or protocol states.

Our policy in Southeast Asia has been consistent and unchanged since 1954. I summarized it on June 2 in four simple propositions:

1. *America keeps her word.* Here as elsewhere, we must and shall honor our commitments.

2. *The issue is the future of Southeast Asia as a whole.* A threat to any nation in that region is a threat to all, and a threat to us.

3. *Our purpose is peace.* We have no military, political or territorial ambitions in the area.

4. *This is not just a jungle war, but a struggle for freedom on every front of human activity.* Our military and economic assistance to South Vietnam and Laos in particular has the purpose of helping these countries to repel aggression and strengthen their independence.

The threat to the free nations of Southeast Asia has long been clear. The North Vietnamese regime has constantly sought to take over South Vietnam and Laos. This Communist regime has violated the Geneva Accords for Vietnam. It has systematically conducted a campaign of subversion, which includes the direction, training, and supply of personnel and arms for the conduct of guerrilla warfare in South Vietnamese territory. In Laos, the North Vietnamese regime has maintained military forces, used Laotian territory for infiltration into South Vietnam, and most recently carried out combat operations—all in direct violation of the Geneva Agreements of 1962.

In recent months, the actions of the North Vietnamese regime have become steadily more threatening. In May, following new acts of Communist aggression in Laos, the United States undertook reconnaissance flights over Laotian territory, at the request of the Government of Laos. These flights had the essential mission of determining the situation in territory where Communist forces were preventing inspection by the International Control Commission. When the Communists attacked these aircraft, I responded by furnishing escort fighters with instructions to fire when fired upon. Thus, these latest North Vietnamese attacks on our naval vessels are not the first direct attack on armed forces of the United States.

As President of the United States I have concluded that I should now ask the Congress, on its part, to join in affirming the national determination that all such attacks will be met, and that the U.S. will continue in its basic policy of assisting the free nations of the area to defend their freedom.

As I have repeatedly made clear, the United States intends no rashness, and seeks no wider war. We must make it clear to all that the United States is united in its determination to bring about the end of Communist subversion and aggression in the area. We seek the full and effective restoration of the international agreements signed in Geneva in 1954, with respect to South Vietnam, and again in Geneva in 1962, with respect to Laos.

I recommend a Resolution expressing the support of the Congress for all necessary action to protect our armed forces and to assist nations covered by the SEATO Treaty. At the same time, I assure the Congress that we shall continue readily to explore any avenues of political solution that will effectively guarantee the removal of Communist subversion and the preservation of the independence of the nations of the area.

The Resolution could well be based upon similar resolutions enacted by the Congress in the past—to meet the threat to Formosa in 1955, to meet the threat to the Middle East in 1957, and to meet the threat in Cuba in 1962. It could state in the simplest terms the resolve and support of the Congress for action to deal appropriately with attacks against our armed forces and to defend freedom and preserve peace in southeast Asia in accordance with the obligations of the United States under the Southeast Asia Treaty. I urge the Congress to enact such a Resolution promptly and thus to give convincing evidence to the aggressive Communist nations, and to the world as a whole, that our policy in Southeast Asia will be carried forward—and that the peace and security of the area will be preserved.

The events of this week would in any event have made the passage of a Congressional Resolution essential. But there is an additional reason for doing so at a time when we are entering on three months of political campaigning. Hostile nations must understand that in such a period the United States will continue to protect its national interests, and that in these matters there is no division among us.

Richard Nixon's China Trip Announcement
(1971)

R ICHARD NIXON'S ELECTION as president in 1968 marked the
greatest political comeback in American history. After losing the
1960 presidential election to John F. Kennedy, Nixon was defeated two
years later in a bid to become governor of California. The day after his
defeat, Nixon angrily declared his retirement from politics. "You won't
have Nixon to kick around anymore," he told a stunned audience of reporters, "because, gentlemen, this is my last press conference." In 1968
Nixon won the Republican presidential nomination with a series of primary victories that convinced party leaders he could still appeal to voters. On election day he eked out a victory over Vice President Hubert
H. Humphrey, the Democratic nominee, that was almost as narrow as
his defeat by Kennedy eight years earlier.

Nixon's political career had been constructed on a foundation of anticommunism. In his first election to the House of Representatives in
1946, Nixon accused incumbent Democrat Jerry Voorhis of being a so-
cialist. Four years later, running for the Senate, Nixon called his opponent, Helen Gahagan Douglas, the "pink lady." In 1952 Nixon ran for
vice president on the ticket headed by Dwight D. Eisenhower by charg-
ing that the Democrats were soft on communism. Most notably, Nixon
gained national fame when, after becoming chair of a subcommittee of
the House Un-American Activities Committee in 1948, he uncovered
evidence that Alger Hiss, a former high-ranking official of the State Department, was a Communist spy.

Nixon's rise to political prominence on the basis of anticommunism
reflected (and contributed to) the tenor of the times. In the late 1940s
the United States and the Soviet Union had ended their World War II
alliance by entering into the Cold War. A long-standing friendship between the United States and China also came to an end when, in 1949, a
Communist revolution led by Mao Zedong overthrew the government
of Chiang Kai-shek. Even after Chiang and his supporters fled to the

offshore island of Formosa, the United States continued to recognize his regime as the legitimate government of China. Relations between the United States and the Maoist government of mainland China were virtually nonexistent; the rhetoric of the two nations was mutually hostile.

Politically, few Democrats or liberal Republicans during the 1950s and 1960s dared broach the subject of better relations with China, for fear of bringing down the wrath of conservatives such as Nixon. It was all the more surprising, then, when on July 15, 1971, President Nixon appeared on national television to announce in a three-and-one-half minute statement that he would be traveling to China sometime in early 1972 at the invitation of the Communist government. The purpose of the visit, Nixon said, would be "to seek the normalization of relations" between the United States and China. The president also revealed that the trip had been arranged at his direction through a series of secret visits to China by his national security adviser, Henry Kissinger, during the preceding two years. Nixon made the China trip, which was politically and diplomatically successful, in February 1972.

Many analysts believe that only a staunch anti-Communist like Nixon could have ended American hostility to such a bitter enemy without provoking widespread political opposition. Part of his motive seems to have been to take advantage of the developing hostility between China and the Soviet Union by forging a relationship between the United States and China. Playing each Communist nation against the other, Nixon also was welcomed to the Soviet Union by Leonid Brezhnev in May 1972. The two leaders concluded their meeting by signing a strategic arms limitation treaty.

Nixon's trips to both China and the Soviet Union were the first by an American president. "Summit" meetings (Winston Churchill coined the term in 1953) between the president and the leader of one or more other nations were rare until World War II but have become common since then.

蕭 蕭 蕭

Good evening.

I have requested this television time tonight to announce a major development in our efforts to build a lasting peace in the world.

As I have pointed out on a number of occasions over the past three years, there can be no stable and enduring peace without the participation of the Peoples [sic] Republic of China and its 750 million people. That is why I have undertaken initiatives in several areas to open the door for more normal relations between our two countries.

In pursuance of that goal, I sent Dr. Kissinger, my Assistant for National Security Affairs, to Peking during his recent world tour for the purpose of having talks with Premier Chou En-lai. The announcement I shall now read is being issued simultaneously in Peking and in the United States.

"Premier Chou En-lai and Dr. Henry Kissinger, President Nixon's Assistant for National Security Affairs, held talks in Peking from July 9 to 11, 1971. Knowing of President Nixon's expressed desire to visit the Peoples Republic of China, Premier Chou En-lai, on behalf of the Government of the Peoples Republic of China, has extended an invitation to President Nixon to visit China at an appropriate date before May 1972. President Nixon has accepted the invitation with pleasure."

The meeting between the leaders of China and the United States is to seek the normalization of relations between the two countries and also to exchange views on questions of concern to the two sides. In anticipation of the inevitable speculation which will follow this announcement, I want to put our policy in the clearest possible context.

Our action in seeking a new relationship with the Peoples Republic of China will not be at the expense of our old friends. It is not directed against any other nation. We seek friendly relations with all nations. Any nation can be our friend without being any other nation's enemy.

I have taken this action because of my profound conviction that all nations will gain from a reduction of tensions and a better relationship between the United States and the Peoples Republic of China.

It is in that spirit that I will undertake what I deeply hope will become a journey for peace, peace not just for our generation, but for future generations on this earth we share together.

Thank you and good night.

The McGovern-Fraser Commission Report

(1971)

ONE OF THE MAJOR COMPLAINTS of Vice President Hubert H. Humphrey's defeated opponents at the 1968 Democratic National Convention was that they had not been given a fair chance to compete in the delegate selection process. Only about one-third of the convention's delegates were chosen in primaries, and many of the remaining two-thirds were appointed by state party leaders before the election year even began.

Although the 1968 convention made no changes in its own structure, it voted to approve the minority report of its rules committee, which required that all Democratic voters receive "full, meaningful and timely opportunity to participate in the selection of delegates" to the 1972 convention.

In February 1969, in order to implement the convention's decision, the Democratic National Committee created the Commission on Party Structure and Delegate Selection, chaired by Sen. George McGovern of South Dakota and, later, by Rep. Donald Fraser of Minnesota. The McGovern-Fraser Commission, as it came to be known, issued its report, *Mandate for Change,* in September 1971. The report included eighteen detailed guidelines that the state parties were obliged to follow in choosing delegates to the 1972 convention.

The McGovern-Fraser Commission transformed the presidential nominating process. The commission banned a number of traditional practices, including the "unit rule" that allowed each state party to award all of its votes to the candidate who had a majority of its delegation. The commission required that racial minorities, women, and young voters be represented at the national convention in proportion to their share of the population in each state. Most important, the commission demanded that all convention delegates be chosen in an open, participatory process, either a presidential primary or a caucus in which any Democrat could vote and be heard.

To the surprise and dismay of the McGovern-Fraser Commission, most states decided to go the simpler, primary route: by the end of the decade, the number of presidential primaries had doubled from seventeen to thirty-five. Because new primaries required changes in state laws, state Republican parties usually followed the Democrats' lead.

Not just the process but also the politics of presidential nominations was affected by the McGovern-Fraser reforms. In 1960 John F. Kennedy, a Democrat, and eight years later, Richard Nixon, a Republican, had entered primaries, but only as a strategy to persuade party leaders to nominate them. In 1968, after Lyndon B. Johnson withdrew from the presidential race in March, Humphrey received the Democratic nomination without entering a single primary. But, beginning in 1972, the first election to be governed by the McGovern-Fraser rules, party leaders have had no choice but to accept the verdict of the primaries. No one has been nominated for president by either of the two major parties without defeating the other candidates at the ballot box.

Subsequent Democratic rules commissions—including the Mikulski Commission (1976), the Winograd Commission (1980), the Hunt Commission (1984), and the Fairness Commission (1988)—further modified the procedures for presidential nominations. But none has substantially undone the radical changes wrought by the McGovern-Fraser Commission.

༈ ༈ ༈

On November 19 and 20, 1969, the Commission, meeting in open session in Washington, D.C., adopted the following Guidelines for delegate selection. . . .

<h3 style="text-align:center">A-1 Discrimination on the basis of race,
color, creed, or national origin</h3>

The 1964 Democratic National Convention adopted a resolution which conditioned the seating of delegations at future conventions on the assurance that discrimination in any State Party affairs on the grounds of race, color, creed or national origin did not occur. The 1968 Convention adopted the 1964 Convention resolution for inclusion in the Call to the 1972 Convention. In 1966, the Special Equal Rights Committee, which had been created in 1964, adopted six anti-discrimination standards—designated as the "six basic elements"—for the State Parties to meet. These standards were adopted by the Democratic National Committee in January 1968 as its official policy statement.

These actions demonstrate the intention of the Democratic Party to ensure a full opportunity for all minority group members to participate in the delegate selection process. To supplement the requirements of the 1964 and 1968 Conventions, the Commission requires that:

1. State Parties add the six basic elements of the Special Equal Rights Committee to their Party rules and take appropriate steps to secure their implementation;

2. State Parties overcome the effects of past discrimination by affirmative steps to encourage minority group participation, including representation of minority groups on the national convention delegation in reasonable relationship to the group's presence in the population of the State.

A-2 Discrimination on the basis of age or sex

The Commission believes that discrimination on the grounds of age or sex is inconsistent with full and meaningful opportunity to participate in the delegate selection process. Therefore, the Commission requires State Parties to eliminate all vestiges of discrimination on these grounds. Furthermore, the Commission requires State Parties to overcome the effects of past discrimination by affirmative steps to encourage representation on the national convention delegation of young people—defined as people of not more than thirty nor less than eighteen years of age—and women in reasonable relationship to their presence in the population of the State. Moreover, the Commission requires State Parties to amend their Party rules to allow and encourage any Democrat of eighteen years or more to participate in all party affairs.

When State law controls, the Commission requires State Parties to make all feasible efforts to repeal, amend, or otherwise modify such laws to accomplish the stated purpose. . . .

A-5 Existence of party rules

In order for rank-and-file Democrats to have a full and meaningful opportunity to participate in the delegate selection process, they must have access to the substantive and procedural rules which govern the process. In some States the process is not regulated by law or rule, but by resolution of the State Committee and by tradition. In other States, the rules exist, but generally are inaccessible. In still others, rules and laws regulate only the formal aspects of the selection process (e.g., date and place of the State convention) and leave to Par-

ty resolution or tradition the more substantive matters (e.g., intrastate apportionment of votes; rotation of alternates; nomination of delegates).

The Commission believes that any of these arrangements is inconsistent
with the spirit of the Call in that they permit excessive discretion on the part
of Party officials, which may be used to deny or limit full and meaningful opportunity to participate. Therefore, the Commission requires State Parties to
adopt and make available readily accessible statewide Party rules and statutes
which prescribe the State's delegate selection process with sufficient details and
clarity. . . .

Furthermore, the Commission requires State Parties to adopt rules which
will facilitate maximum participation among interested Democrats in the
processes by which National Convention delegates are selected. Among other
things, these rules should provide for dates, times, and public places which
would be most likely to encourage interested Democrats to attend all meetings
involved in the delegate selection process.

The Commission requires State Parties to adopt explicit written Party rules
which provide for uniform times and dates of all meetings involved in the delegate selection process. These meetings and events include caucuses, conventions, committee meetings, primaries, filing deadlines, and Party enrollment
periods. Rules regarding time and date should be uniform in two senses. First,
each stage of the delegate selection process should occur at a uniform time and
date throughout the State. Second, the time and date should be uniform from
year to year. . . .

B-2 Clarity of purpose

An opportunity for full participation in the delegate selection process is not
meaningful unless each Party member can clearly express his preference for
candidates for delegates to the National Convention, or for those who will
select such delegates. In many States, a Party member who wishes to affect
the selection of the delegation must do so by voting for delegates or Party
officials who will engage in many activities unrelated to the delegate selection
process.

Whenever other Party business is mixed, without differentiation, with the
delegate selection process, the Commission requires State Parties to make it
clear to voters how they are participating in a process that will nominate their
Party's candidate for President. Furthermore, in States which employ a convention or committee system, the Commission requires State Parties to clearly
designate the delegate selection procedures as distinct from other Party business. . . .

B-5 Unit rule

In 1968, many States used the unit rule at various stages in the processes by which delegates were selected to the National Convention. The 1968 Convention defined unit rule, did not enforce the unit rule on any delegate in 1968, and added language to the 1972 Call requiring that "the unit rule not be used in any stage of the delegate selection process." In light of the Convention action, the Commission requires State Parties to add to their explicit written rules provisions which forbid the use of the unit rule or the practice of instructing delegates to vote against their stated preferences at any stage of the delegate selection process.

B-6 Adequate representation of minority views on presidential candidates at each stage in the delegate selection process

The Commission believes that a full and meaningful opportunity to participate in the delegate selection process is precluded unless the presidential preference of each Democrat is fairly represented at all levels of the process. Therefore, the Commission urges each State Party to adopt procedures which will provide fair representation of minority views on presidential candidates and recommends that the 1972 Convention adopt a rule requiring State Parties to provide for the representation of minority views to the highest level of the nominating process.

The Commission believes that there are at least two different methods by which a State Party can provide for such representation. First, in at-large elections it can divide delegate votes among presidential candidates in proportion to their demonstrated strength. Second, it can choose delegates from fairly apportioned districts no larger than congressional districts. . . .

C-2 Automatic (ex-officio) delegates. . . .

In some States, certain public or Party officeholders are delegates to county, State and National Conventions by virtue of their official position. The Commission believes that State laws, Party rules and Party resolutions which so provide are inconsistent with the Call to the 1972 Convention for three reasons:

1. The Call requires all delegates to be chosen by primary, convention or committee procedures. Achieving delegate status by virtue of public or Party office is not one of the methods sanctioned by the 1968 Convention.

2. The Call requires all delegates to be chosen by a process which begins within the calendar year of the Convention. Ex-officio delegates usually were elected (or appointed) to their positions before the calendar year of the Convention.

3. The Call requires all delegates to be chosen by a process in which all Democrats have a full and meaningful opportunity to participate. Delegate selection by a process in which certain places on the delegation are not open to competition among Democrats is inconsistent with a full and meaningful opportunity to participate.

Accordingly, the Commission requires State Parties to repeal Party rules or resolutions which provide for ex-officio delegates. When State law controls, the Commission requires State Parties to make all feasible efforts to repeal, amend or otherwise modify such laws to accomplish the stated purpose. . . .

C-4 Premature delegate selection (timeliness)

The 1968 Convention adopted language adding to the Call to the 1972 Convention the requirement that the delegate selection process must begin within the calendar year of the Convention. In many States, Governors, State Chairmen, State, district and county committees who are chosen before the calendar year of the Convention, select—or choose agents to select—the delegates. These practices are inconsistent with the Call.

The Commission believes that the 1968 Convention intended to prohibit any untimely procedures which have any direct bearing on the process by which National Convention delegates are selected. The process by which delegates are nominated is such a procedure. Therefore, the Commission requires State Parties to prohibit any practices by which officials elected or appointed before the calendar year choose nominating committees or propose or endorse a slate of delegates—even when the possibility for a challenge to such slate or committee is provided.

When State law controls, the Commission requires State Parties to make all feasible efforts to repeal, amend, or modify such laws to accomplish the stated purposes. . . .

Conclusion

The Guidelines that we have adopted are designed to open the door to all Democrats who seek a voice in their Party's most important decision: the choice of its presidential nominee. We are concerned with the opportunity to participate, rather than the actual level of participation, although the number of Democrats who vote in their caucuses, meetings and primaries is an important index of the opportunities available to them.

As members of the Commission, we are less concerned with the product of the meetings than the process, although we believe that the product will be improved in the give and take of open fairly conducted meetings.

We believe that popular participation is more than a proud heritage of our party, more even than a first principle. We believe that popular control of the Democratic Party is necessary for its survival.

We do not believe this is an idle threat. When we view our past history and present policies alongside that of the Republican Party, we are struck by one unavoidable fact: our Party is the only major vehicle for peaceful, progressive change in the United States.

If we are not an open party; if we do not represent the demands of change, then the danger is not that people will go to the Republican Party; it is that there will no longer be a way for people committed to orderly change to fulfill their needs and desires within our traditional political system. It is that they will turn to third and fourth party politics or the anti-politics of the street.

We believe that our Guidelines offer an alternative for these people. We believe that the Democratic Party can meet the demands for participation with their adoption. We trust that all Democrats will give the Guidelines their careful consideration.

We are encouraged by the response of state Parties to date. In 40 states and territories the Democratic Party has appointed reform commissions (or sub-committees of the state committee) to investigate ways of modernizing party procedures. Of these, 17 have already issued reports and recommendations. In a number of states, party rules and state laws have already been revised, newly written or amended to insure the opportunity for participation in Party matters by all Democrats. . . .

All of these efforts lead us to the conclusion that the Democratic Party is bent on meaningful change. A great European statesman once said, "All things are possible, even the fact that an action in accord with honor and honesty ultimately appears to be a prudent political investment." We share this sentiment. We are confident that party reform, dictated by our Party's heritage and principles, will insure a strong, winning and united Party.

The War Powers Resolution*

(1973)

THE AMERICAN FAILURE in the Vietnam War belied the belief, widely accepted in the post–World War II era, that the executive branch, with its superior sources of information, its unity of command, and its ability to act with dispatch, should be responsible for determining when and how the nation will go to war. In 1973 Congress passed the War Powers Resolution and, after President Richard Nixon vetoed the act, overrode his veto on November 7 by a margin of 284–135 in the House of Representatives and 75–18 in the Senate.

The War Powers Resolution requires the president to consult with Congress "in every possible instance" before committing American armed forces to hostile or dangerous situations. After committing the armed forces, the president is then charged to report his actions in writing to congressional leaders. Within sixty (or, by special presidential request, ninety) days, the forces must be withdrawn unless Congress votes to authorize their continued involvement. Even within that period, Congress can vote to withdraw the forces.

Despite the act's overwhelming support in Congress, both conservative and liberal opponents proved to be prescient in their criticisms. Conservatives echoed Nixon, who vetoed the act as being "both unconstitutional and dangerous to the best interest of the nation." A few liberals, led by Democratic senator Thomas F. Eagleton of Missouri, noted that the act effectively sanctions virtually any presidential use of force for ninety days. Although Congress has the legal power to force a withdrawal, charged Frank Church, a Democratic senator from Idaho, "I cannot imagine a situation where a President would take us into a foreign war of major proportions under circumstances that would not cause both the public and Congress to rally around the flag, at least for sixty days."

Since 1973, every president has questioned the constitutionality of

Go to *http://www.msstate.edu:80/Archives/History/USA/20th_C./warpowers.973*

the War Powers Resolution. A number of military operations have been undertaken by presidents Gerald R. Ford (the Vietnam evacuation and *Mayaguez* rescue), Jimmy Carter (the attempted Iranian hostage rescue), Ronald Reagan (the Lebanon mission, Grenada invasion, bombing of Libya, and naval escort of oil tankers in the Persian Gulf), George Bush (the Panama invasion and Persian Gulf War), and Bill Clinton (the bombing of Iraq and ordering of troops to Somalia, Haiti, and Bosnia). In few instances has the president complied with the letter, much less the spirit, of the act. Prior consultation with Congress (usually a few congressional leaders) has been perfunctory or nonexistent. Written reports often have not been filed.

Congress has seldom voted to start the sixty-day clock, and never when it mattered. In 1983, for example, Congress decreed that the clock had started ticking when Reagan invaded Grenada. (He did not consult with Congress before launching the invasion.) But the troops returned home victorious in a few days, making the time requirement irrelevant.

To be sure, because of the War Powers Resolution, a president would find it more difficult to involve the United States in a drawn-out, Vietnam-style war. But the main lesson of more than two decades of experience under the act is that law cannot substitute for political will if Congress intends to curb the president's role in war making.

※ ※ ※

SECTION 1. This joint resolution may be cited as the "War Powers Resolution."

SECTION 2. (a) It is the purpose of this joint resolution to fulfill the intent of the framers of the Constitution of the United States and insure that the collective judgment of both the Congress and the president will apply to the introduction of United States armed forces into hostilities, or into situations where imminent involvement in hostilities is clearly indicated by the circumstances, and to the continued use of such forces in hostilities or in such situations.

(b) Under article 1, section 8, of the Constitution, it is specifically provided that the Congress shall have the power to make all laws necessary and proper for carrying into execution, not only its own powers but also all other powers vested by the Constitution in the government of the United States, or in any department or officer thereof.

(c) The constitutional powers of the president as commander-in-chief to introduce United States armed forces into hostilities, or into situations where imminent involvement in hostilities is clearly indicated by the circumstances, are exercised only pursuant to (1) a declaration of war, (2) specific statutory authorization, or (3) a national emergency created by attack upon the United States, its territories or possessions, or its armed forces.

SECTION 3. The president in every possible instance shall consult with Congress before introducing United States armed forces into hostilities or into situations where imminent involvement in hostilities is clearly indicated by the circumstances, and after every such introduction shall consult regularly with the Congress until United States armed forces are no longer engaged in hostilities or have been removed from such situations.

SECTION 4. (a) In the absence of a declaration of war, in any case in which United States armed forces are introduced—

(1) into hostilities or into situations where imminent involvement in hostilities is clearly indicated by the circumstances;

(2) into the territory, airspace, or waters of a foreign nation, while equipped for combat, except for deployments which relate solely to supply, replacement, repair, or training of such forces; or

(3) in numbers which substantially enlarge United States armed forces equipped for combat already located in a foreign nation;

the President shall submit within 48 hours to the Speaker of the House of Representatives and to the president pro tempore of the Senate a report, in writing, setting forth—

(A) the circumstances necessitating the introduction of United States armed forces;

(B) the constitutional and legislative authority under which such introduction took place; and

(C) the estimated scope and duration of the hostilities or involvement.

(b) The president shall provide such other information as the Congress may request in the fulfillment of its constitutional responsibilities with respect to committing the nation to war and to the use of United States armed forces abroad.

(c) Whenever United States armed forces are introduced into hostilities or into any situation described in subsection (a) of this section, the president shall, so long as such armed forces continue to be engaged in such hostilities or situation, report to the Congress periodically on the status of such hostilities or situation as well as on the scope and duration of such hostilities or situation, but in no event shall he report to the Congress less often than once every six months.

SECTION 5. (a) Each report submitted pursuant to section 4(a) (1) shall be transmitted to the Speaker of the House of Representatives and to the president pro tempore of the Senate on the same calendar day. Each report so transmitted shall be referred to the Committee on Foreign Affairs of the House of Representatives and to the Committee on Foreign Relations of the Senate for appropriate action. If, when the report is transmitted, the Congress has adjourned sine die or has adjourned for any period in excess of three calendar days, the Speaker of the House of Representatives and the president pro tempore of the Senate, if they deem it advisable (or if petitioned by at least 30 percent of the membership of their respective houses) shall jointly request the president to convene Congress in order that it may consider the report and take appropriate action pursuant to this section.

(b) Within sixty calendar days after a report is submitted or is required to be submitted pursuant to section 4(a) (1), whichever is earlier, the president shall terminate any use of United States armed forces with respect to which such report was submitted (or required to be submitted), unless the Congress (1) has declared war or has enacted a specific authorization for such use of United States armed forces, (2) has extended by law such sixty-day period, or (3) is physically unable to meet as a result of an armed attack upon the United States. Such sixty-day period shall be extended for not more than an additional thirty days if the president determines and certifies to the Congress in writing that unavoidable military necessity respecting the safety of the United States armed forces requires the continued use of such armed forces in the course of bringing about a prompt removal of such forces.

(c) Notwithstanding subsection (b), at any time that United States armed forces are engaged in hostilities outside the territory of the United States, its possessions and territories without a declaration of war or specific statutory authorization, such forces shall be removed by the president if the Congress so directs by concurrent resolution.

SECTION 6. (a) Any joint resolution or bill introduced pursuant to section 5(b) at least thirty calendar days before the expiration of the sixty-day period specified in such section shall be referred to the Committee on Foreign Affairs of the House of Representatives or the Committee on Foreign Relations of the Senate, as the case may be, and such committee shall report one such joint resolution or bill, together with its recommendations, not later than twenty-four calendar days before the expiration of the sixty-day period specified in such section, unless such house shall otherwise determine by the yeas and nays.

(b) Any joint resolution or bill so reported shall become the pending business of the house in question (in the case of the Senate the time for debate shall be equally divided between the proponents and the opponents), and shall be voted on within three calendar days thereafter, unless such house shall otherwise determine by yeas and nays.

(c) Such a joint resolution or bill passed by one house shall be referred to the committee of the other house named in subsection (a) and shall be reported out not later than fourteen calendar days before the expiration of the sixty-day period specified in section 5(b). The joint resolution or bill so reported shall become the pending business of the house in question and shall be voted on within three calendar days after it has been reported, unless such house shall otherwise determine by yeas and nays.

(d) In the case of any disagreement between the two houses of Congress with respect to a joint resolution or bill passed by both houses, conferees shall be promptly appointed and the committee of conference shall make and file a report with respect to such resolution or bill not later than four calendar days before the expiration of the sixty-day period specified in section 5(b). In the event the conferees are unable to agree within forty-eight hours, they shall report back to their respective houses in disagreement. Notwithstanding any rule in either house concerning the printing of conference reports in the Record or concerning any delay in the consideration of such reports, such report shall be acted on by both houses not later than the expiration of such sixty-day period.

SECTION 7. (a) Any concurrent resolution introduced pursuant to section 5(c) shall be referred to the Committee on Foreign Affairs of the House of Representatives or the Committee on Foreign Relations of the Senate, as the case may be, and one such concurrent resolution shall be reported out by such committee together with its recommendations within fifteen calendar days, unless such house shall otherwise determine by the yeas and nays.

(b) Any concurrent resolution so reported shall become the pending business of the house in question (in the case of the Senate the time for debate shall be equally divided between the proponents and the opponents) and shall be voted on within three calendar days thereafter, unless such house shall otherwise determine by yeas and nays.

(c) Such a concurrent resolution passed by one house shall be referred to the committee of the other house named in subsection (a) and shall be reported out by such committee together with its recommendations within fifteen calendar days and shall thereupon become the pending business of such house and shall be voted upon within three calendar days, unless such house shall otherwise determine by yeas and nays.

(d) In the case of any disagreement between the two houses of Congress with respect to a concurrent resolution passed by both houses, conferees shall be promptly appointed and the committee of conference shall make and file a report with respect to such concurrent resolution within six calendar days after the legislation is referred to the committee of conference. Notwithstanding any rule in either house concerning the printing of conference reports in the Record or concerning any delay in the consideration of such reports, such report shall be acted on by both houses not later than six calendar days after the conference report is filed. In the event the conferees are unable to agree within forty-eight hours, they shall report back to their respective houses in disagreement.

SECTION 8. (a) Authority to introduce United States armed forces into hostilities or into situations wherein involvement in hostilities is clearly indicated by the circumstances shall not be inferred—

(1) from any provision of law (whether or not in effect before the date of the enactment of this joint resolution), including any provision contained in any appropriation act, unless such provision specifically authorizes the introduction of United States armed forces into hostilities or into such situations and states that it is intended to constitute specific statutory authorization within the meaning of this joint resolution; or

(2) from any treaty heretofore or henceafter ratified unless such treaty is implemented by legislation specifically authorizing the introduction of United States armed forces into hostilities or into such situations and stating that it is intended to constitute specific statutory authorization within the meaning of this joint resolution.

(b) Nothing in this joint resolution shall be construed to require any further specific statutory authorization to permit members of United States armed forces to participate jointly with members of the armed forces of one or more foreign countries in the headquarters operations of high-level military commands which were established prior to the date of enactment of this joint resolution and pursuant to the United Nations Charter or any treaty ratified by the United States prior to such date.

(c) For purposes of this joint resolution, the term "introduction of United States armed forces" includes the assignment of members of such armed forces to command, coordinate, participate in the movement of, or accompany the regular or irregular military forces of any foreign country or government when such military forces are engaged, or there exists an imminent threat that such forces will become engaged, in hostilities.

(d) Nothing in this joint resolution—

(1) is intended to alter the constitutional authority of the Congress or of the president, or the provisions of existing treaties; or

(2) shall be construed as granting any authority to the president with respect to the introduction of United States armed forces into hostilities or into situations wherein involvement in hostilities is clearly indicated by the circumstances which authority he would not have had in the absence of this joint resolution.

SECTION 9. If any provision of this joint resolution or the application thereof to any person or circumstance is held invalid, the remainder of the joint resolution and the application of such provision to any other person or circumstance shall not be affected thereby.

SECTION 10. This joint resolution shall take effect on the date of its enactment.

Passed over presidential veto Nov. 7, 1973.

✎ 35 ✎

Proposed Articles of Impeachment against Richard Nixon

(1974)

O N JULY 17, 1972, five burglars secretly employed by the Committee to Re-elect the President (better known by its acronym, CREEP) were caught breaking into the offices of the Democratic National Committee in Washington, D.C.'s Watergate hotel. The chain of command that had authorized the break-in, as well as a host of other illegal and unethical campaign activities, reached high into the administration of President Richard Nixon. In an effort to avoid embarrassing revelations, Nixon and some of his closest aides in the White House responded to news of the burglary by trying to obstruct official investigations into what had happened.

A combination of activities brought to light evidence of Nixon's involvement in the Watergate coverup, including: diligent investigations by reporters Bob Woodward and Carl Bernstein of the *Washington Post* in late 1972 and 1973; hearings by a special Senate committee chaired by Democratic senator Sam Ervin of North Carolina during the summer of 1973; testimony before the Ervin committee by White House counsel John Dean and other participants in the Watergate affair regarding their own, each other's, and (in Dean's case) the president's culpability; and the release of secret White House tape recordings.

In February 1974 the House Judiciary Committee began to consider impeaching the president for "high Crimes and Misdemeanors," only the second serious presidential impeachment inquiry in American history. (See Document 16, p. 82.) Between July 27 and 29, the committee decided to recommend three articles of impeachment to the full House of Representatives.

Article I, approved by a bipartisan 27–11 vote, charged that Nixon had violated his oath to "preserve, protect, and defend the Constitution" and his constitutional responsibility to "take Care that the Laws be faithfully executed" with actions that obstructed the administration of justice in the Watergate case. These actions included: withholding evidence, condoning perjury, approving the payment of "hush money," interfering with lawful investigations, and making false and misleading statements.

Article II, approved 28–10, contended that the president had misused and abused both his executive authority and the resources of various executive agencies, including the Federal Bureau of Investigation, the Central Intelligence Agency, the Internal Revenue Service, and the Justice Department's Criminal Division and Office of Watergate Special Prosecution Force. This article involved not only the Watergate coverup, but other misdeeds as well, such as a covert break-in, sponsored by White House operatives, into the office of Dr. Lewis Fielding, who was psychiatrist to former Defense Department employee Daniel Ellsberg.

Article III, approved 21–17, charged Nixon with contempt of Congress for not cooperating with the House Judiciary Committee's impeachment investigation.

Because the committee's working standard for an impeachable offense was that it be an indictable crime "to the manifest injury of the people of the United States," it voted down two other proposed articles of impeachment. The first, which faulted the president for secretly bombing Cambodia, was judged not to be criminal. The second, Nixon's evasion of income taxes, was found to be a personal but not a political crime.

❧ ❧ ❧

Resolution

Impeaching Richard M. Nixon, President of the United States, of high crimes and misdemeanors.

Resolved, That Richard M. Nixon, President of the United States, is impeached for high crimes and misdemeanors, and that the following articles of impeachment be exhibited to the Senate:

Articles of impeachment exhibited by the House of Representatives of the United States of America in the name of itself and of all of the people of the United States of America, against Richard M. Nixon, President of the United States of America, in maintenance and support of its impeachment against him for high crimes and misdemeanors.

Article I

In his conduct of the office of President of the United States, Richard M. Nixon, in violation of his constitutional oath faithfully to execute the office of President of the United States and, to the best of his ability, preserve, protect, and defend the Constitution of the United States, and in violation of his constitutional duty to take care that the laws be faithfully executed, has prevented, obstructed, and impeded the administration of justice, in that:

On June 17, 1972, and prior thereto, agents of the Committee for the Re-election of the President committed unlawful entry of the headquarters of the Democratic National Committee in Washington, District of Columbia, for the purpose of securing political intelligence. Subsequent thereto, Richard M. Nixon, using the powers of his high office, engaged personally and through his subordinates and agents, in a course of conduct or plan designed to delay, impede, and obstruct the investigation of such unlawful entry; to cover up, conceal and protect those responsible; and to conceal the existence and scope of other unlawful covert activities.

The means used to implement this course of conduct or plan included one or more of the following:

(1) making or causing to be made false or misleading statements to lawfully authorized investigative officers and employees of the United States;

(2) withholding relevant and material evidence or information from lawfully authorized investigative officers and employees of the United States;

(3) approving, condoning, acquiescing in, and counseling witnesses with

respect to the giving of false or misleading statements to lawfully authorized investigative officers and employees of the United States and false or misleading testimony in duly instituted judicial and congressional proceedings;

(4) interfering or endeavoring to interfere with the conduct of investigations by the Department of Justice of the United States, the Federal Bureau of Investigation, the Office of Watergate Special Prosecution Force, and Congressional Committees;

(5) approving, condoning, and acquiescing in, the surreptitious payment of substantial sums of money for the purpose of obtaining the silence or influencing the testimony of witnesses, potential witnesses or individuals who participated in such unlawful entry and other illegal activities;

(6) endeavoring to misuse the Central Intelligence Agency, an agency of the United States;

(7) disseminating information received from officers of the Department of Justice of the United States to subjects of investigations conducted by lawfully authorized investigative officers and employees of the United States, for the purpose of aiding and assisting such subjects in their attempts to avoid criminal liability;

(8) making false or misleading public statements for the purpose of deceiving the people of the United States into believing that a thorough and complete investigation had been conducted with respect to allegations of misconduct on the part of personnel of the executive branch of the United States and personnel of the Committee to Re-elect the President, and that there was no involvement of such personnel in such misconduct; or

(9) endeavoring to cause prospective defendants, and individuals duly tried and convicted, to expect favored treatment and consideration in return for their silence or false testimony, or rewarding individuals for their silence or false testimony.

In all of this, Richard M. Nixon has acted in a manner contrary to his trust as President and subversive of constitutional government, to the great prejudice of the cause of law and justice and to the manifest injury of the people of the United States.

Wherefore Richard M. Nixon, by such conduct, warrants impeachment and trial, and removal from office.

Article II

Using the powers of the office of President of the United States, Richard M. Nixon, in violation of his constitutional oath faithfully to execute the office of President of the United States and, to the best of his ability, preserve, protect, and defend the Constitution of the United States, and in disregard of his constitutional duty to take care that the laws be faithfully executed, has repeatedly engaged in conduct violating the constitutional rights of citizens, impairing the due and proper administration of justice and the conduct of lawful inquiries, or contravening the laws governing agencies of the executive branch and the purposes of these agencies.

This conduct has included one or more of the following:

(1) He has, acting personally and through his subordinates and agents, endeavored to obtain from the Internal Revenue Service, in violation of the constitutional rights of citizens, confidential information contained in income tax returns for purposes not authorized by law, and to cause, in violation of the constitutional rights of citizens, income tax audits or other income tax investigations to be initiated or conducted in a discriminatory manner.

(2) He misused the Federal Bureau of Investigation, the Secret Service, and other executive personnel, in violation or disregard of the constitutional rights of citizens, by directing or authorizing such agencies or personnel to conduct or continue electronic surveillance or other investigations for purposes unrelated to national security, the enforcement of laws, or any other lawful function of his office; he did direct, authorize, or permit the use of information obtained thereby for purposes unrelated to national security, the enforcement of laws, or any other lawful function of his office; and he did direct the concealment of certain records made by the Federal Bureau of Investigation of electronic surveillance.

(3) He has, acting personally and through his subordinates and agents, in violation or disregard of the constitutional rights of citizens, authorized and permitted to be maintained a secret investigative unit within the office of the President, financed in part with money derived from campaign contributions, which unlawfully utilized the resources of the Central Intelligence Agency, engaged in covert and unlawful activities, and attempted to prejudice the constitutional right of an accused to a fair trial.

(4) He has failed to take care that the laws were faithfully executed by failing to act when he knew or had reason to know that his close subordinates endeavored to impede and frustrate lawful inquiries by duly constituted executive, judicial, and legislative entities concerning the unlawful entry into the headquarters of the Democratic National Committee, and the cover-up thereof, and concerning other unlawful activities, including those relating to the confirmation of Richard Kleindienst as Attorney General of the United States, the electronic surveillance of private citizens, the break-in into the offices of Dr. Lewis Fielding, and the campaign financing practices of the Committee to Re-elect the President.

(5) In disregard of the rule of law, he knowingly misused the executive power by interfering with agencies of the executive branch, including the Federal Bureau of Investigation, the Criminal Division, and the Office of Watergate Special Prosecution Force, of the Department of Justice, and the Central Intelligence Agency, in violation of his duty to take care that the laws be faithfully executed.

In all of this, Richard M. Nixon has acted in a manner contrary to his trust as President and subversive of constitutional government, to the great prejudice of the cause of law and justice and to the manifest injury of the people of the United States.

Wherefore Richard M. Nixon, by such conduct, warrants impeachment and trial, and removal from office.

Article III

In his conduct of the office of President of the United States, Richard M. Nixon, contrary to his oath faithfully to execute the office of President of the United States and, to the best of his ability, preserve, protect, and defend the Constitution of the United States, and in violation of his constitutional duty to take care that the laws be faithfully executed, has failed without lawful cause or excuse to produce papers and things as directed by duly authorized subpoenas issued by the Committee on the Judiciary of the House of Representatives on April 11, 1974, May 15, 1974, May 30, 1974, and June 24, 1974, and willfully disobeyed such subpoenas. The subpoenaed papers and things were deemed necessary by the Committee in order to resolve by direct evidence fundamental, factual questions relating to Presidential direction, knowledge, or approval of actions demonstrated by other evidence to be substantial grounds for impeachment of the President. In refusing to produce these papers and things, Richard M. Nixon, substituting his judgment as to what materials were necessary for the inquiry, interposed the powers of the Presidency against the lawful subpoenas of the House of Representatives, thereby assuming to himself functions and judgments necessary to the exercise of the sole power of impeachment vested by the Constitution in the House of Representatives.

In all of this, Richard M. Nixon has acted in a manner contrary to his trust as President and subversive of constitutional government, to the great prejudice of the cause of law and justice, and to the manifest injury of the people of the United States.

Wherefore Richard M. Nixon, by such conduct, warrants impeachment and trial, and removal from office.

United States v. Nixon*

(1974)

IN JUNE 1973 the special Senate Watergate committee, chaired by
Sen. Sam Ervin of North Carolina, learned in testimony from former
White House aide Alexander P. Butterfield that President Richard
Nixon had installed a secret, voice-activated audiotaping system in the
Oval Office of the White House and in some other presidential offices.
The revelation, which seemed to indicate that conclusive evidence exist-
ed regarding the truth or falsehood of the president's and other adminis-
tration officials' versions of the Watergate affair, marked a turning point
in the investigation. It also touched off a lengthy political and legal battle for control of the tapes.

Several investigating bodies, including the Senate committee, the
House Judiciary Committee, and the Watergate special prosecutor, subpoenaed a number of tapes in late 1973 and early 1974. At various
times, bending to overwhelming political pressure, Nixon released
transcripts of selected taped discussions. But he continued to claim that
the president's right to executive privilege justified his decision not to
comply with any of the subpoenas. Eventually, the request of Special
Watergate Prosecutor Leon Jaworski, who stated that he needed sixty-
four tapes as evidence in the criminal trial of several former Nixon aides,
came before the Supreme Court for review.

On July 24, 1974, the Court ruled by an 8–0 vote that Nixon must
turn over the tapes to Judge John J. Sirica, the judge in the criminal trial. (Justice William Rehnquist, as a former Nixon administration
official, disqualified himself from the case.) Chief Justice Warren E.
Burger, writing for all of his colleagues, conceded the existence of a limited executive privilege under the Constitution, a doctrine the Court

*Go to *http://www.findlaw.com*, click on "U.S. Supreme Court Cases," then type "Nixon"
in the box called "Party Name Search"

To hear the oral arguments in this case, go to *http://oyez.nwu.edu*, click on "Cases," then
type "Nixon" in the box called "Search by Title"

had never before declared. Burger wrote that under the separation of powers, the "President and those who assist him must be free to explore alternatives in the process of shaping policies and making decisions and to do so in a way many would be unwilling to express except privately." But, Burger continued, executive privilege does not outweigh the explicit constitutional rights that defendants have to a fair trial and due process. Thus, "absent a claim of need to protect military, diplomatic or sensitive national security secrets," executive privilege must give way to a proper subpoena. The Court ordered Nixon to turn over the tapes to Jaworski.

Nixon had considered defying the Supreme Court decision if the justices' vote was close. (Four of them were Nixon appointees.) But in the face of a unanimous ruling, he agreed to turn over the tapes to Sirica.

🏇 🏇 🏇

MR. CHIEF JUSTICE BURGER delivered the opinion of the court. . . .

[W]e turn to the claim that the subpoena should be quashed because it demands "confidential conversations between a President and his close advisors that it would be inconsistent with the public interest to produce." The first contention is a broad claim that the separation of powers doctrine precludes judicial review of a President's claim of privilege. The second contention is that if he does not prevail on the claim of absolute privilege, the court should hold as a matter of constitutional law that privilege prevails over the subpoena *duces tecum*.

In the performance of assigned constitutional duties each branch of the Government must initially interpret the Constitution, and the interpretation of its powers by any branch is due great respect from the others. The President's counsel, as we have noted, reads the Constitution as providing the absolute privilege of confidentiality for all presidential communications. Many decisions of this court, however, have unequivocally reaffirmed the holding of *Marbury v. Madison,* (1803), that "it is emphatically the province and duty of the judicial department to say what the law is.". . .

No holding of the Court has defined the scope of judicial power specifically relating to the enforcement of a subpoena for confidential presidential communications for use in a criminal prosecution, but other exercises of powers by the Executive Branch and the Legislative Branch have been found invalid as in conflict with the Constitution. *Powell v. McCormack,* (1967), *Youngstown Sheet and Tube v. Sawyer,* (1952). . . . Since this Court has consistently exercised the power to construe and delineate claims arising under express powers, it must follow that the court has authority to interpret claims with respect to powers alleged to derive from enumerated powers. . . .

In support of his claim of absolute privilege, the President's counsel urges two grounds, one of which is common to all governments and one of which is peculiar to our system of separation of powers. The first ground is the valid need for protection of communications between high government officials and those who advise and assist them in the performance of their manifold duties; the importance of this confidentiality is too plain to require further discussion. Human experience teaches that those who expect public dissemination of their remarks may well temper candor with a concern for appearances and for their own interests to the detriment of the decisionmaking process. Whatever the nature of the privilege of confidentiality of presidential communications in the exercise of Art. II powers the privilege can be said to derive from the supremacy of each branch within its own assigned area of constitutional duties. Certain powers and privileges flow from the nature of enumerated powers; the protection of the confidentiality of presidential communications has similar constitutional underpinnings.

The second ground asserted by the President's counsel in support of the claim of absolute privilege rests on the doctrine of separation of powers. Here it is argued that the independence of the Executive Branch within its own sphere, *Humphrey's Executor v. United States, Kilbourn v. Thompson,* (1880), insulates a president from a judicial subpoena in an ongoing criminal prosecution, and thereby protects confidential presidential communications.

However, neither the doctrine of separation of powers, nor the need for confidentiality of high level communications, without more, can sustain an absolute, unqualified presidential privilege of immunity from judicial process under all circumstances. The President's need for complete candor and objectivity from advisers calls for great deference from the courts. However, when the privilege depends solely on the broad undifferentiated claim of public interest in the confidentiality of such conversations, a confrontation with other values arises. Absent a claim of need to protect military, diplomatic or sensitive national security secrets, we find it difficult to accept the argument that even the very important interest in confidentiality of presidential communications is significantly diminished by production of such material for *in camera* inspection with all the protection that a district court will be obliged to provide.

The impediment that an absolute, unqualified privilege would place in the way of the primary constitutional duty of the Judicial Branch to do justice in criminal prosecutions would plainly conflict with the function of the courts under Art. III. In designing the structure of our Government and dividing and allocating the sovereign power among three coequal branches, the Framers of the Constitution sought to provide a comprehensive system, but the separate powers were not intended to operate with absolute independence.

"While the Constitution diffuses power the better to secure liberty, it also contemplates that practice will integrate the dispersed powers into a workable government. It enjoins upon its branches separateness but interdependence, autonomy but reciprocity." *Youngstown Sheet & Tube Co. v. Sawyer,* (1952) (Jackson, J., concurring).

To read Art. II powers of the President as providing an absolute privilege as against a subpoena essential to enforcement of criminal statutes on no more than a generalized claim of the public interest in confidentiality of nonmilitary and nondiplomatic discussions would upset the constitutional balance of "a workable government" and gravely impair the role of the courts under Art. III.

Since we conclude that the legitimate needs of the judicial process may outweigh presidential privilege, it is necessary to resolve those competing interests in a manner that preserves the essential functions of each branch. The right and indeed the duty to resolve that question does not free the judiciary from according high respect to the representations made on behalf of the President. *United States v. Burr,* (1807).

The expectation of a President to the confidentiality of his conversations and correspondence, like the claim of confidentiality of judicial deliberations, for example, has all the values to which we accord deference for the privacy of all citizens and added to those values the necessity for protection of the public interest in candid, objective, and even blunt or harsh opinions in presidential decisionmaking. A President and those who assist him must be free to explore alternatives in the process of shaping policies and making decisions and to do so in a way many would be unwilling to express except privately. These are the considerations justifying a presumptive privilege for presidential communications. The privilege is fundamental to the operation of government and inextricably rooted in the separation of powers under the Constitution. In *Nixon v. Sirica,* (1973), the Court of Appeals held that such presidential communications are "presumptively privileged," and this position is accepted by both parties in the present litigation. We agree with Mr. Chief Justice Marshall's observation, therefore, that "in no case of this kind would a court be required to proceed against the President as against an ordinary individual." *United States v. Burr,* (CCD Va. 1807).

But this presumptive privilege must be considered in light of our historic commitment to the rule of law. This is nowhere more profoundly manifest than in our view that "the twofold aim [of criminal justice] is that guilt shall not escape or innocence suffer." *Berger v. United States,* (1935). We have elected to employ an adversary system of criminal justice in which the parties contest all issues before a court of law. The need to develop all relevant facts in the adversary system is both fundamental and comprehensive. The ends of criminal justice would be defeated if judgments were to be founded on a partial or speculative presentation of the facts. The very integrity of the judicial system and public confidence in the system depend on full disclosure of all the facts, within the framework of the rules of evidence. To ensure that justice is done, it is imperative to the function of courts that compulsory process be available for the production of evidence needed either by the prosecution or by the defense. . . .

In this case the President challenges a subpoena served on him as a third party requiring the production of materials for use in a criminal prosecution on the claim that he has a privilege against disclosure of confidential communications. He does not place his claim of privilege on the ground they are military or diplomatic secrets. As to these areas of Art. II duties the courts have traditionally shown the utmost deference to presidential responsibilities. . . .

No case of the Court, however, has extended this high degree of deference to a President's generalized interest in confidentiality. Nowhere in the Constitution, as we have noted earlier, is there any explicit reference to a privilege of confidentiality, yet to the extent this interest relates to the effective discharge of a President's powers, it is constitutionally based.

The right to the production of all evidence at a criminal trial similarly has constitutional dimensions. The Sixth Amendment explicitly confers upon every defendant in a criminal trial the right "to be confronted with the witnesses against him" and "to have compulsory process for obtaining witnesses in his favor." Moreover, the Fifth Amendment also guarantees that no person shall be deprived of liberty without due process of law. It is the manifest duty of the courts to vindicate those guarantees and to accomplish that it is essential that all relevant and admissible evidence be produced.

In this case we must weigh the importance of the general privilege of confidentiality of presidential communications in performance of his responsibilities against the inroads of such a privilege on the fair administration of criminal justice. The interest in preserving confidentiality is weighty indeed and entitled to great respect. However we cannot conclude that advisers will be moved to temper the candor of their remarks by the infrequent occasions of disclosure because of the possibility that such conversations will be called for in the context of criminal prosecution.

On the other hand, the allowance of the privilege to withhold evidence that is demonstrably relevant in a criminal trial would cut deeply into the guarantee of due process of law and gravely impair the basic function of the courts. A President's acknowledged need for confidentiality in the communications of his office is general in nature, whereas the constitutional need for production of relevant evidence in a criminal proceeding is specific and central to the fair adjudication of a particular criminal case in the administration of justice. Without access to specific facts a criminal prosecution may be totally frustrated. The President's broad interest in confidentiality of communications will not be vitiated by disclosure of a limited number of conversations preliminarily shown to have some bearing on the pending criminal cases.

We conclude that when the ground for asserting privilege as to subpoenaed materials sought for use in a criminal trial is based only on the generalized interest in confidentiality, it cannot prevail over the fundamental demands of due process of law in the fair administration of criminal justice. The generalized assertion of privilege must yield to the demonstrated, specific need for evidence in a pending criminal trial. . . .

⊰ 37 ⊱

The "Smoking Gun" Watergate Tapes

(1974)

O N AUGUST 2, 1974, responding to the order of the Supreme Court in the case of *United States v. Nixon* (see Document 36, p. 196), Richard Nixon turned over a number of Watergate-related tape recordings to Watergate trial judge John J. Sirica. On August 5 he publicly released transcripts of three of these tapes.

The transcripts, which included three conversations between the president and White House chief of staff H. R. Haldeman on June 23, 1972, destroyed any hope that Nixon could avoid impeachment by the House of Representatives and removal by the Senate. In these conversations, Nixon approved a plan proposed by Haldeman to have top officials at the Central Intelligence Agency (CIA) tell L. Patrick Gray

III, the acting director of the Federal Bureau of Investigation (FBI), not to conduct a serious investigation of the June 17 Watergate burglary on national security grounds. Nixon also reacted to Haldeman's subsequent report on his conversation with CIA director Richard Helms and deputy director Vernon A. Walters.

The June 23 tape transcripts were the "smoking gun" in the Watergate investigation—that is, the first piece of evidence that indisputably demonstrated Nixon's active role in the coverup. After their release, Vice President Gerald R. Ford announced that he would no longer proclaim the president's innocence. Republicans in Congress, including the ten members of the House Judiciary Committee who had voted against every proposed article of impeachment, publicly denounced Nixon, all but guaranteeing that a near-unanimous House would impeach the president and that the Senate would overwhelmingly vote to convict. (See Document 35, p. 190.)

Nixon announced in a televised address to the nation on the evening of August 8, 1974, that he would resign the presidency effective noon the following day. On the morning of August 9, Nixon wrote a letter of resignation to Secretary of State Henry Kissinger before bidding an emotional farewell to the White House staff. The letter read, in its entirety: "I hereby resign the Office of President of the United States."

Meeting: The President and Haldeman

Oval Office, June 23, 1972
(10:04–11:39 a.m.)

H. Now, on the investigation, you know the Democratic break-in thing, we're back in the problem area because the FBI is not under control, because Gray doesn't exactly know how to control it and they have—their investigation is now leading into some productive areas—because they've been able to trace the money—not through the money itself—but through the bank sources—the banker. And, and it goes in some directions we don't want it to go. Ah, also there have been some things—like an informant came in off the street to the FBI in Miami who was a photographer or has a friend who is a photographer who developed some films through this guy [Bernard] Barker [one of the burglars] and the films had pictures of Democratic National Committee letterhead documents and things. So it's things like that that are filtering in. [Nixon campaign manager John] Mitchell came up with yesterday, and [White House counsel] John Dean analyzed very carefully last night and concludes, concurs now with Mitchell's recommendation that the only way to solve this, and we're set up beautifully to do it, ah, in that and that—the only network that paid any attention to it last night was NBC—they did a massive story on the Cuban thing.

P. That's right.

H. That's the way to handle this now is for us to have Walters call Pat Gray and just say, "Stay to hell out of this—this is ah, business here we don't want you to go any further on it." That's not an unusual development, and ah, that would take care of it.

P. What about Pat Gray—you mean Pat Gray doesn't want to?

H. Pat does want to. He doesn't know how to, and he doesn't have, he doesn't have any basis for doing it. Given this, he will then have the basis. He'll call Mark Felt in [W. Mark Felt, FBI deputy associate director in 1972], and the two of them—and Mark Felt wants to cooperate because he's ambitious—

P. Yeah.

H. He'll call him in and say, "We've got the signal from across the river to put the hold on this." And that will fit rather well because the FBI agents who are working the case, at this point, feel that's what it is.

P. This is CIA? They've traced the money? Who'd they trace it to?

H. Well they've traced it to a name, but they haven't gotten to the guy yet.

P. Would it be somebody here?

H. Ken Dahlberg.

P. Who the hell is Ken Dahlberg?

H. He gave $25,000 in Minnesota and, ah, the check went directly to this guy Barker.

P. It isn't from the Committee [to Re-elect the President], though, from [campaign treasurer Maurice] Stans?

H. Yeah. It is. It's directly traceable and there's some more through some Texas people that went to the Mexican bank which can also be traced to the Mexican bank—they'll get their names today.

H. —And (pause)

P. Well, I mean, there's no way—I'm just thinking if they don't cooperate, what do they say? That they were approached by the Cubans. That's what Dahlberg has to say, the Texans too, that they—

H. Well, if they will. But then we're relying on more and more people all the time. That's the problem and they'll stop if we could take this other route.

P. All right.

H. And you seem to think the thing to do is get them to stop?

P. Right, fine.

H. They say the only way to do that is from White House instructions. And it's got to be to Helms and to—ah, what's his name. . . . ? Walters.

P. Walters.

H. And the proposal would be that [Nixon aide John] Ehrlichman and I call them in, and say, ah—

P. All right, fine. How do you call him in—I mean you just—well, we protected Helms from one hell of a lot of things.

H. That's what Ehrlichman says.

P. Of course, this Hunt [E. Howard Hunt, the chief burglar], that will uncover a lot of things. You open that scab there's a hell of a lot of things and we just feel that it would be very detrimental to have this thing go any further. This involves these Cubans, Hunt, and a lot of hanky-panky that we have nothing to do with ourselves. Well what the hell, did Mitchell know about this?

H. I think so. I don't think he knew the details, but I think he knew.

P. He didn't know how it was going to be handled though—with Dahlberg and the Texans and so forth? Well who was the asshole that did? Is it Liddy [G. Gordon Liddy, a Nixon campaign operative]? Is that the fellow? He must be a little nuts!

H. He is.

P. I mean he just isn't well screwed on is he? Is that the problem?

H. No, but he was under pressure, apparently, to get more information, and as he got more pressure, he pushed the people harder to move harder—

P. Pressure from Mitchell?

H. Apparently.

P. Oh, Mitchell. Mitchell was at the point (unintelligible).

H. Yeah.

P. All right, fine, I understand it all. We won't second-guess Mitchell and the rest. Thank God it wasn't [Nixon aide Charles] Colson.

H. The FBI interviewed Colson yesterday. They determined that would be a good thing to do. To have him take an interrogation, which he did, and that—the FBI guys working the case concluded that there were one or two possibilities—one, that this was a White House—they don't think that there is anything at the Election Committee—they think it was either a White House operation and they had some obscure reasons for it—non-political, or it was a—Cuban and the CIA. And after their interrogation of Colson yesterday, they concluded it was not the White House, but are now convinced it is a CIA thing, so the CIA turnoff would—

P. Well, not sure of their analysis, I'm not going to get that involved. I'm (unintelligible).

H. No, sir, we don't want you to.

P. You call them in.

H. Good deal.

P. Play it tough. That's the way they play it and that's the way we are going to play it.

H. O.K.

P. When I saw that news summary, I questioned whether it's a bunch of crap, but I thought, er, well it's good to have them off us awhile, because when they start bugging us, which they have, our little boys will not know how to handle it. I hope they will though.

H. You never know.

P. Good.

(Other matters are discussed. Then the conversation returns to the break-in coverup strategy.)

P. When you get in—when you get in (unintelligible) people, say, Look the problem is that this will open the whole, the whole Bay of Pigs thing, and the President just feels that ah, without going into the details—don't, don't lie to them to the extent to say there is no involvement, but just say this is a comedy of errors, without getting into it, the President believes that it is going to open the whole Bay of Pigs thing up again. And, ah, because these people are plugging for (unintelligible) and that they should call the FBI in and (unintelligible) don't go any further into this case period!

P. (Inaudible) our cause—

H. Get more done for our cause by the opposition than by us.

P. Well, can you get it done?

H. I think so.

Meeting: The President and Haldeman

Oval Office, June 23, 1972
(1:04–1:13 p.m.)

P. O.K., just postpone (scratching noises) (unintelligible) Just say (unintelligible) very bad to have this fellow Hunt, ah, he knows too damned much, if he was involved—you happen to know that? If it gets out that this is all involved, the Cuba thing it would be a fiasco. It would make the CIA look bad, it's going to make Hunt look bad, and it is likely to blow the whole Bay of Pigs thing which we think would be very unfortunate—both for CIA, and for the country, at this time, and for American foreign policy. Just tell him to lay off. Don't you?

H. Yep. That's the basis to do it on. Just leave it at that.

P. I don't know if he'll get any ideas for doing it because our concern political (unintelligible). Helms is not one to (unintelligible)—I would just say, lookit, because of the Hunt involvement, whole cover basically this.

H. Yep. Good move. . . .

Meeting: The President and Haldeman

Executive Office Building,
June 23, 1972 (2:20–2:45 p.m.)

H. Well, it was kind of interesting. Walters made the point and I didn't mention Hunt, I just said that the thing was leading into directions that were going to create potential problems because they were exploring leads that led back into areas that would be harmful to the CIA and harmful to the government (unintelligible) didn't have anything to do (unintelligible). . . .

H. (unintelligible) I think Helms did to (unintelligible) said, I've had no—

P. God (unintelligible).

H. Gray called and said, yesterday, and said that he thought—

P. Who did? Gray?

H. Gray called Helms and said I think we've run right into the middle of a CIA covert operation.

P. Gray said that?

H. Yeah. And (unintelligible) said nothing we've done at this point and ah (unintelligible) says well it sure looks to me like it is (unintelligible) and ah, that was the end of that conversation (unintelligible) the problem is it tracks back to the Bay of Pigs and it tracks back to some other the leads run out to people who had no involvement in this, except by contacts and connection, but it gets to areas that are liable to be raised? The whole problem (unintelligible) Hunt. So at that point he kind of got the picture. He said, he said we'll be very happy to be helpful (unintelligible) handle anything you want. I would like to know the reason for being helpful, and I made it clear to him he wasn't going to get explicit (unintelligible) generality, and he said fine. And Walters (unintelligible). Walters is going to make a call to Gray. That's the way we put it and that's the way it was left.

P. How does that work though, how, they've got to (unintelligible) somebody from the Miami bank.

H. (unintelligible). The point John [Ehrlichman? Dean?] makes—the Bureau is going on and on this because they don't know what they are uncovering (unintelligible) continue to pursue it. They don't need to because they already have their case as far as the charges against these men (unintelligible) and ah, as they pursue it (unintelligible) exactly, but we didn't in any way say we (unintelligible). One thing Helms did raise. He said, Gray—he asked Gray why they thought they had run into a CIA thing and Gray said because of the characters involved and the amount of money involved, a lot of dough. (unintelligible) and ah, (unintelligible)

P. (Unintelligible)

H. Well, I think they will. . . .

❧ 38 ❧

Gerald R. Ford's Pardon of Richard Nixon

(1974)

SINCE THE ENACTMENT of the Twenty-fifth Amendment in 1967, the president has been charged to fill any vacancy that might arise in the vice presidency by nominating a new vice president, subject to confirmation by a majority of both houses of Congress. When Vice President Spiro T. Agnew resigned in the face of federal bribery and tax evasion charges in October 1973, President Richard Nixon nominated House Minority Leader Gerald R. Ford of Michigan, a fellow Republican, to be vice president. Congress confirmed the nomination overwhelmingly. On August 9, 1974, Ford became president when Nixon resigned.

Resignation left Nixon subject to indictment, trial, and possible conviction for obstructing justice in the Watergate investigation. On Sunday morning, September 8, 1974, Ford announced to a national television audience that he was exercising his constitutional power to grant Nixon a "full, free and absolute pardon . . . for all offenses against the United States which he . . . has committed or may have committed" as president. Ford's exercise of the pardon power—the only constitutional power of the presidency that may not be checked by Congress or the

Supreme Court—effectively freed Nixon from prosecution for any federal crime.

In announcing the pardon, Ford noted several reasons for his decision, including the former president's health and mental anguish and the difficulty of securing a fair trial. More than anything else, however, Ford believed that "someone must write 'The End'" to the Watergate affair, lest "ugly passions . . . again be aroused."

Nixon received the pardon with a statement conceding only "mistakes and misjudgments" in his handling of the Watergate affair. Responding to critics who complained that Ford should have insisted on a stronger apology, administration officials said that the very act of accepting the pardon was, in effect, a confession of guilt by the former president.

Ford paid a severe political price for the Nixon pardon. He was roundly criticized in Congress and the media, and his public approval rating instantly dropped twenty percentage points in the polls. When the House Judiciary Committee conducted hearings to investigate why the pardon was granted, Ford appeared personally before the committee—the first time in history that a president testified under oath to a congressional committee—to deny that he and Nixon had made any secret arrangement to exchange the promise of a pardon for Nixon's agreement to resign.

Ford's loss of public support enfeebled his presidency in the face of severe foreign and domestic problems. At home, inflation and unemployment rose steadily, producing an unprecedented "stagflation" that standard economic remedies did not address. Abroad, South Vietnam fell to the Communists, and the Soviet Union, taking advantage of weakened American resolve, successfully aided revolutions throughout the Third World. Congressional Republicans suffered severe losses in the 1974 elections. Ford himself was the victim of two assassination attempts in September 1975. In addition, he nearly lost the 1976 Republican presidential nomination to Ronald Reagan, the former governor of California. In the course of beating back the challenge from the conservative Reagan, Ford dropped his own appointed vice president, the liberal former New York governor Nelson A. Rockefeller, from the ticket, in favor of Kansas senator Robert Dole.

Ford waged a hard and generally effective campaign against the

Democratic presidential nominee, former Georgia governor Jimmy Carter, in the 1976 election. But he was defeated narrowly, bringing his two-and-one-half-year presidency to an end.

※ ※ ※

Ladies and gentlemen, I have come to a decision which I felt I should tell you, and all of my fellow American citizens, as soon as I was certain in my own mind and in my own conscience that it was the right thing to do.

I have learned already in this office that the difficult decisions always come to this desk. I must admit that many of them do not look at all the same as the hypothetical questions that I have answered freely and perhaps too fast on previous occasions. My customary policy is to try and get all the facts and to consider the opinions of my countrymen and to take counsel with my most valued friends. But these seldom agree, and in the end the decision is mine.

To procrastinate, to agonize and to wait for a more favorable turn of events that may never come, or more compelling external pressures that may as well be wrong as right, is itself a decision of sorts and a weak course for a President to follow.

I have promised to uphold the Constitution, to do what is right as God gives me to see the right, and to do the very best that I can for America. I have asked your help and your prayers not only when I became President, but many times since.

The Constitution is the supreme law of our land and it governs our actions as citizens. Only the laws of God, which govern our consciences, are superior to it. As we are a nation under God, so I am sworn to uphold our laws with the help of God. And I have sought such guidance and searched my own conscience with special diligence to determine the right thing for me to do with respect to my predecessor in this place, Richard Nixon, and his loyal wife and family.

Theirs is an American tragedy in which we all have played a part. It could go on and on and on, or someone must write "The End" to it.

I have concluded that only I can do that. And if I can, I must.

There are no historic or legal precedents to which I can turn in this matter, none that precisely fit the circumstances of a private citizen who has resigned the presidency of the United States. But it is common knowledge that serious allegations and accusations hang like a sword over our former President's head, threatening his health, as he tries to reshape his life, a great part of which was spent in the service of this country and by the mandate of its people.

After years of bitter controversy and divisive national debate, I have been advised and I am compelled to conclude that many months and perhaps more years will have to pass before Richard Nixon could obtain a fair trial by jury in any jurisdiction of the United States under governing decisions of the Supreme Court.

I deeply believe in equal justice for all Americans, whatever their station or former station. The law, whether human or divine, is no respecter of persons but the law is a respecter of reality. The facts as I see them are that a former President of the United States, instead of enjoying equal treatment with any other citizen accused of violating the law, would be cruelly and excessively penalized either in preserving the presumption of his innocence or in obtaining a speedy determination of his guilt in order to repay a legal debt to society.

During this long period of delay and potential litigation, ugly passions would again be aroused, and our people would again be polarized in their opinions, and the credibility of our free institutions of government would again be challenged at home and abroad. In the end, the courts might well hold that Richard Nixon had been denied due process and the verdict of history would even more be inconclusive with respect to those charges arising out of the period of his presidency of which I am presently aware.

But it is not the ultimate fate of Richard Nixon that most concerns me— though surely it deeply troubles every decent and every compassionate person. My concern is the immediate future of this great country. In this I dare not depend upon my personal sympathy as a longtime friend of the former President nor my professional judgment as a lawyer. And I do not.

As President, my primary concern must always be the greatest good of all the people of the United States, whose servant I am.

As a man, my first consideration is to be true to my own convictions and my own conscience.

My conscience tells me clearly and certainly that I cannot prolong the bad dreams that continue to reopen a chapter that is closed. My conscience tells me that only I, as President, have the constitutional power to firmly shut and seal this book. My conscience says it is my duty, not merely to proclaim domestic tranquility, but to use every means that I have to ensure it.

I do believe that the buck stops here, that I cannot rely upon public opinion polls to tell me what is right. I do believe that right makes might, and that if I am wrong 10 angels swearing I was right would make no difference. I do believe with all my heart and mind and spirit that I, not as President, but as a humble servant of God, will receive justice without mercy if I fail to show mercy.

Finally, I feel that Richard Nixon and his loved ones have suffered enough, and will continue to suffer no matter what I do, no matter what we as a great and good nation can do together to make his goal of peace come true.

Now, therefore, I, Gerald R. Ford, President of the United States, pursuant to the pardon power conferred upon me by Article II, Section 2, of the Constitution, have granted and by these presents do grant a full, free, and absolute pardon unto Richard Nixon for all offenses against the United States which he, Richard Nixon, has committed or may have committed or taken part in during the period from January 20, 1969, through August 9, 1974.

In witness whereof, I have hereunto set my hand this 8th day of September in the year of our Lord Nineteen Hundred Seventy Four, and of the independence of the United States of America the 199th.

❧ 39 ❧

Jimmy Carter's "Crisis of Confidence" Speech*

(1979)

FORMER GEORGIA GOVERNOR Jimmy Carter's narrow victory over Gerald R. Ford in the 1976 election marked the first time that a challenger had unseated an incumbent president since Franklin D. Roosevelt defeated Herbert C. Hoover in 1932. Carter, a Democrat, stressed domestic issues in his campaign but, as president, was generally unsuccessful in enacting his policies into law. By the summer of 1979, the nation was plagued by gasoline shortages, raging inflation, and soaring interest rates. The president's public approval rating sank like a stone.

On July 5, 1979, Carter began an unprecedented effort to revive his presidency. Convinced by his advisers that most people would not watch, he canceled a televised address on energy that was scheduled for that evening. The next day, Carter went to Camp David, the presiden-

*Go to *http://hs1.hst.msu.edu/~hst306/documents/carter.html*

tial retreat in Maryland's Catoctin Mountains, to reflect on the underlying causes of the energy crisis and the nation's other problems. During the week that followed, Carter met with more than one hundred invited visitors, including political, business, labor, and religious leaders, to discuss politics, public policy, and philosophy. He also made some unannounced helicopter trips to visit families in their homes.

On the evening of July 15 Carter returned to Washington and gave a nationally televised speech from the Oval Office that, although dealing in part with energy (he proposed a ten-year, $142 billion program to obtain national energy independence), dwelt on the "crisis of confidence" that he believed was enfeebling the American spirit.

Carter's speech began with an extended *mea culpa,* quoting criticisms of his leadership from some of the people with whom he had spoken during his retreat. He then described his perception of "a fundamental threat to American democracy," namely, a "crisis of the American spirit" that was marked by loss of faith in the country and confidence in the future. "Restoring that faith and that confidence to America is now the most important task we face," the president concluded.

Although Carter never spoke the word, his address soon became known as the "malaise" speech. Critics charged that the president, who had been elected by praising the American people as "good and honest and decent and competent and compassionate and filled with love," was now blaming them for his own failure to solve soluble problems. The public's reaction was initially more positive, but Carter quickly dissipated whatever political gains he had made by firing five cabinet members during the week following the speech. To a nation unused to having its president undertake soul-searching retreats, the firings reinforced doubts about the stability and competence of Carter's leadership.

❧ ❧ ❧

Good evening.

This is a special night for me. Exactly three years ago on July 15, 1976, I accepted the nomination of my party to run for President of the United States. I promised you a President who is not isolated from the people, who feels your pain and who shares your dreams and who draws his strength and his wisdom from you.

During the past 3 years I have spoken to you on many occasions about national concerns, the energy crisis, reorganizing the Government, our Nation's economy and issues of war and especially peace. But over those years the subjects of the speeches, the talks and the press conferences have become increasingly narrow, focused more and more on what the isolated world of Washington thinks is important. Gradually you have heard more and more about what the Government thinks or what the Government should be doing and less and less about our Nation's hopes, our dreams and our vision of the future.

Ten days ago I had planned to speak to you again about a very important subject—energy. For the fifth time I would have described the urgency of the problem and laid out a series of legislative recommendations to the Congress. But as I was preparing to speak, I began to ask myself the same question that I now know has been troubling many of you. Why have we not been able to get together as a nation to resolve our serious energy problem?

It's clear that the true problems of our Nation are much deeper—deeper than gasoline lines or energy shortages, deeper even than inflation or recession. And I realize more than ever that as President I need your help. So, I decided to reach out and to listen to the voices of America.

I invited to Camp David people from almost every segment of our society—business and labor, teachers and preachers, Governors, mayors and private citizens. And then I left Camp David to listen to other Americans, men and women like you. It has been an extraordinary 10 days, and I want to share with you what I've heard.

First of all, I got a lot of personal advice. Let me quote a few of the typical comments that I wrote down.

This from a Southern governor: "Mr. President, you are not leading this Nation—you're just managing the Government."

"You don't see the people enough any more."

"Some of your Cabinet members don't seem loyal. There is not enough discipline among your disciples."

"Don't talk to us about politics or the mechanics of government, but about an understanding of our common good."

"Mr. President, we're in trouble. Talk to us about blood and sweat and tears."

"If you lead, Mr. President, we will follow."

Many people talked about themselves and about the condition of our Nation. This from a young woman in Pennsylvania: "I feel so far from government. I feel like ordinary people are excluded from political power."

And this from a young Chicano: "Some of us have suffered from recession all our lives."

"Some people have wasted energy, but others haven't had anything to waste."

And this from a religious leader: "No material shortage can touch the important things like God's love for us or our love for one another."

And I like this one particularly from a black woman who happens to be the mayor of a small Mississippi town: "The big shots are not the only ones who are important. Remember, you can't sell anything on Wall Street unless someone digs it up somewhere else first."

This kind of summarized a lot of other statements: "Mr. President, we are confronted with a moral and a spiritual crisis."

Several of our discussions were on energy and I have a notebook full of comments and advice. I'll read just a few.

"We can't go on consuming 40 percent more energy than we produce. When we import oil we are also importing inflation plus unemployment."

"We've got to use what we have. The Middle East has only 5 percent of the world's energy, but the United States has 24 percent."

And this is one of the most vivid statements: "Our neck is stretched over the fence and OPEC [Organization of Petroleum Exporting Countries] has the knife."

"There will be other cartels and other shortages. American wisdom and courage right now can set a path to follow in the future."

This was a good one: "Be bold, Mr. President. We may make mistakes, but we are ready to experiment."

And this one from a labor leader got to the heart of it: "The real issue is freedom. We must deal with the energy problem on a war footing."

And the last that I'll read: "When we enter the moral equivalent of war, Mr. President, don't issue us BB guns."

These 10 days confirmed my belief in the decency and the strength and the wisdom of the American people, but it also bore out some of my longstanding concerns about our Nation's underlying problems.

I know, of course, being President, that government actions and legislation can be very important. That is why I've worked hard to put my campaign promises into law—and I have to admit, with just mixed success. But after listening to the American people I have been reminded again that all the legislation in the world can't fix what's wrong with America. So, I want to speak to you first tonight about a subject even more serious than energy or inflation. I want to talk to you right now about a fundamental threat to American democracy.

I do not mean our political and civil liberties. They will endure. And I do not refer to the outward strength of America, a nation that is at peace tonight everywhere in the world, with unmatched economic power and military might.

The threat is nearly invisible in ordinary ways. It is a crisis of confidence. It is a crisis that strikes at the very heart and soul and spirit of our national will. We can see this crisis in the growing doubt about the meaning of our own lives and in the loss of a unity of purpose for our Nation.

The erosion of our confidence in the future is threatening to destroy the social and the political fabric of America.

The confidence that we have always had as a people is not simply some romantic dream or a proverb in a dusty book that we read just on the Fourth of July. It is the idea we founded our Nation on and has guided our development as a people. Confidence in the future has supported everything else—public institutions and private enterprise, our own families, and the very Constitution of the United States. Confidence has defined our course and has served as a link between generations. We've always believed in something called progress. We've always had a faith that the days of our children would be better than our own.

Our people are losing that faith, not only in government itself, but in the ability as citizens to serve as the ultimate rulers and shapers of our democracy. As a people we know our past and we are proud of it. Our progress has been part of the living history of America, even the world. We always believed that we were part of a great movement of humanity itself called democracy, involved in the search for freedom and that belief has always strengthened us in our purpose. But just as we are losing our confidence in the future, we are also beginning to close the door on our past.

In a Nation that was proud of hard work, strong families, close knit communities, and our faith in God, too many of us now tend to worship self-indulgence and consumption. Human identity is no longer defined by what one does, but by what one owns. But we've discovered that owning things and consuming things does not satisfy our longing for meaning. We've learned that piling up material goods cannot fill the emptiness of lives which have no confidence or purpose.

The symptoms of this crisis of the American spirit are all around us. For the first time in the history of our country the majority of our people believe that the next 5 years will be worse than the past 5 years. Two-thirds of our people do not even vote. The productivity of American workers is actually dropping and the willingness of Americans to save for the future has fallen below that of all other people in the Western world.

As you know, there is a growing disrespect for government and for churches and for schools, the news media, and other institutions. This is not a message of happiness or reassurance, but it is the truth and it is a warning.

These changes did not happen overnight. They've come upon us gradually over the last generation, years that were filled with shocks and tragedy.

We were sure that ours was a nation of the ballot, not the bullet, until the murders of John Kennedy and Robert Kennedy and Martin Luther King Jr. We were taught that our armies were always invincible and our causes were always just, only to suffer the agony of Vietnam. We respected the Presidency as a place of honor until the shock of Watergate.

We remember when the phrase "sound as a dollar" was an expression of absolute dependability, until 10 years of inflation began to shrink our dollars and our savings. We believed that our Nation's resources were limitless until 1973 when we had to face a growing dependence on foreign oil.

These wounds are still very deep. They have never been healed.

Looking for a way out of this crisis, our people have turned to the Federal Government and found it isolated from the mainstream of our Nation's life. Washington, D.C., has become an island. The gap between our citizens and our government has never been so wide. The people are looking for honest answers, not easy answers; clear leadership, not false claims and evasiveness and politics as usual.

What you see too often in Washington and elsewhere around the country is a system of government that seems incapable of action. You see a Congress twisted and pulled in every direction by hundreds of well-financed and powerful special interests.

You see every extreme position defended to the last vote, almost to the last breath by one unyielding group or another. You often see a balanced and a fair approach that demands sacrifice, a little sacrifice from everyone, abandoned like an orphan without support and without friends.

Often you see paralysis and stagnation and drift. You don't like it, and neither do I. What can we do?

First of all, we must face the truth and then we can change our course. We simply must have faith in each other, faith in our ability to govern ourselves and faith in the future of this Nation.

Restoring that faith and that confidence to America is now the most important task we face. It is a true challenge of this generation of Americans.

One of the visitors to Camp David last week put it this way: "We've got to stop crying and start sweating, stop talking and start walking, stop cursing and start praying. The strength we need will not come from the White House, but from every house in America."

We know the strength of America. We are strong. We can regain our unity. We can regain our confidence. We are the heirs of generations who survived threats much more powerful and awesome than those that challenge us now. Our fathers and mothers were strong men and women who shaped a new society during the Great Depression, who fought world wars and who carved out a new charter of peace for the world.

We ourselves are the same Americans who just 10 years ago put a man on the moon. We are the generation that dedicated our society to the pursuit of human rights and equality. And we are the generation that will win the war on the energy problem and in that process rebuild the unity and confidence of America.

We are at a turning point in our history. There are two paths to choose. One is a path I warned about tonight, the path that leads to fragmentation and self-interest. Down that road lies a mistaken idea of freedom, the right to grasp for ourselves some advantage over others. That path would be one of constant conflict between narrow interests ending in chaos and immobility. It is a certain route to failure.

All the traditions of our past, all the lessons of our heritage, all the promises of our future point to another path, the path of common purpose and the restoration of American values. That path leads to true freedom for our Nation and ourselves. We can take the first steps down that path as we begin to solve our energy problem.

Energy will be the immediate test of our ability to unite this Nation and it can also be the standard around which we rally. On the battlefield of energy we can win for our Nation a new confidence, and we can seize control again of our common destiny.

In little more than two decades we've gone from a position of energy independence to one in which almost half the oil we use comes from foreign countries, at prices that are going through the roof. Our excessive dependence on OPEC has already taken a tremendous toll on our economy and our people. This is the direct cause of the long lines which have made millions of you spend aggravating hours waiting for gasoline. It's a cause of the increased inflation and unemployment that we now face. This intolerable dependence on foreign oil threatens our economic independence and the very security of our Nation.

The energy crisis is real. It is worldwide. It is a clear and present danger to our Nation. These are facts and we simply must face them. . . .

Twelve hours from now I will speak again in Kansas City, to expand and to explain further our energy program. Just as the search for solutions to our energy shortages has now led us to a new awareness of our Nation's deeper problems, so our willingness to work for those new solutions in energy can strengthen us to attack those deeper problems.

I will continue to travel this country, to hear the people of America. You can help me to develop a national agenda for the 1980s. I will listen and I will act. We will act together. These were the promises I made three years ago and I intend to keep them.

Little by little we can and we must rebuild our confidence. We can spend until we empty our treasuries, and we may summon all the wonders of science. But we can succeed only if we tap our greatest resources—America's people, America's values, and America's confidence.

I have seen the strength of America in the inexhaustible resources of our people. In the days to come, let us renew that strength in the struggle for an energy-secure nation.

In closing, let me say this: I will do my best, but I will not do it alone. Let your voice be heard. Whenever you have a chance, say something good about our country. With God's help and for the sake of our Nation, it is time for us to join hands in America. Let us commit ourselves together to a rebirth of the American spirit. Working together with our common faith we cannot fail.

Thank you and good night.

❧ 40 ❧

Ronald Reagan's First Inaugural Address*

(1981)

RONALD REAGAN was a professional movie and television actor and a New Deal Democrat for most of his life. In 1966, four years after changing his party registration, Reagan entered elective politics by running successfully for governor of California as a conservative Republican. After leaving the governorship in 1975, Reagan challenged incumbent Gerald R. Ford for the party's 1976 presidential nomination. He was defeated, but came very close to winning. Reagan's strong

*Go to *http://www.cc.columbia.edu/acis/bartleby/inaugural/pres61.html*

conservative credentials and exceptional ability as a television orator, which had been honed throughout his career in show business, made him a formidable candidate in any election he entered.

In 1980 Reagan swept easily to the Republican nomination. His main rival was former United Nations ambassador George Bush, whom he tapped at the convention as his vice-presidential running mate. Capitalizing on severe economic conditions and on the year-long seizure of more than fifty American hostages by militant revolutionaries in Iran, Reagan defeated President Jimmy Carter by the largest electoral vote majority in history against an incumbent president: 489 votes for Reagan to 49 for Carter.

Reagan's inauguration as president also was unprecedented in some ways. Two weeks shy of his seventieth birthday, Reagan was the oldest person ever to take the oath of office. (Previously, at sixty-eight, William Henry Harrison had been.) He was inaugurated on the West Front of the Capitol, not the traditional East Front, and coordinated part of his speech with television cameras that showed viewers the Washington Monument, the Jefferson and Lincoln Memorials, and Arlington National Cemetery as he spoke of them.

Reagan's first inaugural address advanced the two main themes of his political career, of his 1980 campaign, and, subsequently, of his presidency: the failings of big government ("government is not the solution to our problem; government is the problem") and a fervent optimism that national problems could be overcome with conservative policies. "The economic ills we suffer . . . will go away," Reagan proclaimed. "They will go away because we as Americans have the capacity now, as we've had it in the past, to do whatever needs to be done to preserve this last and greatest bastion of freedom."

Congress passed Reagan's program of tax cuts, budget reductions for social welfare, and spending increases for defense in 1981. During the course of his eight years as president inflation, interest rates, and unemployment fell. After a severe recession in 1982, the economy grew rapidly. But the combination of reduced tax revenues and soaring defense spending caused the national debt to triple from approximately $1 billion to $3 trillion.

🐎 🐎 🐎

To a few of us here today this is a solemn and most momentous occasion. And, yet, in the history of our Nation it is a commonplace occurrence. The orderly transfer of authority as called for in the Constitution routinely takes place, as it has for almost two centuries, and few of us stop to think how unique we really are. In the eyes of many in the world, this every-4-year ceremony we accept as normal is nothing less than a miracle.

Mr. President [Carter], I want our fellow citizens to know how much you did to carry on this tradition. By your gracious cooperation in the transition process you have shown a watching world that we are a united people pledged to maintaining a political system which guarantees individual liberty to a greater degree than any other, and I thank you and your people for all your help in maintaining the continuity which is the hallmark of our Republic.

The business of our Nation goes forward. These United States are confronted with an economic affliction of great proportions. We suffer from the longest and one of the worst sustained inflations in our national history. It distorts our economic decisions, penalizes thrift and crushes the struggling young and the fixed-income elderly alike. It threatens to shatter the lives of millions of our people.

Idle industries have cast workers into unemployment, human misery, and personal indignity. Those who do work are denied a fair return for their labor by a tax system which penalizes successful achievement and keeps us from maintaining full productivity.

But great as our tax burden is, it has not kept pace with public spending. For decades we have piled deficit upon deficit, mortgaging our future and our children's future for the temporary convenience of the present. To continue this long trend is to guarantee tremendous social, cultural, political, and economic upheavals.

You and I, as individuals, can, by borrowing, live beyond our means, but for only a limited period of time. Why, then, should we think that collectively, as a nation, we're not bound by that same limitation? We must act today in order to preserve tomorrow. And let there be no misunderstanding—we are going to begin to act, beginning today.

The economic ills we suffer have come upon us over several decades. They will not go away in days, weeks, or months, but they will go away. They will go away because we as Americans have the capacity now, as we've had in the past, to do whatever needs to be done to preserve this last and greatest bastion of freedom.

In this present crisis, government is not the solution to our problem; government is the problem. From time to time we've been tempted to believe that society has become too complex to be managed by self-rule, that government by an elite group is superior to government for, by, and of the people. Well, if no one among us is capable of governing himself, then who among us has the capacity to govern someone else? All of us together—in and out of government—must bear the burden. The solutions we seek must be equitable with no one group singled out to pay a higher price.

We hear much of special interest groups. Well, our concern must be for a special interest group that has been too long neglected. It knows no sectional boundaries or ethnic and racial divisions, and it crosses political party lines. It is made up of men and women who raise our food, patrol our streets, man our mines and factories, teach our children, keep our homes, and heal us when we're sick—professionals, industrialists, shopkeepers, clerks, cabbies, and truck drivers. They are, in short, "We the people," this breed called Americans.

Well, this administration's objective will be a healthy, vigorous, growing economy that provides equal opportunities for all Americans with no barriers born of bigotry or discrimination. Putting America back to work means putting all Americans back to work. Ending inflation means freeing all Americans from the terror of runaway living costs. All must share in the productive work of this "new beginning," and all must share in the bounty of a revived economy. With the idealism and fair play which are the core of our system and our strength, we can have a strong and prosperous America at peace with itself and the world.

So, as we begin, let us take inventory. We are a nation that has a government—not the other way around. And this makes us special among the nations of the Earth. Our government has no power except that granted it by the people. It is time to check and reverse the growth of government which shows signs of having grown beyond the consent of the governed.

It is my intention to curb the size and influence of the Federal establishment and to demand recognition of the distinction between the powers granted to the Federal Government and those reserved to the States or to the people. All of us need to be reminded that the Federal Government did not create the States; the States created the Federal Government.

Now so there will be no misunderstanding, it's not my intention to do away with government. It is rather to make it work—work with us, not over us; to stand by our side, not ride on our back. Government can and must provide opportunity, not smother it; foster productivity, not stifle it.

If we look to the answer as to why for so many years we achieved so much, prospered as no other people on Earth, it was because here in this land we unleashed the energy and individual genius of man to a greater extent than has ever been done before. Freedom and the dignity of the individual have been more available and assured here than in any other place on Earth. The price for this freedom at times has been high. But we have never been unwilling to pay that price.

It is no coincidence that our present troubles parallel and are proportionate to the intervention and intrusion in our lives that result from unnecessary and excessive growth of government. It is time for us to realize that we're too great a nation to limit ourselves to small dreams. We're not, as some would have us believe, doomed to an inevitable decline. I do not believe in a fate that will fall on us no matter what we do. I do believe in a fate that will fall on us if we do nothing. So, with all the creative energy at our command, let us begin an era of national renewal. Let us renew our determination, our courage, and our strength. And let us renew our faith and our hope.

We have every right to dream heroic dreams. Those who say we're in a time when there are no heroes, they just don't know where to look. You can see heroes every day going in and out of factory gates. Others, a handful in number, produce food enough to feed all of us and much of the world beyond. You meet heroes across a counter. And they're on both sides of that counter. There are entrepreneurs with faith in themselves and faith in an idea who create new jobs, new wealth and opportunity. They're individuals and families whose taxes support the government and whose voluntary gifts support church, charity, culture, art, and education. Their patriotism is quiet but deep. Their values sustain our national life.

Now, I have used the words "they" and "their" in speaking of these heroes. I could say "you" and "your," because I'm addressing the heroes of whom I speak—you, the citizens of this blessed land. Your dreams, your hopes, your goals are going to be the dreams, the hopes, and the goals of this administration, so help me God.

We shall reflect the compassion that is so much a part of your makeup. How can we love our country and not love our countrymen; and loving them, reach out a hand when they fall, heal them when they're sick, and provide opportunity to make them self-sufficient so they will be equal in fact and not just in theory?

Can we solve the problems confronting us? Well, the answer is an unequivocal and emphatic "yes." To paraphrase Winston Churchill, I do not take the oath I've just taken with the intention of presiding over the dissolution of the world's strongest economy.

In the days ahead I will propose removing the roadblocks that have slowed our economy and reduced productivity. Steps will be taken aimed at restoring the balance between the various levels of government. Progress may be slow, measured in inches and feet, not miles, but we will progress. It is time to reawaken this industrial giant, to get government back within its means, and to lighten our punitive tax burden. And these will be our first priorities, and on these principles, there will be no compromise.

On the eve of our struggle for independence a man who might have been one of the greatest among the Founding Fathers, Dr. Joseph Warren, president of the Massachusetts Congress, said to his fellow Americans, "Our country is in danger, but not to be despaired of. . . . On you depend the fortunes of America. You are to decide the important question on which rests the happiness and liberty of millions yet unborn. Act worthy of yourselves."

Well, I believe we, the Americans of today, are ready to act worthy of ourselves, ready to do what must be done to ensure happiness and liberty for ourselves, our children, and our children's children. And as we renew ourselves here in our own land, we will be seen as having greater strength throughout the world. We will again be the exemplar of freedom and a beacon of hope for those who do not now have freedom.

To those neighbors and allies who share our ideal of freedom, we will strengthen our historic ties and assure them of our support and firm commitment. We will match loyalty with loyalty. We will strive for mutually beneficial relations. We will not use our friendship to impose on their sovereignty, for our own sovereignty is not for sale.

As for the enemies of freedom, those who are potential adversaries, they will be reminded that peace is the highest aspiration of the American people. We will negotiate for it, sacrifice for it; we will not surrender it now or ever.

Our forbearance should never be misunderstood. Our reluctance for conflict should not be misjudged as a failure of will. When action is required to preserve our national security, we will act. We will maintain sufficient strength to prevail if need be, knowing that if we do so we have the best chance of never having to use that strength.

Above all we must realize that no arsenal or no weapon in the arsenals of the world is so formidable as the will and moral courage of free men and women. It is a weapon our adversaries in today's world do not have. It is a weapon that we as Americans do have. Let that be understood by those who practice terrorism and prey upon their neighbors.

I'm told that tens of thousands of prayer meetings are being held on this day, and for that I'm deeply grateful. We are a nation under God, and I believe God intended for us to be free. It would be fitting and good, I think, if each Inaugural Day in future years should be declared a day of prayer.

This is the first time in our history that this ceremony has been held, as you've been told, on this West Front of the Capitol. Standing here, one faces a magnificent vista, opening up on this city's special beauty and history. At the end of this open mall are those shrines to the giants on whose shoulders we stand.

Directly in front of me, the monument to a monumental man. George Washington, father of our country. A man of humility who came to greatness reluctantly. He led America out of revolutionary victory into infant nationhood. Off to one side, the stately memorial to Thomas Jefferson. The Declaration of Independence flames with his eloquence. And then, beyond the Reflecting Pool, the dignified columns of the Lincoln Memorial. Whoever would understand in his heart the meaning of America will find it in the life of Abraham Lincoln.

Beyond these monuments to heroism is the Potomac River, and on the far shore the sloping hills of Arlington National Cemetery, with its row upon row of simple white markers bearing crosses or Stars of David. They add up to only a tiny fraction of the price that has been paid for our freedom.

Each one of those markers is a monument to the kind of hero I spoke of earlier. Their lives ended in places called Belleau Wood, The Argonne, Omaha Beach, Salerno, and halfway around the world on Guadalcanal, Tarawa, Pork Chop Hill, the Chosin Reservoir, and in a hundred rice paddies and jungles of a place called Vietnam. Under one such marker lies a young man, Martin Treptow, who left his job in a small town barbershop in 1917 to go to France with the famed Rainbow Division. There, on the western front, he was killed trying to carry a message between battalions under heavy artillery fire.

We're told that on his body was found a diary. On the flyleaf under the heading, "My Pledge," he had written these words: "America must win this war. Therefore I will work, I will save, I will sacrifice, I will endure, I will fight cheerfully and do my utmost, as if the issue of the whole struggle depended on me alone."

The crisis we are facing today does not require of us the kind of sacrifice that Martin Treptow and so many thousands of others were called upon to make. It does require, however, our best effort, and our willingness to believe in ourselves and to believe in our capacity to perform great deeds, to believe that together and with God's help we can and will resolve the problems which confront us.

And after all, why shouldn't we believe that? We are Americans.

God bless you, and thank you.

❧ 41 ❧

Immigration and Naturalization
Service v. Chadha*

(1983)

SINCE THE NEW DEAL dramatically expanded the scope of federal activity, Congress often has dealt with complex problems of public policy by writing laws in broad language and granting wide discretion to the executive branch about how to implement them. To prevent federal agencies (or even the president) from either abusing this discretion or exercising it in ways that Congress disapproves, Congress also has included in many laws a provision that enables it to pass judgment on what the executive branch has done. This provision, known as the legislative veto, permits Congress, in some fashion or other, to overturn an executive regulation or action within a prescribed length of time, often ninety days. In all cases, a legislative veto is final—the president, who can veto ordinary bills that are passed by Congress, has no power to overturn a legislative veto.

The first legislative veto provision was written into a 1932 law that empowered President Herbert C. Hoover to reorganize the executive branch, subject to a veto of any of his plans by either the House of Representatives or the Senate. Afterward, other laws were passed with legislative veto requirements that ranged in difficulty from a concurrent resolution of both houses to an objection by a single designated committee in either house. From 1932 to 1982, the legislative veto was included in more than 250 laws, including the War Powers Resolution of 1973. (See Document 34, p. 184.)

On June 23, 1983, the Supreme Court decided by a 7–2 vote to declare the legislative veto unconstitutional. The case in which it did so,

---

*Go to *http://www.findlaw.com*, click on "U.S. Supreme Court Cases," then type "Chadha" in the box called "Party Name Search"

To hear the oral arguments in this case, go to *http://oyez.nwu.edu*, click on "Cases," then type "Chadha" in the box called "Search by Title"

Immigration and Naturalization Service v. Chadha, originated in 1974 when a Kenyan student who had overstayed his visa received permission from the Immigration and Naturalization Service to remain in the United States. Relying on the legislative veto provision of the Immigration and Naturalization Act of 1952, the House voted in 1975 to deport the student, whose name was Jagdish Rai Chadha. Chadha sued, challenging the constitutional basis of the House action.

Writing for a majority of justices, Chief Justice Warren E. Burger argued that the legislative veto violated the Constitution's separation of powers in general and, in particular, the presentment clause of Article I, section 7, which says that binding actions emanating from Congress must be presented to the president for signature or veto. "The Constitution sought to divide the delegated powers of the new federal government into three defined categories, legislative, executive and judicial," Burger wrote, "to assure, as nearly as possible, that each Branch of government would confine itself to its assigned responsibility." In a blistering dissent, Justice Byron R. White complained that, having allowed the legislature to delegate substantial authority to the executive branch ever since the legal controversy over the New Deal, the Court was foolish to deny Congress its best tool for overseeing the exercise of that authority. (See the headnote to Document 23, p. 123.)

Despite the *Chadha* decision, the legislative veto is still in use, albeit in slightly modified form. Since the Court's ruling, more than two hundred new laws have been passed containing legislative veto provisions, most of which require the executive to obtain the approval of the House and Senate appropriations committees. In addition, a number of de facto legislative vetoes have been implemented through informal agreements between Congress and the executive.

⁂ ⁂ ⁂

CHIEF JUSTICE BURGER delivered the opinion of the Court. . . .

Explicit and unambiguous provisions of the Constitution prescribe and define the respective functions of the Congress and of the Executive in the legislative process. Since the precise terms of those familiar provisions are critical to the resolution of this case, we set them out verbatim. Art. I provides:

"All legislative Powers herein granted shall be vested in a Congress of the United States, which shall consist of a Senate *and* a House of Representatives." Art. I, § 1. (Emphasis added).

"Every Bill which shall have passed the House of Representatives *and* the Senate, *shall,* before it become a Law, be presented to the President of the United States: . . ." Art. I, § 7, cl. 2. (Emphasis added).

"*Every* Order, Resolution, or Vote to which the Concurrence of the Senate and House of Representatives may be necessary (except on a question of Adjournment) *shall be* presented to the President of the United States; and before the Same shall take effect, *shall be* approved by him, or being disapproved by him, *shall be* repassed by two thirds of the Senate and House of Representatives, according to the Rules and Limitations prescribed in the Case of a Bill." Art. I, § 7, cl. 3. (Emphasis added). . . .

[W]e find that the purposes underlying the Presentment Clauses, Art. I, § 7, cls. 2, 3, and the bicameral requirement of Art. I, § 1 and § 7, cl. 2, guide our resolution of the important question presented in this case. The very structure of the articles delegating and separating powers under Arts. I, II, and III exemplify the concept of separation of powers and we now turn to Art. I.

The records of the Constitutional Convention reveal that the requirement that all legislation be presented to the President before becoming law was uniformly accepted by the Framers. Presentment to the President and the Presidential veto were considered so imperative that the draftsmen took special pains to assure that these requirements could not be circumvented. During the final debate on Art. I, § 7, cl. 2, James Madison expressed concern that it might easily be evaded by the simple expedient of calling a proposed law a "resolution" or "vote" rather than a "bill."

The decision to provide the President with a limited and qualified power to nullify proposed legislation by veto was based on the profound conviction of the Framers that the powers conferred on Congress were the powers to be most carefully circumscribed. It is beyond doubt that lawmaking was a power to be shared by both Houses and the President. . . .

The bicameral requirement of Art. I, § § 1, 7 was of scarcely less concern to the Framers than was the Presidential veto and indeed the two concepts are interdependent. By providing that no law could take effect without the concurrence of the prescribed majority of the Members of both Houses, the Framers reemphasized their belief, already remarked upon in connection with the Presentment Clauses, that legislation should not be enacted unless it has been carefully and fully considered by the Nation's elected officials. In the Constitutional Convention debates on the need for a bicameral legislature, James Wilson, later to become a Justice of this Court, commented:

"Despotism comes on mankind in different shapes. Sometimes in an Executive, sometimes in a military, one. Is there danger of a Legislative despotism? Theory & practice both proclaim it. If the Legislative authority be not restrained, there can be neither liberty nor stability; and it can only be restrained by dividing it within itself, into distinct and independent branches. In a single house there is no check, but the inadequate one, of the virtue & good sense of those who compose it."

We see therefore that the Framers were acutely conscious that the bicameral requirement and the Presentment Clauses would serve essential constitutional functions. The President's participation in the legislative process was to protect the Executive Branch from Congress and to protect the whole people from improvident laws. The division of the Congress into two distinctive bodies assures that the legislative power would be exercised only after opportunity for full study and debate in separate settings. The President's unilateral veto power, in turn, was limited by the power of two thirds of both Houses of Congress to overrule a veto thereby precluding final arbitrary action of one person. It emerges clearly that the prescription for legislative action in Art. I, §§ 1, 7 represents the Framers' decision that the legislative power of the Federal government be exercised in accord with a single, finely wrought and exhaustively considered, procedure.

The Constitution sought to divide the delegated powers of the new federal government into three defined categories, legislative, executive and judicial, to assure, as nearly as possible, that each Branch of government would confine itself to its assigned responsibility. The hydraulic pressure inherent within each of the separate branches to exceed the outer limits of its power, even to accomplish desirable objectives, must be resisted.

Although not "hermetically" sealed from one another, *Buckley v. Valeo* [1976], the power delegated to the three Branches are functionally identifiable. When any Branch acts, it is presumptively exercising the power the Constitution has delegated to it. See *Hampton & Co. v. United States* (1928). When the Executive acts, it presumptively acts in an executive or administrative capacity as defined in Art. II. And when, as here, one House of Congress purports to act, it is presumptively acting within its assigned sphere.

Beginning with this presumption, we must nevertheless establish that the challenged action under § 244 (c) (2) [of the Immigration and Nationality Act] is of the kind to which the procedural requirements of Art. I, § 7 apply. Not every action taken by either House is subject to the bicameralism and presentment requirements of Art. I. Whether actions taken by either House are, in law and fact, an exercise of legislative power depends not on their form but upon "whether they contain matter which is properly to be regarded as legislative in its character and effect."

Examination of the action taken here by one House pursuant to § 244 (c) (2) reveals that it was essentially legislative in purpose and effect. In purporting to exercise power defined in Art. I, § 8, cl. 4 to "establish an uniform Rule of

Naturalization," the House took action that had the purpose and effect of altering the legal rights, duties and relations of persons, including the Attorney General, Executive Branch officials and Chadha, all outside the legislative branch. Section 244 (c) (2) purports to authorize one House of Congress to require the Attorney General to deport an individual alien whose deportation otherwise would be cancelled under § 244. The one-House veto operated in this case to overrule the Attorney General and mandate Chadha's deportation; absent the House action, Chadha would remain in the United States. Congress has *acted* and its action has altered Chadha's status.

The legislative character of the one-House veto in this case is confirmed by the character of the Congressional action it supplants. Neither the House of Representatives nor the Senate contends that, absent the veto provision in § 244 (c) (2), either of them, or both of them acting together, could effectively require the Attorney General to deport an alien once the Attorney General, in the exercise of legislatively delegated authority, had determined the alien should remain in the United States. Without the challenged provision in § 244 (c) (2), this could have been achieved, if at all, only by legislation requiring deportation. Similarly, a veto by one House of Congress under § 244 (c) (2) cannot be justified as an attempt at amending the standards set out in § 244 (a) (1), or as a repeal of § 244 as applied to Chadha. Amendment and repeal of statutes, no less than enactment, must conform with Art. I.

The nature of the decision implemented by the one-House veto in this case further manifests its legislative character. After long experience with the clumsy, time consuming private bill procedure, Congress made a deliberate choice to delegate to the Executive Branch, and specifically to the Attorney General, the authority to allow deportable aliens to remain in this country in certain specified circumstances. It is not disputed that this choice to delegate authority is precisely the kind of decision that can be implemented only in accordance with the procedures set out in Art. I. Disagreement with the Attorney General's decision on Chadha's deportation—that is, Congress' decision to deport Chadha—no less than Congress' original choice to delegate to the Attorney General the authority to make that decision, involves determinations of policy that Congress can implement in only one way; bicameral passage followed by presentment to the President. Congress must abide by its delegation of authority until that delegation is legislatively altered or revoked.

Finally, we see that when the Framers intended to authorize either House of Congress to act alone and outside of its prescribed bicameral legislative role, they narrowly and precisely defined the procedure for such action. There are but four provisions in the Constitution, explicit and unambiguous, by which one House may act alone with the unreviewable force of law, not subject to the President's veto:

(a) The House of Representatives alone was given the power to initiate impeachments. Art. I, § 2, cl. 6;

(b) The Senate alone was given the power to conduct trials following impeachment on charges initiated by the House and to convict following trial. Art. I, § 3, cl. 5;

(c) The Senate alone was given final unreviewable power to approve or to disapprove presidential appointments. Art. II, § 2, cl. 2;

(d) The Senate alone was given unreviewable power to ratify treaties negotiated by the President. Art. II, § 2, cl. 2.

Clearly, when the Draftsmen sought to confer special powers on one House, independent of the other House, or of the President, they did so in explicit, unambiguous terms. These carefully defined exceptions from presentment and bicameralism underscore the difference between the legislative functions of Congress and other unilateral but important and binding one-House acts provided for in the Constitution. These exceptions are narrow, explicit, and separately justified; none of them authorize the action challenged here. On the contrary, they provide further support for the conclusion that the veto provided for in § 244 (c) (2) is not authorized by the constitutional design of the powers of the Legislative Branch.

Since it is clear that the action by the House under § 244 (c) (2) was not within any of the express constitutional exceptions authorizing one House to act alone, and equally clear that it was an exercise of legislative power, that action was subject to the standards prescribed in Article I. . . .

The veto authorized by § 244 (c) (2) doubtless has been in many respects a convenient shortcut; the "sharing" with the Executive by Congress of its authority over aliens in this manner is, on its face, an appealing compromise. In purely practical terms, it is obviously easier for action to be taken by one House without submission to the President; but it is crystal clear from the records of the Convention, contemporaneous writings and debates, that the Framers ranked other values higher than efficiency. The records of the Convention and debates in the States preceding ratification underscore the common desire to define and limit the exercise of the newly created federal powers affecting the states and the people. There is unmistakable expression of a determination that legislation by the national Congress be a step-by-step, deliberate and deliberative process.

The choices we discern as having been made in the Constitutional Convention impose burdens on governmental processes that often seem clumsy, inefficient, even unworkable, but those hard choices were consciously made by men who had lived under a form of government that permitted arbitrary governmental acts to go unchecked. There is no support in the Constitution or decisions of this Court for the proposition that the cumbersomeness and delays often encountered in complying with explicit Constitutional standards may be avoided, either by the Congress or by the President. See *Youngstown Sheet & Tube Co. v. Sawyer* (1952). With all the obvious flaws of delay, untidiness, and potential for abuse, we have not yet found a better way to preserve freedom than by making the exercise of power subject to the carefully crafted restraints spelled out in the Constitution.

We hold that the Congressional veto provision in § 244 (c) (2) is severable from the Act and that it is unconstitutional. Accordingly, the judgment of the Court of Appeals is Affirmed.

JUSTICE WHITE, dissenting.

Today the Court not only invalidates § 244 (c) (2) of the Immigration and Nationality Act, but also sounds the death knell for nearly 200 other statutory provisions in which Congress has reserved a "legislative veto." For this reason, the Court's decision is of surpassing importance. . . .

[T]he legislative veto is more than "efficient, convenient, and useful." It is an important if not indispensable political invention that allows the President and Congress to resolve major constitutional and policy differences, assures the accountability of independent regulatory agencies, and preserves Congress' control over lawmaking. Perhaps there are other means of accommodation and accountability, but the increasing reliance of Congress upon the legislative veto suggests that the alternatives to which Congress must now turn are not entirely satisfactory.

The history of the legislative veto also makes clear that it has not been a sword with which Congress has struck out to aggrandize itself at the expense of the other branches—the concerns of Madison and Hamilton. Rather, the veto has been a means of defense, a reservation of ultimate authority necessary if Congress is to fulfill its designated role under Article I as the nation's lawmaker. While the President has often objected to particular legislative vetoes, generally those left in the hands of congressional committees, the Executive has more often agreed to legislative review as the price for a broad delegation of authority. To be sure, the President may have preferred unrestricted power, but that could be precisely why Congress thought it essential to retain a check on the exercise of delegated authority.

For all these reasons, the apparent sweep of the Court's decision today is regrettable. The Court's Article I analysis appears to invalidate all legislative vetoes irrespective of form or subject. Because the legislative veto is commonly found as a check upon rulemaking by administrative agencies and upon broad-based policy decisions of the Executive Branch, it is particularly unfortunate that the Court reaches its decision in a case involving the exercise of a veto over deportation decisions regarding particular individuals. Courts should always be wary of striking statutes as unconstitutional; to strike an entire class of statutes based on consideration of a somewhat atypical and more-readily in-dictable exemplar of the class is irresponsible. It was for cases such as this one that Justice Brandeis wrote:

"The Court has frequently called attention to the 'great gravity and delicacy' of its function in passing upon the validity of an act of Congress. . . . The Court will not 'formulate a rule of constitutional law broader than is required by the precise facts to which it is to be applied.' *Liverpool, N.Y. & P.S.S. Co. v. Emigration Commissioners, supra.*" *Ashwander v. Tennessee Valley Authority* (1936) (concurring opinion).

Unfortunately, today's holding is not so limited.

If the legislative veto were as plainly unconstitutional as the Court strives to suggest, its broad ruling today would be more comprehensible. But, the constitutionality of the legislative veto is anything but clearcut. The issue divides scholars, courts, attorneys general, and the two other branches of the National Government. If the veto devices so flagrantly disregarded the re-quirements of Article I as the Court today suggests, I find it incomprehensible that Congress, whose members are bound by oath to uphold the Constitution, would have placed these mechanisms in nearly 200 separate laws over a period of 50 years.

The reality of the situation is that the constitutional question posed today is one of immense difficulty over which the executive and legislative branches— as well as scholars and judges—have understandably disagreed. That disagree-ment stems from the silence of the Constitution on the precise question: The Constitution does not directly authorize or prohibit the legislative veto. Thus, our task should be to determine whether the legislative veto is consistent with the purposes of Art. I and the principles of Separation of Powers which are reflected in that Article and throughout the Constitution. We should not find the lack of a specific constitutional authorization for the legislative veto sur-prising, and I would not infer disapproval of the mechanism from its absence. From the summer of 1787 to the present the government of the United States has become an endeavor far beyond the contemplation of the Framers. Only within the last half century has the complexity and size of the Federal Govern-ment's responsibilities grown so greatly that the Congress must rely on the legislative veto as the most effective if not the only means to insure their role as the nation's lawmakers. But the wisdom of the Framers was to anticipate that the nation would grow and new problems of governance would require different solutions. Accordingly, our Federal Government was intentionally chartered with the flexibility to respond to contemporary needs without losing sight of fundamental democratic principles. . . .

This is the perspective from which we should approach the novel constitutional questions presented by the legislative veto. In my view, neither Article I of the Constitution nor the doctrine of separation of powers is violated by this mechanism by which our elected representatives reserve their voice in the governance of the nation.

The Court holds that the disapproval of a suspension of deportation by the resolution of one House of Congress is an exercise of legislative power without compliance with the prerequisites for lawmaking set forth in Art. I of the Constitution. Specifically, the Court maintains that the provisions of § 244 (c) (2) are inconsistent with the requirement of bicameral approval, implicit in Art. I, § 1, and the requirement that all bills and resolutions that require the concurrence of both Houses be presented to the President, Art. I, § 7, cl. 2 and 3.

I do not dispute the Court's truismatic exposition of these clauses. . . .

It does not, however, answer the constitutional question before us. The power to exercise a legislative veto is not the power to write new law without bicameral approval or presidential consideration. The veto must be authorized by statute and may only negative what an Executive department or independent agency has proposed. On its face, the legislative veto no more allows one House of Congress to make law than does the presidential veto confer such power upon the President. . . .

When the Convention did turn its attention to the scope of Congress' lawmaking power, the Framers were expansive. The Necessary and Proper Clause, Art. I, § 8, cl. 18, vests Congress with the power "to make all laws which shall be necessary and proper for carrying into Execution the foregoing Powers [the enumerated powers of § 8], and all other Powers vested by this Constitution in the government of the United States, or in any Department or Officer thereof." It is long-settled that Congress may "exercise its best judgment in the selection of measures, to carry into execution the constitutional powers of the government," and "avail itself of experience, to exercise its reason, and to accommodate its legislation to circumstances," *McCulloch v. Maryland* (1819).

The Court heeded this counsel in approving the modern administrative state. The Court's holding today that all legislative-type action must be enacted through the lawmaking process ignores that legislative authority is routinely delegated to the Executive branch, to the independent regulatory agencies, and to private individuals and groups. . . .

The wisdom and the constitutionality of these broad delegations are matters that still have not been put to rest. But for present purposes, these cases establish that by virtue of congressional delegation, legislative power can be exercised by independent agencies and Executive departments without the passage of new legislation. For some time, the sheer amount of law—the substantive rules that regulate private conduct and direct the operation of government—made by the agencies has far outnumbered the lawmaking engaged in by Congress through the traditional process. There is no question but that agency rulemaking is lawmaking in any functional or realistic sense of the term. . . .

If Congress may delegate lawmaking power to independent and executive agencies, it is most difficult to understand Article I as forbidding Congress from also reserving a check on legislative power for itself. Absent the veto, the agencies receiving delegations of legislative or quasi-legislative power may issue regulations having the force of law without bicameral approval and without the President's signature. It is thus not apparent why the reservation of a veto over the exercise of that legislative power must be subject to a more exacting test. In both cases, it is enough that the initial statutory authorizations comply with the Article I requirements. . . .

I do not suggest that all legislative vetoes are necessarily consistent with separation of powers principles. A legislative check on an inherently executive function, for example that of initiating prosecutions, poses an entirely different question. But the legislative veto device here—and in many other settings—is far from an instance of legislative tyranny over the Executive. It is a necessary check on the unavoidably expanding power of the agencies, both executive and independent, as they engage in exercising authority delegated by Congress.

I regret that I am in disagreement with my colleagues on the fundamental questions that this case presents. But even more I regret the destructive scope of the Court's holding. It reflects a profoundly different conception of the Constitution than that held by the courts which sanctioned the modern administrative state. Today's decision strikes down in one fell swoop provisions in more laws enacted by Congress than the Court has cumulatively invalidated in its history. I fear it will now be more difficult "to insure that the fundamental policy decisions in our society will be made not by an appointed official but by the body immediately responsible to the people," *Arizona v. California* (1963) (Harlan, J., dissenting). I must dissent.

✧ 42 ✧

George Bush's Persian Gulf War Address

(1991)

N O DECISION WEIGHS MORE HEAVILY on a president than one to commit American troops to war. The president must bear not only the moral burden of ordering young soldiers into harm's way but also the political burden of doing so. The Vietnam experience taught that no president can sustain foreign military operations for long without the support of the American people and Congress.

War seemed unlikely at the advent of the 1990s. The Soviet empire, the United States' Cold War nemesis since the late 1940s, collapsed in 1989 and 1990 as the Communist governments of Eastern Europe fell and nations such as Poland and East Germany spun free of Soviet domination. In late 1991, the Soviet Union itself dissolved.

Yet new threats to peace arose. George Bush was president on August 1, 1990, when Iraqi troops invaded neighboring Kuwait, an oil-rich ally of the United States. Bush, who served as vice president in the Reagan administration, had won the presidency in the 1988 election, thus becoming the first incumbent vice president since Martin Van Buren in 1836 to be elected president. Focused throughout his term on foreign affairs, Bush quickly denounced the Iraqi invasion as "naked aggression" and vowed that it would not stand.

In the five months that followed the invasion, Bush pursued a two-track strategy: he tried through bilateral and multilateral diplomatic initiatives to convince Iraqi leader Saddam Hussein to withdraw his troops voluntarily, while simultaneously preparing the American military, the American people, and the international community for war. In news conferences and public addresses, Bush repeatedly stated the case for intervention in moral terms, downplaying his more practical concern that Iraq not gain control of the Middle East's vast oil supplies. "In the life of a nation, we're called upon to define who we are and what we believe," Bush said in a televised speech on August 8. "Sometimes these decisions are not easy. But today as President, I ask for your support in a decision I've made to stand for what's right and condemn what's wrong, all in the cause of peace." Bush buttressed his rhetoric with Operation Desert Shield, dispatching half a million American troops to Saudi Arabia, another oil-rich ally imperiled by Iraq.

Meanwhile, behind the scenes, Bush worked the telephone to rally the leaders (all of whom he knew well) of the Soviet Union, China, Japan, Western European nations, and several Arab countries to help the United States bring diplomatic, economic, and military pressure to bear on Iraq. Several of these countries participated in the military buildup; collectively, they contributed $54 billion of the $61 billion cost of the operation.

By January 15, 1991—the deadline set, at Bush's urging, by United Nations Resolution 678 for Iraqi withdrawal from Kuwait—the president had secured a narrow congressional endorsement of his policies, along with the support of a majority of the American people. (Bush did not comply with the War Powers Resolution, however [see Document 34, p. 184].) On January 16 the United States, in coalition with twenty-seven other nations, went to war with Iraq: Desert Shield became Desert Storm. Less than two hours after the first aircraft began the attack, Bush addressed the nation. Speaking from the Oval Office, he sought to assure the American people and the international community that the war's aims were just, necessary, and limited. He also pledged that "this will not be another Vietnam."

The Persian Gulf War was won quickly. After thirty-eight days of aerial bombing, the allied ground offensive was launched on February 23. In four days of fighting, Iraq was driven out of Kuwait and its capacity to threaten neighboring nations was severely weakened. Nevertheless, Saddam Hussein remained in power, much to Bush's surprise and disappointment. (He had expected the Iraqis themselves to overthrow their leader.) The Iraqi dictator has sparked several international confrontations in the years since the war.

In the aftermath of victory, Bush's approval rating in public opinion polls soared to 90 percent, the highest in history. Less than two years later, however, the president's concentration on foreign affairs at the expense of domestic policy caught up with him. In the midst of an economic recession, Bush was defeated for reelection by the Democratic governor of Arkansas, Bill Clinton, in 1992.

🐟 🐟 🐟

Just 2 hours ago, allied air forces began an attack on military targets in Iraq and Kuwait. These attacks continue as I speak. Ground forces are not engaged.

This conflict started August 2d when the dictator of Iraq invaded a small and helpless neighbor. Kuwait—a member of the Arab League and a member of the United Nations—was crushed; its people, brutalized. Five months ago, Saddam Hussein started this cruel war against Kuwait. Tonight, the battle has been joined.

This military action, taken in accord with United Nations resolutions and with the consent of the United States Congress, follows months of constant and virtually endless diplomatic activity on the part of the United Nations, the United States, and many, many other countries. Arab leaders sought what became known as an Arab solution, only to conclude that Saddam Hussein was unwilling to leave Kuwait. Others traveled to Baghdad in a variety of efforts to restore peace and justice. Our Secretary of State, James Baker, held an historic meeting in Geneva, only to be totally rebuffed. This past weekend, in a last-ditch effort, the Secretary-General of the United Nations went to the Middle East with peace in his heart—his second such mission. And he came back from Baghdad with no progress at all in getting Saddam Hussein to withdraw from Kuwait.

Now the 28 countries with forces in the Gulf area have exhausted all reasonable efforts to reach a peaceful resolution—have no choice but to drive Saddam from Kuwait by force. We will not fail.

As I report to you, air attacks are underway against military targets in Iraq. We are determined to knock out Saddam Hussein's nuclear bomb potential. We will also destroy his chemical weapons facilities. Much of Saddam's artillery and tanks will be destroyed. Our operations are designed to best protect the lives of all the coalition forces by targeting Saddam's vast military arsenal. Initial reports from General [Norman] Schwarzkopf are that our operations are proceeding according to plan.

Our objectives are clear: Saddam Hussein's forces will leave Kuwait. The legitimate government of Kuwait will be restored to its rightful place, and Kuwait will once again be free. Iraq will eventually comply with all relevant United Nations resolutions, and then, when peace is restored, it is our hope that Iraq will live as a peaceful and cooperative member of the family of nations, thus enhancing the security and stability of the Gulf.

Some may ask: Why act now? Why not wait? The answer is clear: The world could wait no longer. Sanctions, though having some effect, showed no signs of accomplishing their objective. Sanctions were tried for well over 5 months, and we and our allies concluded that sanctions alone would not force Saddam from Kuwait.

While the world waited, Saddam Hussein systematically raped, pillaged, and plundered a tiny nation, no threat to his own. He subjected the people of Kuwait to unspeakable atrocities—and among those maimed and murdered, innocent children.

While the world waited, Saddam sought to add to the chemical weapons arsenal he now possesses, an infinitely more dangerous weapon of mass destruction—a nuclear weapon. And while the world waited, while the world talked peace and withdrawal, Saddam Hussein dug in and moved massive forces into Kuwait.

While the world waited, while Saddam stalled, more damage was being done to the fragile economies of the Third World, emerging democracies of Eastern Europe, to the entire world, including to our own economy. The United States, together with the United Nations, exhausted every means at our disposal to bring this crisis to a peaceful end. However, Saddam clearly felt that by stalling and threatening and defying the United Nations, he could weaken the forces arrayed against him.

While the world waited, Saddam Hussein met every overture of peace with open contempt. While the world prayed for peace, Saddam prepared for war.

I had hoped that when the United States Congress, in historic debate, took its resolute action, Saddam would realize he could not prevail and would move out of Kuwait in accord with the United Nations resolutions. He did not do that. Instead, he remained intransigent, certain that time was on his side.

Saddam was warned over and over again to comply with the will of the United Nations: Leave Kuwait, or be driven out. Saddam has arrogantly rejected all warnings. Instead, he tried to make this a dispute between Iraq and the United States of America.

Well, he failed. Tonight, 28 nations—countries from 5 continents, Europe and Asia, Africa, and the Arab League—have forces in the Gulf area standing shoulder to shoulder against Saddam Hussein. These countries had hoped the use of force could be avoided. Regrettably, we now believe that only force will make him leave.

Prior to ordering our forces into battle, I instructed our military commanders to take every necessary step to prevail as quickly as possible, and with the greatest degree of protection possible for American and allied servicemen and women. I've told the American people before that this will not be another Vietnam, and I repeat this here tonight. Our troops will have the best possible support in the entire world, and they will not be asked to fight with one hand tied behind their back. I'm hopeful that this fighting will not go on for long and that casualties will be held to an absolute minimum.

This is an historic moment. We have in this past year made great progress in ending the long era of conflict and cold war. We have before us the opportunity to forge for ourselves and for future generations a new world order—a world where the rule of law, not the law of the jungle, governs the conduct of nations. When we are successful—and we will be— we have a real chance at this new world order, an order in which a credible United Nations can use its peacekeeping role to fulfill the promise and vision of the U.N.'s founders.

We have no argument with the people of Iraq. Indeed, for the innocents caught in this conflict, I pray for their safety. Our goal is not the conquest of Iraq. It is the liberation of Kuwait. It is my hope that somehow the Iraqi people can, even now, convince their dictator that he must lay down his arms, leave Kuwait and let Iraq itself rejoin the family of peace-loving nations.

Thomas Paine wrote many years ago: "These are the times that try men's souls." Those well-known words are so very true today. But even as planes of the multinational forces attack Iraq, I prefer to think of peace, not war. I am convinced not only that we will prevail but that out of the horror of combat will come the recognition that no nation can stand against a world united. No nation will be permitted to brutally assault its neighbor.

No president can easily commit our sons and daughters to war. They are the Nation's finest. Ours is an all-volunteer force, magnificently trained, highly motivated. The troops know why they're there. And listen to what they say, for they've said it better than any President or Prime Minister ever could.

Listen to Hollywood Huddleston, Marine lance corporal. He says, "Let's free these people, so we can go home and be free again." And he's right. The terrible crimes and tortures committed by Saddam's henchmen against the innocent people of Kuwait are an affront to mankind and a challenge to the freedom of all.

Listen to one of our great officers out there, Marine Lieutenant General Walter Boomer. He said: "There are things worth fighting for. A world in which brutality and lawlessness are allowed to go unchecked isn't the kind of world we're going to want to live in."

Listen to Master Sergeant J. P. Kendall of the 82d Airborne: "We're here for more than just the price of a gallon of gas. What we're doing is going to chart the future of the world for the next 100 years. It's better to deal with this guy now than 5 years from now."

And finally, we should all sit up and listen to Jackie Jones, an Army lieutenant, when she says, "If we let him get away with this, who knows what's going to be next?"

I have called upon Hollywood and Walter and J. P. and Jackie and all their courageous comrades-in-arms to do what must be done. Tonight, America and the world are deeply grateful to them and to their families. And let me say to everyone listening or watching tonight: When the troops we've sent in finish their work, I am determined to bring them home as soon as possible.

Tonight, as our forces fight, they and their families are in our prayers. May God bless each and every one of them, and the coalition forces at our side in the Gulf, and may He continue to bless our nation, the United States of America.

❧ 43 ❧

Bill Clinton's State of the Union Address*

(1998)

BILL CLINTON'S FIRST TWO YEARS in office were among the rockiest of any newly inaugurated president in history. Clinton's problems had several sources. He had been elected in 1992 without a mandate, winning only 43 percent of the popular vote in a three-way contest with Republican incumbent George Bush and independent candidate H. Ross Perot. The new president, who had served for ten years as governor of Arkansas, was inexperienced in the ways of Washington. In addition, liberal Democrats in Congress, who had controlled the House of Representatives for the past forty years and the Senate for almost as long, were unsympathetic to his goal of moving the party toward the political center.

Clinton's difficulties manifested themselves in a number of ways, including bad press relations, an undisciplined staff, controversial appointments, and a host of political scandals. In 1994, his major first-term legislative initiative, a sweeping overhaul of the nation's health care system, was defeated in Congress. The Republicans took control of both the House and Senate in that year's midterm elections. In early 1995, they seized the policy initiative so firmly that Clinton was forced to assert plaintively, "The president is relevant here."

*Go to *http://www.law.ou.edu/hist/state98.html*

Clinton's political comeback was grounded mainly in his adoption of *triangulation,* the strategy introduced in 1995 by Dick Morris, the president's new political adviser. Morris thought that it was important for the president not only to stake out a position at the political center, midway between liberal congressional Democrats and conservative congressional Republicans, but also to find new issues that would allow him to rise above the conventional left-right political spectrum. The three points of the new political triangle would then be occupied by orthodox Democrats and Republicans at opposite ends of the baseline, with Clinton hovering at a point above and between them.

Triangulation animated, for example, Clinton's approach to the defining controversy of his third year as president—the budget battle with Congress. Riding high, the Republicans committed themselves to cut spending and taxes dramatically. Congressional Democrats opposed them on both counts. In mid-1995 Clinton angered Democrats by boldly embracing the Republican goal of a balanced budget but infuriated Republicans by insisting that Democratic programs such as Medicare and Medicaid be left substantially unaltered. The public strongly supported the president. In 1996, Clinton pursued a similar strategy on welfare reform, this time with the cooperation of a much-chastened Republican Party.

Although the Republicans maintained control of Congress in the 1996 elections, Clinton was reelected against former Republican Senate leader Robert Dole and Perot. Unlike most second-term presidents, he remained popular during his fifth year in office, mostly on the strength of a surging economy. Then, on January 21, 1998, political disaster struck. News organizations reported that Clinton, whose marital fidelity had long been doubted, had had an affair with a twenty-one-year-old White House intern, Monica Lewinsky, then urged her to lie in sworn testimony about their relationship. Clinton forcefully denied the allegations, but most political pundits predicted that he would either have to resign from the presidency or face impeachment.

Six days later, Clinton faced Congress and a prime-time national television audience to deliver his long-scheduled State of the Union address. Ignoring the Lewinsky affair, the president reminded listeners of the progress the nation had made during his administration, especially in the economy, and declared that it had done so by moving "past the sterile debate between those who say government is the enemy and those who say government is the answer." The confidently delivered speech, with its message of peace, prosperity, and moderation, struck an overwhelmingly responsive chord with the national audience, arresting at least temporarily Clinton's political free-fall. (See Document 45, p. 252.)

(See Document 45, p. 252.)

⁂ ⁂ ⁂

. . . For 209 years it has been the president's duty to report to you on the state of the union. Because of the hard work and high purpose of the American people, these are good times for America. We have more than 14 million new jobs, the lowest unemployment in 24 years, the lowest inflation in 30 years, incomes are rising, and we have the highest home ownership in history. Crime has dropped for a record five years in a row, and the welfare rolls are at their lowest levels in 27 years. Our leadership in the world is unrivaled. Ladies and gentlemen, the state of our union is strong.

But with barely 700 days left in the 20th century, this is not a time to rest. It is a time to build—to build the America within reach, an America where everybody has a chance to get ahead, with hard work; where every citizen can live in a safe community; where families are strong, schools are good, and all our young people can go on to college; an America where scientists find cures for diseases from diabetes to Alzheimer's to AIDS; an America where every child can stretch a hand across a keyboard and reach every book ever written, every painting ever painted, every symphony ever composed; where government provides opportunity and citizens honor the responsibility to give something back to their communities; an America which leads the world to new heights of peace and prosperity.

This is the America we have begun to build. This is the America we can leave to our children—if we join together to finish the work at hand. Let us strengthen our nation for the 21st century.

Rarely have Americans lived through so much change in so many ways in so short a time. Quietly, but with gathering force, the ground has shifted beneath our feet as we have moved into an information age, a global economy, a truly new world.

For five years now, we have met the challenge of these changes as Americans have at every turning point in our history, by renewing the very idea of America, widening the circle of opportunity, deepening the meaning of our freedom, forging a more perfect union. We shaped a new kind of government for the information age. . . .

We have moved past the sterile debate between those who say government is the enemy and those who say government is the answer. My fellow Americans, we have found a third way. We have the smallest government in 35 years, but a more progressive one. We have a smaller government but a stronger nation.

We are moving steadily toward an even stronger America in the 21st century—an economy that offers opportunity, a society rooted in responsibility, and a nation that lives as a community.

First, Americans in this chamber and across this nation have pursued a new strategy for prosperity: fiscal discipline to cut interest rates and spur growth; investments in education and skills, in science and technology and transportation, to prepare our people for the new economy; new markets for American products and American workers.

When I took office, the deficit for 1998 was projected to be $357 billion, and heading higher. This year, our deficit is projected to be $10 billion, and heading lower.

For three decades, six presidents have come before you to warn of the damage deficits pose to our nation. Tonight I come before you to announce that the federal deficit, once so incomprehensibly large that it had 11 zeros, will be simply zero. I will submit to Congress, for 1999, the first balanced budget in 30 years.

And if we hold fast to fiscal discipline, we may balance the budget this year—four years ahead of schedule. You can all be proud of that, because turning a sea of red ink into black is no miracle. It is the product of hard work by the American people, and of two visionary actions in Congress: the courageous vote in 1993 that led to a cut in the deficit of 90 percent and the truly historic bipartisan balanced-budget agreement passed by this Congress.

Here's the really good news. If we maintain our resolve, we will produce balanced budgets as far as the eye can see. We must not go back to unwise spending or untargeted tax cuts that risk reopening the deficit.

Last year, together we enacted targeted tax cuts so that the typical middle-class family will now have the lowest tax rates in 20 years.

My plan to balance the budget next year includes both new investments and new tax cuts targeted to the needs of working families, for education, for child care, for the environment. But whether the issue is tax cuts or spending, I ask all of you to meet this test: approve only those priorities that can actually be accomplished without adding a dime to the deficit.

Now, if we balance the budget for next year, it is projected that we'll then have a sizable surplus in the years that immediately follow. What should we do with this projected surplus? I have a simple four-word answer: Save Social Security first.

Tonight I propose that we reserve 100 percent of the surplus—that's every penny of any surplus—until we have taken all the necessary measures to strengthen the Social Security system for the 21st century.

Let us say to all Americans watching tonight, whether you're 70 or 50, or whether you just started paying into the system, Social Security will be there when you need it. Let us make this commitment: Social Security first. Let's do that—together. . . .

A strong nation rests on the rock of responsibility. A society rooted in responsibility must first promote the value of work, not welfare. We could be proud that after decades of finger-pointing and failure, together we ended the old welfare system. And we're now replacing welfare checks with paychecks. Last year, after a record four-year decline in welfare rolls, I challenged our nation to move 2 million more Americans off welfare by the year 2000. I'm pleased to report we have also met that goal two full years ahead of schedule. This is a grand achievement, the sum of many acts of individual courage, persistence and hope.

For 13 years, Elaine Kinslow of Indianapolis, Ind., was on and off welfare. Today she's a dispatcher with a van company. She's saved enough money to move her family into a good neighborhood. And she's helping other welfare recipients go to work. Elaine Kinslow and all those like her are the real heroes of the welfare revolution. There are millions like her all across America, and I am happy she could join the first lady tonight. Elaine, we're very proud of you. Please stand up.

We still have a lot more to do, all of us, to make welfare reform a success—providing child care, helping families move closer to available jobs, challenging more companies to join our Welfare to Work Partnership, increasing child-support collections from deadbeat parents who have a duty to support their own children. . . .

Next, we must help parents protect their children from the gravest health threat that they face: an epidemic of teen smoking spread by multimillion-dollar marketing campaigns. I challenge Congress: Let's pass bipartisan, comprehensive legislation that will improve public health, protect our tobacco farmers, and change the way tobacco companies do business forever. Let's do what it takes to bring teen smoking down. Let's raise the price of cigarettes by up to $1.50 a pack over the next 10 years, with penalties on the tobacco industry if it keeps marketing to our children.

Now tomorrow, like every day, 3,000 children will start smoking, and a thousand will die early as a result. Let this Congress be remembered as the Congress that saved their lives. . . .

Our communities are only as healthy as the air our children breathe, the water they drink, the Earth they will inherit. . . .

Our overriding environmental challenge tonight is the worldwide problem of climate change, global warming, the gathering crisis that requires worldwide action. The vast majority of scientists have concluded unequivocally that if we don't reduce the emission of greenhouse gases at some point in the next century, we'll disrupt our climate and put our children and grandchildren at risk. This past December, America led the world to reach a historic agreement committing our nation to reduce greenhouse gas emissions through market forces, new technologies, energy efficiency.

We have it in our power to act right here, right now. I propose $6 billion in tax cuts, in research and development, to encourage innovation, renewable energy, fuel-efficient cars, energy-efficient homes. Every time we have acted to heal our environment, pessimists have told us it would hurt the economy. Well, today our economy is the strongest in a generation, and our environment is the cleanest in a generation. We have always found a way to clean the environment and grow the economy at the same time. And when it comes to global warming, we'll do it again.

Finally, community means living by the defining American value, the ideal heard 'round the world: that we're all created equal. Throughout our history, we haven't always honored that ideal, and we've never fully lived up to it. Often it's easier to believe that our differences matter more than what we have in common. It may be easier, but it's wrong. . . .

In our day and generation to make sure that America truly becomes one nation, what do we have to do? We're becoming more and more and more diverse. Do you believe we can become one nation? The answer cannot be to dwell on our differences, but to build on our shared values. And we all cherish family and faith, freedom and responsibility. We all want our children to grow up in the world where their talents are matched by their opportunities. I've launched this national initiative on race to help us recognize our common interests and to bridge the opportunity gaps that are keeping us from becoming one America. Let us begin by recognizing what we still must overcome: Discrimination against any American is un-American. . . .

We must work together, learn together, live together, serve together. On the forge of common enterprise, Americans of all backgrounds can hammer out a common identity.

We see it today in the United States military, in the Peace Corps, in Ameri-

Corps. Wherever people of all races and backgrounds come together in a shared endeavor and get a fair chance, we do just fine. With shared values and meaningful opportunities and honest communications and citizen service, we can unite a diverse people in freedom and mutual respect. We are many; we must be one. . . .

And while we honor the past, let us imagine the future. Now, think about this. The entire store of human knowledge now doubles every five years. In the 1980s, scientists identified the gene causing cystic fibrosis; it took nine years. Last year, scientists located the gene that causes Parkinson's disease—in only nine days! Within a decade, "gene chips" will offer a road map for prevention of illnesses throughout a lifetime. Soon, we'll be able to carry all the phone calls on Mother's Day on a single strand of fiber the width of a human hair. A child born in 1998 may well live to see the 22nd century. Tonight, as part of our gift to the millennium, I propose a 21st century research fund for pathbreaking scientific inquiry, the largest funding increase in history for the National Institutes of Health, the National Science Foundation, and the National Cancer Institute. We have already discovered genes for breast cancer and diabetes. I ask you to support this initiative so ours will be the generation that finally wins the war against cancer and begins a revolution in our fight against all deadly diseases.

As important as all this scientific progress is, we must continue to see that science serves humanity, not the other way around. We must prevent the misuse of genetic tests to discriminate against any American; and we must ratify the ethical consensus of the scientific and religious communities and ban the cloning of human beings.

We should enable all the world's people to explore the far reaches of cyberspace. Think of this: The first time I made a State of the Union speech to you, only a handful of physicists used the World Wide Web—literally just a handful of people. Now in schools and libraries, homes and businesses, millions and millions of Americans surf the Net every day.

We must give parents the tools they need to help protect their children from inappropriate material on the Net, but we also must make sure that we protect the exploding, global commercial potential of the Internet. We can do the kinds of things that we need to do and still protect our kids. For one thing, I ask Congress to step up support for building the next generation Internet. It's getting kind of clogged, you know. And the next generation Internet will operate at speeds up to a thousand times faster than today.

Even as we explore this inner space, in the new millennium we're going to open new frontiers in outer space. Throughout all history, humankind has had only one place to call home—our planet Earth. Beginning this year, 1998, men and women from 16 countries will build a foothold in the heavens—the international space station. With its vast expanses, scientists and engineers will actually set sail on an uncharted sea of limitless mystery and unlimited potential. And this October, a true American hero, a veteran pilot of 149 combat missions and one five-hour space flight that changed the world, will return to the heavens. Godspeed, John Glenn! . . .

God bless you, and God bless the United States.

⋯ 44 ⋯
Clinton v. City of New York*
(1998)

THE PRECEDENT ESTABLISHED by George Washington that after Congress legislates a president must "approve all the parts of a bill, or reject it in toto" has been a long-standing irritant to political conservatives and to presidents themselves, who object that Congress often lards up important bills with extraneous and wasteful "pork-barrel" programs. During the 1980s, as federal budget deficits soared, President Ronald Reagan urged Congress to empower presidents with a line-item veto that would enable them to sign some parts of a newly enacted money bill while vetoing others. Republican candidates made the line-item veto a prominent part of their "Contract with America" in the 1994 elections and enacted it into law after they won control of Congress. President Bill Clinton, who along with forty-two other state governors had enjoyed the line-item veto as governor of Arkansas, enthusiastically signed the legislation, even though Congress had delayed its effective date until January 1997 in hopes that a new Republican president would take power.

*Go to *http://www.findlaw.com*, click on "U.S. Supreme Court Cases," then type "Clinton, President of the United States" in the box called "Party Name Search"

The law allowed the president to cancel any new spending projects, narrowly targeted tax breaks, and entitlement programs within five days of signing a money bill. Should Congress want to restore a canceled provision, it would have to pass a "disapproval" bill. If the president vetoed the disapproval bill, a two-thirds majority of both houses was required to override the veto. Between January 1997 and June 1998, Clinton used the line-item veto to cancel eighty-two provisions in eleven laws, ranging from $15,000 for a new police training center in Arab, Alabama, to $30 million for an air force program to intercept an asteroid in space. Congress overrode thirty-eight of the cancellations, all of them in a single military construction bill. In all, Clinton's use of the line-item veto saved $869 million in spending and tax breaks.

The line-item veto was controversial from the start, especially among liberal Democrats. Critics charged that it had done little to curb wasteful government spending in the states. Instead, state legislatures often forestalled vetoes of favored spending programs by granting governors some of theirs in return. Constitutional scholars argued that Article I, section 7 allows the president only to veto a "bill," not "part of a bill."

The critics lost their case in the political arena but won on constitutional grounds. On June 25, 1998, a six-member majority of the Supreme Court overturned the Line Item Veto Act in response to lawsuits filed by the City of New York, which objected to Clinton's veto of a tax break tied to the Medicaid program, and by the Snake River (Idaho) Potato Growers, who had a lost capital gains tax advantage for farmers' cooperatives. Relying on the same "presentment" clause in Article I, section 7 that the Court had invoked in overturning the legislative veto in 1983 (see Document 41, p. 225), Justice John Paul Stevens wrote that line-item vetoes are "the functional equivalent of partial repeal of acts of Congress," even though "there is no provision in the Constitution that authorizes the president to enact, to amend or to repeal statutes." In dissent, Justice Antonin Scalia argued that the Court's interpretation of the presentment clause was too narrow and doctrinaire.

❧ ❧ ❧

JUSTICE STEVENS delivered the opinion of the Court.

The Line Item Veto Act was enacted in April 1996 and became effective on January 1, 1997. . . . [In June] the President exercised his authority to cancel one provision in the Balanced Budget Act of 1997 and two provisions in the Taxpayer Relief Act of 1997. Appellees, claiming that they had been injured by two of those cancellations, filed these cases in the District Court. That Court again held the statute invalid, and we again expedited our review. We now hold that these appellees have standing to challenge the constitutionality of the Act and, reaching the merits, we agree that the cancellation procedures set forth in the Act violate the Presentment Clause, Art. I, §7, cl. 2, of the Constitution. . . .

The Line Item Veto Act gives the President the power to "cancel in whole" three types of provisions that have been signed into law: "(1) any dollar amount of discretionary budget authority; (2) any item of new direct spending; or (3) any limited tax benefit." It is undisputed that the New York case involves an "item of new direct spending" and that the Snake River case involves a "limited tax benefit" as those terms are defined in the Act. It is also undisputed that each of those provisions had been signed into law pursuant to Article I, §7, of the Constitution before it was canceled.

The Act requires the President to adhere to precise procedures whenever he exercises his cancellation authority. In identifying items for cancellation he must consider the legislative history, the purposes, and other relevant information about the items. He must determine, with respect to each cancellation, that it will "(i) reduce the Federal budget deficit; (ii) not impair any essential Government functions; and (iii) not harm the national interest." Moreover, he must transmit a special message to Congress notifying it of each cancellation within five calendar days (excluding Sundays) after the enactment of the canceled provision. It is undisputed that the President meticulously followed these procedures in these cases.

A cancellation takes effect upon receipt by Congress of the special message from the President. If, however, a "disapproval bill" pertaining to a special message is enacted into law, the cancellations set forth in that message become "null and void." The Act sets forth a detailed expedited procedure for the consideration of a "disapproval bill," but no such bill was passed for either of the cancellations involved in these cases.

A majority vote of both Houses is sufficient to enact a disapproval bill. The Act does not grant the President the authority to cancel a disapproval bill, but he does, of course, retain his constitutional authority to veto such a bill.

The effect of a cancellation is plainly stated in §691e [of the Line Item Veto Act], which defines the principal terms used in the Act. With respect to both an item of new direct spending and a limited tax benefit, the cancellation prevents the item "from having legal force or effect."

Thus, under the plain text of the statute, the two actions of the President that are challenged in these cases prevented one section of the Balanced Budget Act of 1997 and one section of the Taxpayer Relief Act of 1997 "from having legal force or effect." The remaining provisions of those statutes, with the exception of the second canceled item in the latter, continue to have the same force and effect as they had when signed into law.

In both legal and practical effect, the President has amended two Acts of Congress by repealing a portion of each. "[R]epeal of statutes, no less than enactment, must conform with Art. I." *INS v. Chadha* (1983). There is no provision in the Constitution that authorizes the President to enact, to amend, or to repeal statutes. Both Article I and Article II assign responsibilities to the President that directly relate to the lawmaking process, but neither addresses the issue presented by these cases. The President "shall from time to time give to the Congress Information on the State of the Union, and recommend to their Consideration such Measures as he shall judge necessary and expedient. . . ." Art. II, §3. Thus, he may initiate and influence legislative proposals. Moreover, after a bill has passed both Houses of Congress, but "before it become[s] a Law," it must be presented to the President. If he approves it, "he shall sign it, but if not he shall return it, with his Objections to that House in which it shall have originated, who shall enter the Objections at large on their Journal, and proceed to reconsider it." Art. I, §7, cl. 2.

His "return" of a bill, which is usually described as a "veto," is subject to being overridden by a two-thirds vote in each House.

There are important differences between the President's "return" of a bill pursuant to Article I, §7, and the exercise of the President's cancellation authority pursuant to the Line Item Veto Act. The constitutional return takes place before the bill becomes law; the statutory cancellation occurs after the bill becomes law. The constitutional return is of the entire bill; the statutory cancellation is of only a part. Although the Constitution expressly authorizes the President to play a role in the process of enacting statutes, it is silent on the subject of unilateral Presidential action that either repeals or amends parts of duly enacted statutes.

There are powerful reasons for construing constitutional silence on this profoundly important issue as equivalent to an express prohibition. The procedures governing the enactment of statutes set forth in the text of Article I were the product of the great debates and compromises that produced the Constitution itself. Familiar historical materials provide abundant support for the conclusion that the power to enact statutes may only "be exercised in accord with a single, finely wrought and exhaustively considered, procedure." *INS v. Chadha*. Our first President understood the text of the Presentment

Clause as requiring that he either "approve all the parts of a Bill, or reject it in toto.". . . .

If the Line Item Veto Act were valid, it would authorize the President to create a different law, one whose text was not voted on by either House of Congress or presented to the President for signature. Something that might be known as "Public Law 105-33 as modified by the President" may or may not be desirable, but it is surely not a document that may "become a law" pursuant to the procedures designed by the Framers of Article I, §7, of the Constitution. . . .

JUSTICE SCALIA, dissenting.

. . . [T]he crux of the matter [is] whether Congress's authorizing the President to cancel an item of spending gives him a power that our history and traditions show must reside exclusively in the Legislative Branch. I may note, to begin with, that the Line Item Veto Act is not the first statute to authorize the President to "cancel" spending items. In *Bowsher v. Synar* (1986), we addressed the constitutionality of the Balanced Budget and Emergency Deficit Control Act of 1985, which required the President, if the federal budget deficit exceeded a certain amount, to issue a "sequestration" order mandating spending reductions specified by the Comptroller General. The effect of sequestration was that "amounts sequestered . . . shall be permanently cancelled." We held that the Act was unconstitutional, not because it impermissibly gave the Executive legislative power, but because it gave the Comptroller General, an officer of the Legislative Branch over whom Congress retained removal power, "the ultimate authority to determine the budget cuts to be made," "functions . . . plainly entailing execution of the law in constitutional terms." The President's discretion under the Line Item Veto Act is certainly broader than the Comptroller General's discretion was under the 1985 Act, but it is no broader than the discretion traditionally granted the President in his execution of spending laws.

Insofar as the degree of political, "law-making" power conferred upon the Executive is concerned, there is not a dime's worth of difference between Congress's authorizing the President to cancel a spending item, and Congress's authorizing money to be spent on a particular item at the President's discretion. And the latter has been done since the Founding of the Nation. From 1789–1791, the First Congress made lump-sum appropriations for the entire Government—"sum[s] not exceeding" specified amounts for broad purposes. From a very early date Congress also made permissive individual appropriations, leaving the decision whether to spend the money to the President's unfettered discretion. . . .

The short of the matter is this: Had the Line Item Veto Act authorized the President to "decline to spend" any item of spending contained in the Balanced Budget Act of 1997, there is not the slightest doubt that authorization would have been constitutional. What the Line Item Veto Act does instead—authorizing the President to "cancel" an item of spending—is technically different. But the technical difference does not relate to the technicalities of the Presentment Clause, which have been fully complied with; and the doctrine of unconstitutional delegation, which is at issue here, is preeminently not a doctrine of technicalities. The title of the Line Item Veto Act, which was perhaps designed to simplify for public comprehension, or perhaps merely to comply with the terms of a campaign pledge, has succeeded in faking out the Supreme Court. The President's action it authorizes in fact is not a line item veto and thus does not offend Art. I, §7; and insofar as the substance of that action is concerned, it is no different from what Congress has permitted the President to do since the formation of the Union. . . .

❦ 45 ❦

Bill Clinton's "Apology" Address

(1998)

On the evening of August 17, 1998, Bill Clinton delivered a televised address to the nation unlike any other in the history of the presidency. In the opening seconds of the four-minute speech, which he gave from the Map Room of the White House, Clinton admitted that his personal relationship with former presidential intern Monica Lewinsky "was not appropriate. In fact, it was wrong." He devoted the rest of his remarks to denying that he had violated any laws and to attacking independent counsel Kenneth Starr's conduct of the investigation into his behavior.

Starr owed his authority to the Ethics of Government Act of 1973, which had been renewed at Clinton's urging in 1993. Under the act, an independent counsel is to be appointed whenever the attorney general concludes that a high-level executive official may have committed a crime. The counsel is then appointed by a panel of federal judges and can be removed only for cause. In 1994, Starr had been appointed by Attorney General Janet Reno to investigate Clinton's possible involvement during the late 1970s in a real estate investment scheme known as Whitewater. In subsequent years, Starr's investigation had broadened, eventually centering on the president's testimony in a sexual harassment lawsuit brought by former Arkansas state employee Paula Jones. Although the suit was thrown out of federal court, Clinton had already testified in a sworn deposition that he had never had "sexual relations" or "an affair" with Lewinsky. Starr regarded this testimony as possible perjury and also suspected the president of having persuaded Lewinsky to perjure herself in her own deposition in the Jones case.

Matters came to a head on August 6, 1998, when Lewinsky, in exchange for a promise of immunity from prosecution, testified to Starr's Whitewater grand jury that she and the president had had a number of sexual encounters. When the federal courts ruled that Starr had the authority to subpoena Clinton to testify before the grand jury, the president agreed to appear voluntarily. He did so on the afternoon preceding his public apology, in the very Map Room from which he addressed the nation.

Reaction to Clinton's speech on this most personal of subjects was mixed, even within his own party. Three days later, Clinton returned from vacation to the White House and again addressed the nation, this time on a subject more typical of such a forum (national security) and this time from the Oval Office. Clinton explained that earlier in the day he had ordered a missile attack on sites in Afghanistan and Sudan that, intelligence officials had concluded, were occupied by terrorists who had recently bombed two American embassies in Africa. Response to this second speech was generally favorable, providing a vivid illustration of the president's ability to rally public support around the flag against foreign threats.

※ ※ ※

Good evening.

This afternoon in this room, from this chair, I testified before the Office of Independent Counsel and the grand jury.

I answered their questions truthfully, including questions about my private life, questions no American citizen would ever want to answer.

Still, I must take complete responsibility for all my actions, both public and private. And that is why I am speaking to you tonight.

As you know, in a deposition in January, I was asked questions about my relationship with Monica Lewinsky. While my answers were legally accurate, I did not volunteer information.

Indeed, I did have a relationship with Miss Lewinsky that was not appropriate. In fact, it was wrong. It constituted a critical lapse in judgment and a personal failure on my part for which I am solely and completely responsible.

But I told the grand jury today and I say to you now that at no time did I ask anyone to lie, to hide or destroy evidence or to take any other unlawful action.

I know that my public comments and my silence about this matter gave a false impression. I misled people, including even my wife. I deeply regret that.

I can only tell you I was motivated by many factors. First, by a desire to protect myself from the embarrassment of my own conduct.

I was also very concerned about protecting my family. The fact that these questions were being asked in a politically inspired lawsuit, which has since been dismissed, was a consideration, too.

In addition, I had real and serious concerns about an independent counsel investigation that began with private business dealings 20 years ago, dealings I might add about which an independent federal agency found no evidence of any wrongdoing by me or my wife over two years ago.

The independent counsel investigation moved on to my staff and friends, then into my private life. And now the investigation itself is under investigation.

This has gone on too long, cost too much and hurt too many innocent people.

Now, this matter is between me, the two people I love most—my wife and our daughter—and our God. I must put it right, and I am prepared to do whatever it takes to do so.

Nothing is more important to me personally. But it is private, and I intend to reclaim my family life for my family. It's nobody's business but ours.

Even presidents have private lives. It is time to stop the pursuit of personal destruction and the prying into private lives and get on with our national life.

Our country has been distracted by this matter for too long, and I take my responsibility for my part in all of this. That is all I can do.

Now it is time—in fact, it is past time to move on.

We have important work to do—real opportunities to seize, real problems to solve, real security matters to face.

And so tonight, I ask you to turn away from the spectacle of the past seven months, to repair the fabric of our national discourse, and to return our attention to all the challenges and all the promise of the next American century.

Thank you for watching. And good night.

Topical Guide to the Documents

	Constitution & history	Pres. elect.	Pres. & public	W.H. staff	Pres. & burcry	Pres. & Congress	Pres. & courts	Pres. & dom. pol.	Pres. & econ. pol.	Pres. & nat'l sec.
1. The Constitution: Provisions Concerning the Presidency	×	×			×	×	×	×	×	×
2. Letters of Cato, Nos. 4 and 5	×	×		×		×				
3. *The Federalist Papers*, Nos. 69 and 70	×	×		×	×	×				×
4. George Washington's First Inaugural Address	×		×							
5. James Madison's Defense of the President's Removal Power	×				×	×				
6. The Pacificus-Helvidius Letters	×	×	×			×				×
7. Thomas Jefferson's First Inaugural Address	×	×	×							
8. Thomas Jefferson's Letter to the Vermont Legislature	×	×								
9. The Monroe Doctrine	×					×				×
10. The Tennessee General Assembly's Protest against the Caucus System	×	×								
11. Andrew Jackson's First Message to Congress	×	×	×		×			×		
12. Andrew Jackson's Veto of the Bank Bill	×					×	×		×	
13. Abraham Lincoln's Letter to Albert G. Hodges	×					×				×

(guide continues)

Topical Guide to the Documents (*continued*)

	Constitution & history	Pres. elect.	Pres. & public	W.H. staff	Pres. & burcrcy	Pres. & Congress	Pres. & courts	Pres. & dom. pol.	Pres. & econ. pol.	Pres. & nat'l sec.
14. The Gettysburg Address	X		X							
15. *Ex Parte Milligan*	X						X			X
16. Articles of Impeachment against Andrew Johnson	X		X		X	X				
17. Theodore Roosevelt's and William Howard Taft's Theories of Presidential Power	X							X		
18. Woodrow Wilson's First State of the Union Address	X		X			X			X	
19. The Teapot Dome Resolution						X				
20. Franklin D. Roosevelt's First Inaugural Address			X					X	X	
21. *Humphrey's Executor v. United States*	X				X	X	X			
22. *United States v. Curtiss-Wright Export Corp.*	X					X	X			X
23. Franklin D. Roosevelt's Court-packing Address			X			X	X			
24. Report of the Brownlow Committee				X	X					
25. *Youngstown Sheet and Tube Co. v. Sawyer*	X					X	X			X

Topical Guide to the Documents *(continued)*

	Constitution & history	Pres. elect.	Pres. & public	W.H. staff	Pres. & burcrcy	Pres. & Congress	Pres. & courts	Pres. & dom. pol.	Pres. & econ. pol.	Pres. & nat'l sec.
26. Dwight D. Eisenhower's Little Rock Executive Order	X						X	X		
27. The First Kennedy-Nixon Debate		X	X							
28. John F. Kennedy's Inaugural Address			X							X
29. The Cuban Missile Crisis: John F. Kennedy's Letter to Soviet Premier Nikita Khrushchev				X	X					X
30. Lyndon B. Johnson's "Great Society" Speech			X			X		X		
31. Lyndon B. Johnson's Gulf of Tonkin Message	X					X				X
32. Richard Nixon's China Trip Announcement			X							X
33. The McGovern-Fraser Commission Report		X								
34. The War Powers Resolution	X					X				X
35. Proposed Articles of Impeachment against Richard Nixon	X			X		X				
36. *United States v. Nixon*	X			X			X			X
37. The "Smoking Gun" Watergate Tapes	X			X	X					

(guide continues)

Topical Guide to the Documents (continued)

	Constitution & history	Pres. elect.	Pres. & public	W.H. staff	Pres. & burrcry	Pres. & Congress	Pres. & courts	Pres. & dom. pol.	Pres. & econ. pol.	Pres. & nat'l sec.
38. Gerald R. Ford's Pardon of Richard Nixon	X		X							
39. Jimmy Carter's "Crisis of Confidence" Speech			X					X		
40. Ronald Reagan's First Inaugural Address			X					X	X	
41. *Immigration and Naturalization Service v. Chadha*	X				X	X	X	X		
42. George Bush's Persian Gulf War Address	X		X			X				X
43. Bill Clinton's State of the Union Address			X			X		X	X	
44. *Clinton v. City of New York*	X					X	X	X	X	
45. Bill Clinton's "Apology" Address			X				X			